Understanding Privacy

Understanding Privacy

Daniel J. Solove

HARVARD UNIVERSITY PRESS

Cambridge, Massachusetts
London, England

First Harvard University Press paperback edition, 2009

Library of Congress Cataloging-in-Publication Data
Solove, Daniel J., 1972–
  Understanding privacy / Daniel J. Solove.
    p.   cm.
  Includes bibliographical references (p.   ) and index.
  ISBN 978-0-674-02772-5 (cloth : alk. paper)
  ISBN 978-0-674-03507-2 (pbk.)
  1. Privacy.   I. Title.
  BF637.P74S65 2008
  155.9'2—dc22   2007032776

To my grandfather, Curtis

Contents

Preface

For over a decade, the topic of privacy has had a hold on me. I was attracted to privacy issues because of their immense complexity, philosophical richness, and contemporary relevance. When I first began exploring privacy issues, I sought to reach a definitive conclusion about what "privacy" is, but after delving into the question, I was humbled by it. I could not reach a satisfactory answer. This struggle ultimately made me recognize that privacy is a plurality of different things and that the quest for a singular essence of privacy leads to a dead end. There is no overarching conception of privacy—it must be mapped like terrain, by painstakingly studying the landscape. In my initial years of studying privacy, I was not yet ready to do the mapping. The only way to do so would be to become fully immersed in the issues.

Over the years, my understanding of privacy grew, and I now believe that I am ready to set forth my theory of privacy. Although I feel that my theory is mature enough to take form in this book, it is but a snapshot of one point in an ongoing evolutionary process. Theories are not lifeless pristine abstractions but organic and dynamic beings. They are meant to live, breathe, and grow. Throughout their lifetimes, they will, it is hoped, be tested, doubted, criticized, amended, supported, and reinterpreted. Theories, in short, are not meant to be the final word, but a new chapter in an ongoing conversation.

This book is the product of many years of conversations. Countless people have helped me shape my ideas, and this book would not have been possible without them. A project such as this—one that attempts to make sense of the sprawling and complex concept of privacy—cannot be created by one individual alone. Many people helped by providing insightful comments on the manuscript or portions thereof. Deserving special mention is Michael Sullivan, who has been a great friend and teacher. His comments on this book have truly been indispensable. Many others contributed greatly to all or part of this project: Michelle Adams, Anita Allen, Francesca Bignami, Julie Cohen, Deven Desai, Howard Erichson, Jim Freeman, Robert Gellman, Timothy Glynn, Rachel Godsil, Stan Karas, Orin Kerr, Raymond Ku, Erik Lillquist, Chip Lupu, Jon Michaels, Larry Mitchell, Marc Poirier, Robert Post, Neil Richards, Michael Risinger, Peter Sand, Heidi Schooner, Paul Schwartz, Richard St. John, Lior Strahilevitz, Charles Sullivan, Peter Swire, Robert Tsai, Robert Tuttle, Sarah Waldeck, Richard Weisberg, and James Whitman. I would also like to thank my research assistants, Jessica Kahn, Romana Kaleem, Poornima Ravishankar, Erica Ruddy, Sheerin Shahinpoor, John Spaccarotella, and Tiffany Stedman, for their excellent work. Matthew Braun deftly assisted me in the library, quickly tracking down any books and articles I needed. Additionally, I benefited from helpful comments on parts of this book at workshops at Washington University Law School, the International Association of Privacy Professionals, and the American Philosophical Association Pacific Division Annual Meeting. And lastly, Dean Fred Lawrence of the George Washington University Law School graciously provided me with all the resources I asked for.

Portions of this book were adapted from the following articles: "Conceptualizing Privacy," 90 *California Law Review* 1087 (2002); "The Virtues of Knowing Less: Justifying Privacy Protections against Disclosure," 53 *Duke Law Journal* 967 (2003); and "A Taxonomy of Privacy," 154 *University of Pennsylvania Law Review* 477 (2006). In some cases, I have used only selected passages from the articles; in many cases, the text and argument of the articles have been significantly reworked.

Understanding Privacy

~ 1

Privacy: A Concept in Disarray

Privacy. U.S. Supreme Court Justice Louis Brandeis pronounced it "the most comprehensive of rights and the right most valued by civilized men."[1] Commentators have declared it "essential to democratic government," critical to "our ability to create and maintain different sorts of social relationships with different people," necessary for "permitting and protecting an autonomous life," and important for "emotional and psychological tranquility."[2] It has been hailed as "an integral part of our humanity," the "heart of our liberty," and "the beginning of all freedom."[3]

Privacy, however, is a concept in disarray. Nobody can articulate what it means. Currently, privacy is a sweeping concept, encompassing (among other things) freedom of thought, control over one's body, solitude in one's home, control over personal information, freedom from surveillance, protection of one's reputation, and protection from searches and interrogations. Philosophers, legal theorists, and jurists have frequently lamented the great difficulty in reaching a satisfying conception of privacy.[4] Legal scholar Arthur Miller has declared that privacy is "difficult to define because it is exasperatingly vague and evanescent."[5] "On closer examination," author Jonathan Franzen observes, "privacy proves to be the Cheshire cat of values: not much substance, but a very winning smile."[6] According to philosopher Julie Inness, the legal and philosophical discourse of privacy is in a state of "chaos."[7] Professor Hyman Gross asserts that "the concept of privacy is infected with pernicious ambiguities."[8] Political scientist Colin Bennett declares that "[a]ttempts to define the concept of 'privacy' have generally not met with any success."[9] According to legal theorist Robert Post, "Privacy is a value so complex, so entangled in competing and contradictory dimensions, so engorged with various and distinct meanings, that I sometimes despair whether it can be usefully addressed at all."[10]

Widespread discontent over conceptualizing privacy persists even though privacy is an essential issue for freedom and democracy. To begin to solve some of the problems of privacy, we must develop an approach to conceptualizing privacy to guide policymaking and legal interpretation. Although a large body of law pertains to privacy, it thus far has suffered numerous failures and difficulties in resolving privacy problems. Judges, politicians, businesspeople, government officials, and scholars have often failed to adequately conceptualize the problems that privacy law is asked to redress. Privacy problems are often not well articulated, and as a result, we frequently lack a compelling account of what is at stake when privacy is threatened and what precisely the law must do to solve these problems. The difficulty in articulating what privacy is and why it is important has often made privacy law ineffective and blind to the larger purposes it must serve. Thus the need to conceptualize privacy is significant, but the discourse about conceptualizing privacy remains deeply dissatisfying.

In this book, I aim to bring clarity to privacy's current conceptual muddle. I develop a new understanding of privacy that strives to account for privacy's breadth and complexities without dissipating into vagueness. I endeavor to set forth a theory of privacy that will guide our understanding of privacy issues and the crafting of effective laws and policies to address them.

Privacy: An Issue of Global Concern

Privacy is an issue of profound importance around the world. In nearly every nation, numerous statutes, constitutional rights, and judicial decisions seek to protect privacy. In the constitutional law of countries around the globe, privacy is enshrined as a fundamental right. Although the U.S. Constitution does not explicitly mention the word "privacy," it safeguards the sanctity of the home and the confidentiality of communications from government intrusion. The Supreme Court has concluded that the Fourth Amendment protects against government searches whenever a person has a "reasonable expectation of privacy."[11] Additionally, the Supreme Court has held that the Constitution preserves a "zone of privacy" encompassing decisions people make about their sexual conduct, birth control, and health, as well as protects their personal information against unwarranted disclosures by the government.[12] Many states explicitly protect privacy in their constitutions.[13]

Beyond the United States, the vast majority of nations protect privacy in their constitutions. For example, Brazil proclaims that "the privacy, private life, honor and image of people are inviolable"; South Africa declares that "[e]veryone has the right to privacy"; and South Korea announces that "the privacy of no citizen shall be infringed."[14] When privacy is not directly mentioned in constitutions, the courts of many countries have recognized implicit constitutional rights to privacy, such as Canada, France, Germany, Japan, and India.[15]

In addition, thousands of laws protect privacy around the world. Multinational privacy guidelines, directives, and frameworks have influenced the passage of privacy laws in a vast number of nations. In 1980, the Organization for Economic Cooperation and Development (OECD) issued its Privacy Guidelines.[16] In 1995, the European Union's Directive on Data Protection specified fundamental principles for privacy protection in Europe.[17] The Asia-Pacific Economic Cooperation (APEC), with over twenty member nations, set forth a Privacy Framework in 2004.[18] Numerous countries have enacted extensive privacy protections, such as Canada's Personal Information Protection and Electronic Documents Act of 2000, Japan's Personal Information Protection Law of 2003, Australia's Privacy Act of 1988, and Argentina's Law for the Protection of Personal Data of 2000, to name just a few. In the United States, hundreds of laws at state and federal levels protect privacy. Courts in most states recognize four torts to remedy privacy wrongs.[19] Since 1970, the U.S. Congress has passed several dozen statutes to protect the privacy of government records, student records, financial information, electronic communications, video rental data, and drivers' records, among other things.[20]

Furthermore, privacy is recognized as a fundamental human right. According to the United Nations Universal Declaration of Human Rights of 1948, "No one shall be subjected to arbitrary interference with his privacy, family, home or correspondence, nor to attacks upon his honor and reputation."[21] The European Convention of Human Rights of 1950 provides that "[e]veryone has the right to respect for his private and family life, his home and his correspondence."[22] Thus there appears to be worldwide consensus about the importance of privacy and the need for its protection.

Beyond this outer layer of consensus, however, lurks an underworld of confusion. What exactly is privacy? Why is it worth protecting? How valuable is it? Legal protections of privacy depend upon a conception of privacy that informs what matters are protected and the nature and scope of the particular protections employed, but this underlying conception of privacy is often poorly theorized and rarely examined.

Technology and the Rising Concern over Privacy

Since antiquity, people in nearly all societies have debated issues of privacy, ranging from gossip to eavesdropping to surveillance. The development of new technologies kept concern about privacy smoldering for centuries, but the profound proliferation of new information technologies during the twentieth century—especially the rise of the computer—made privacy erupt into a frontline issue around the world. Starting in the 1960s, the topic of privacy received steadily increasing attention.[23] The discourse has ranged from popular writers to journalists to experts in law, philosophy, psychology, sociology, literature, economics, and countless other fields. In 1964, journalist Vance Packard declared in his best-selling book *The Naked Society* that privacy was rapidly "evaporating."[24] That same year, in another best seller, *The Privacy Invaders*, author Myron Brenton declared that "we stand on the threshold of what might be called the Age of the Goldfish Bowl." He asked, "A couple of generations hence, will some automated society look upon privacy with the same air of amused nostalgia we now reserve for, say, elaborate eighteenth-century drawing room manners?"[25] In his 1967 book *Privacy and Freedom*, Professor Alan Westin noted "a deep concern over the preservation of privacy under the new pressures from surveillance technology."[26] Psychologist Bruno Bettelheim observed in 1968, "Everywhere one turns these days it seems that the right to privacy is constantly under assault."[27]

Today, the concern remains largely the same. Philosopher Thomas Nagel notes that there has been "a disastrous erosion of the precious but fragile conventions of personal privacy in the United States over the past ten or twenty years."[28] Countless commentators have declared that privacy is "under siege" and "attack"; that it is in "peril," "distress," or "danger"; that it is "eroding," "evaporating," "dying," "shrinking," "slipping away," "diminishing," or "vanishing"; and that it is "lost" or "dead."[29] Legions of books and articles have warned of the "destruction," "death," or "end" of privacy.[30] As Professor Deborah Nelson has put it, "Privacy, it seems, is not simply dead. It is dying over and over again."[31]

But not everyone is concerned. Some argue that despite what people say, their actions demonstrate that they really do not want privacy at all. Jonathan Franzen notes, "The panic about privacy has all the finger-pointing and paranoia of a good old American scare, but it's missing one vital ingredient: a genuinely alarmed public. Americans care about privacy mainly in the abstract."[32] Although polls indicate that people care deeply about privacy, people routinely give out their personal information and willingly reveal intimate details about their lives on the Internet. Law professor Eric Goldman points out that people's "stated privacy concerns diverge from what [they] do."[33] Canadian scholar Calvin Gotlieb declares that "most people, when other interests are at stake, do not care enough about privacy to value it."[34]

Others contend that privacy can be socially detrimental. According to law professor Richard Epstein, privacy is "a plea for the right to misrepresent one's self to the rest of the world."[35] Judge Richard Posner views privacy as giving individuals "power to conceal information about themselves that others might use to [the individuals'] disadvantage."[36] Legal scholar Fred Cate declares that privacy is "an antisocial construct . . . [that] conflicts with other important values within the society, such as society's interest in facilitating free expression, preventing and punishing crime, protecting private property, and conducting government operations efficiently."[37]

Thus privacy is a fundamental right, essential for freedom, democracy, psychological well-being, individuality, and creativity. It is proclaimed inviolable but decried as detrimental, antisocial, and even pathological. Some claim that privacy is nearing extinction; others argue that the threat to privacy is illusory.[38] It seems as though everybody is talking about "privacy," but it is not clear exactly what they are talking about.

The Concept of Privacy

Privacy violations involve a variety of types of harmful or problematic activities. Consider the following examples of activities typically referred to as privacy violations:

- · A newspaper reports the name of a rape victim.[39]
- · Reporters deceitfully gain entry to a person's home and secretly photograph and record him.[40]
- · New X-ray devices can see through people's clothing, amounting to what some call a "virtual strip-search."[41]
- · The government uses a thermal sensor device to detect heat patterns in a person's home.[42]
- · A company markets a list of five million elderly incontinent women.[43]
- · Despite promising not to sell its members' personal information to others, a company does so anyway.[44]

Although these violations are clearly not the same, courts and policy-makers frequently have a singular view of privacy in mind when they assess whether an activity violates privacy. As a result, they either conflate distinct privacy problems despite significant differences or fail to recognize a problem entirely. In short, privacy problems are frequently misconstrued or inconsistently recognized in the law.

Merely being more contextual about privacy, however, will not be sufficient to develop a fruitful understanding of privacy. In author Jorge Luis Borges's illuminating parable "Everything and Nothing," a gifted playwright creates breathtaking works of literature, populated with an unforgettable legion of characters, one after the other imbued with a unique, unforgettable personality. Despite his spectacular feats of imagination, the playwright lives a life of despair. He can dream up a multitude of characters—become them, think like them, understand the depths of their souls—yet he himself has no core, no way to understand himself, no way to define who he is. His gift of assuming so many different personalities has left him with no identity of his own. At the end of the parable, before he dies, the playwright communicates his despair to God:

"I who have been so many men in vain want to be one and my-self." The voice of the Lord answered from a whirlwind: "Neither am I anyone; I have dreamt the world as you dreamt your work, my Shakespeare, and among the forms in my dream are you, who like myself are many and no one."[45]

Privacy seems to encompass everything, and therefore it appears to be nothing in itself. One commentator observed:

It is apparent that the word "privacy" has proven to be a powerful rhetorical battle cry in a plethora of unrelated contexts. . . . Like the emotive word "freedom," "privacy" means so many different things to so many different people that it has lost any precise legal connotation that it might once have had.[46]

Legal scholar Lillian BeVier writes, "Privacy is a chameleon-like word, used denotatively to designate a wide range of wildly disparate interests—from confidentiality of personal information to reproductive autonomy—and connotatively to generate goodwill on behalf of whatever interest is being asserted in its name."[47] Other commentators have lamented that privacy is "protean" and suffers from "an embarrassment of meanings."[48] "Perhaps the most striking thing about the right to privacy," philosopher Judith Jarvis Thomson has observed, "is that nobody seems to have any clear idea what it is."[49]

Often, privacy problems are merely stated in knee-jerk form: "That violates my privacy!" When we contemplate an invasion of privacy—such as having our personal information gathered by companies in databases—we instinctively recoil. Many discussions of privacy appeal to people's fears and anxieties. Commentators, however, often fail to translate those instincts into a reasoned, well-articulated account of why privacy problems are harmful. When people claim that privacy should be protected, it is unclear precisely what they mean. This lack of clarity creates difficulty when making policy or resolving a case because lawmakers and judges cannot easily articulate the privacy harm. The interests on the other side—free speech, efficient consumer transactions, and security—are often much more readily articulated. Courts and policymakers frequently struggle in recognizing privacy interests, and when this occurs, cases are dismissed or laws are not passed. The result is that privacy is not balanced against countervailing interests. For example, in England, discontent over defining privacy led the Younger Committee on Privacy to recommend in 1972 against recognizing a right to privacy, as was proposed in legislation at the time. The major difficulty in enacting a statutory protection of privacy, the committee's report declared, is the "lack of any clear and generally agreed definition of what privacy itself is." Courts would struggle in dealing with "so ill-defined and unstable a concept."[50] As a result, the legislation failed to pass.

Despite the wide-ranging body of law that addresses privacy issues today, commentators often lament the law's inability to adequately protect privacy.[51] Moreover, abstract incantations of "privacy" are not nuanced enough to capture the problems involved. In the United States, for example, the *9/11 Commission Report* recommended that as government agencies engage in greater information sharing with each other and with businesses, they should "safeguard the privacy of individuals about whom information is shared."[52] But what does safeguarding "privacy" mean? Without an understanding of what the privacy problems are, privacy cannot be addressed in a meaningful way.

A New Theory of Privacy

There is a great need to understand privacy in a clear and comprehensive manner. In this book, I set forth a new theory of privacy. I begin in Chapter 2 by critiquing the existing attempts to conceptualize privacy by a wide array of jurists, legal scholars, philosophers, psychologists, and sociologists. In examining these theories of privacy, I survey the criticisms of various scholars regarding each other's conceptions of privacy and suggest a number of my own criticisms. Almost all the criticisms boil down to claims that the theories are too narrow, too broad, or too vague. More generally, many existing theories of privacy view it as a unitary concept with a uniform value that is unvarying across different situations. I contend that with a few exceptions, traditional accounts of privacy seek to conceptualize it in terms of necessary and sufficient conditions. In other words, most theorists attempt to define privacy by isolating a common denominator in all instances of privacy. I argue that the attempt to locate the "essential" or "core" characteristics of privacy has led to failure.

In Chapter 3, I develop an alternative approach to conceptualizing privacy. There are four dimensions to my approach: (1) method, (2) generality, (3) variability, and (4) focus. Regarding method, I suggest abandoning the traditional way of conceptualizing privacy and instead understanding it with Ludwig Wittgenstein's notion of "family resemblances." Wittgenstein suggests that certain concepts might not have a single common characteristic; rather, they draw from a common pool of similar elements.[53] Privacy, therefore, consists of many different yet related things.

In terms of generality, I argue that privacy should be conceptualized from the bottom up rather than the top down, from particular contexts rather than in the abstract. All conceptions must exist at some level of generality, however, so my theory generalizes beyond the myriad of specific contexts.

Regarding variability, a workable theory of privacy should account for the differing attitudes toward privacy across many cultures. It should recognize that notions about what information or matters are private have evolved throughout history. A theory of privacy, however, should avoid being too variable and contingent, or else it will not have lasting or widespread usefulness.

Finally, an approach to conceptualizing privacy must have a focus. It needs to unravel the complexities of privacy in a consistent manner; otherwise it merely picks at privacy from many angles, becoming a diffuse and discordant mess. Following philosopher John Dewey's view that philosophical inquiry should begin as a response to dealing with life's problems and difficulties, I argue that the focal point should be on privacy *problems*.[54] When we protect privacy, we protect against disruptions to certain activities. A privacy invasion interferes with the integrity of certain activities and even destroys or inhibits some activities. Instead of attempting to locate the common denominator of these activities, we should conceptualize privacy by focusing on the specific types of disruption.

Therefore, my approach to conceptualizing privacy understands it pluralistically rather than as having a unitary common denominator. In focusing on privacy problems, my approach seeks to be contextual without being overly tied to specific contexts, flexible enough to accommodate changing attitudes toward privacy, yet firm enough to remain stable and useful.

In Chapter 4, I contend that the value of privacy must be determined on the basis of its importance to society, not in terms of individual rights. Moreover, privacy does not have a universal value that is the same across all contexts. The value of privacy in a particular context depends upon the social importance of the activities that it facilitates.

In Chapter 5, having laid out the general groundwork for what needs to be done to develop a theory of privacy, I propose a taxonomy of privacy—a framework for understanding privacy in a pluralistic and contextual manner. The taxonomy is grounded in the different kinds of activities that impinge upon privacy. I endeavor to shift the focus away from the vague term "privacy" and toward the specific activities that pose privacy problems. Additionally, the taxonomy is an attempt to identify and understand the different kinds of socially recognized privacy violations, one that I hope will enable courts and policymakers to better balance privacy against countervailing interests. Ultimately, the purpose of this taxonomy is to aid the development of the body of law that addresses privacy.

The taxonomy consists of four principal groups of activities: (1) information collection, (2) information processing, (3) information dissemination, and (4) invasion. Each group encompasses a variety of activities that can create privacy problems. The taxonomy is as follows:

1. Information collection
    Surveillance
    Interrogation
2. Information processing
    Aggregation
    Identification
    Insecurity
    Secondary use
    Exclusion
3. Information dissemination
    Breach of confidentiality
    Disclosure
    Exposure
    Increased accessibility
    Blackmail

      Appropriation
      Distortion
  4. Invasion
      Intrusion
      Decisional interference

In the chapter, I explain in depth each of these types of problems and why they can be problematic.

In Chapter 6, I conclude by explaining the benefits of understanding privacy with the taxonomic framework I have developed. It is my hope that the theory of privacy set forth in this book will clear the fog of confusion that often envelops the concept of privacy. A lucid, comprehensive, and concrete understanding of privacy will aid the creation of law and policy to address privacy issues. Far too often, the effective resolution of privacy issues gets lost in navigating the conceptual labyrinth of privacy. This book endeavors to guide us in understanding this bewildering terrain.

~ 2

Theories of Privacy and Their Shortcomings

What is "privacy"? This question is essential for making legal and policy decisions. Many recognize the importance of privacy for freedom, democracy, social welfare, individual well-being, and other ends. Many also assert that it is worth protecting at significant cost. Society's commitment to privacy often entails restraining or even sacrificing interests of substantial importance, such as freedom of speech and press, efficient law enforcement, and access to information. Balancing privacy against countervailing interests requires having some notion of what privacy is. When we protect "privacy," what are we protecting?

There is a vast literature attempting to address this question. Many philosophers, jurists, sociologists, and scholars in other fields have tried valiantly to develop a theory of privacy, but most of their endeavors have major shortcomings. Traditionally, theorists of privacy have attempted to locate the essential elements common to the aspects of life we deem "private" and then formulate a conception based on these elements. A robust discourse has developed about conceptualizing privacy, and a multitude of different conceptions of privacy have been proposed and critiqued.

Although the extensive scholarly and judicial writing on privacy has produced many different conceptions of privacy, they can be classified into six general types: (1) the right to be let alone—Samuel Warren and Louis Brandeis's famous formulation of the right to privacy; (2) limited access to the self—the ability to shield oneself from unwanted access by others; (3) secrecy—the concealment of certain matters from others; (4) control over personal information—the ability to exercise control over information about oneself; (5) personhood—the protection of one's personality, individuality, and dignity; and (6) intimacy—control over, or limited access to, one's intimate relationships or aspects of life.[1] The conceptions often overlap, but each has a distinctive perspective on privacy. In this chapter, I delve into the extensive literature on the subject, analyzing and critiquing the privacy conceptions set forth in judicial opinions and legal scholarship, as well as in works by philosophers, psychologists, sociologists, and others. I demonstrate that the different conceptions suffer from similar problems.

The most prevalent problem with the conceptions is that they are either too narrow because they fail to include the aspects of life we typically view as private or too broad because they fail to exclude matters that we do not deem private. Some conceptions even suffer from being both too narrow and too broad. These problems stem from the method most theorists use to conceptualize privacy.

Methods of Conceptualizing

A conception of privacy is different from the usage of the word "privacy." The usage of the word "privacy" constitutes the ways in which we employ the word in everyday life and the things we are referring to when we speak of "privacy." A conception of privacy is an abstract mental picture of what privacy is and what makes it unique and distinct.

Under what I will refer to as the "traditional method," conceptualizing privacy is understood as an attempt to articulate what separates privacy from other things and what identifies it in its various manifestations. The purpose of conceptualizing is to define the unique characteristics of privacy. Usage of the word "privacy" must then be cleaned up to match the conceptual category of privacy, because people can use the word "privacy" improperly by referring to things outside the conceptual boundaries. Given the great difficulties of capturing everything referred to by "privacy," the often-disparate ways that the word "privacy" is used, and the lack of agreement over the precise meaning of the word, many scholars seek to establish criteria to distinguish "privacy" from other things. A few things might be left out, but the aim is to establish a conception that encompasses most things that are commonly viewed under the rubric of privacy.

Most attempts to conceptualize privacy thus far have followed the traditional method of conceptualizing. The majority of theorists conceptualize privacy by defining it *per genus et differentiam*. In other words, theorists look for a common set of necessary and sufficient elements that single out privacy as unique from other conceptions.[2] Although the terminologies theorists employ differ, most theorists strive to locate the "essence" of privacy—the core common denominator that makes things private. The traditional method endeavors to conceptualize privacy by constructing a category that is separate from other conceptual categories (such as autonomy or freedom) and that has fixed, clear boundaries so we can know when things fall within or outside the category.

Under the traditional method, conceptions of privacy are evaluated by determining their accuracy in capturing what privacy is and by their coherence—whether they are logical and consistent. Theorists often examine whether a conception of privacy includes the things we view as private and excludes the things we do not. For example, if a conception of privacy were to omit things we commonly view as private—such as medical information, intimate marital secrets, and freedom from surveillance—theorists would likely reject the conception. A successful conception thus aims to get close to the modern usage of the word "privacy," yet maintain coherence by identifying a combination of common elements that are unique to privacy. This is certainly not the only way to evaluate conceptions of privacy, but it is the way most often used by theorists.

In the remainder of this chapter, I will examine the various attempts to conceptualize privacy and will demonstrate the shortcomings of these conceptions. Ultimately, the problem emerges from the fact that theorists are attempting to conceptualize privacy with the traditional method. They are seeking to isolate its core characteristics. Privacy, however, does not lend itself very well to this form of conceptualization.

Conceptions of Privacy

The philosophical and legal discourse about privacy has proposed numerous conceptions in an attempt to capture the common denominator of privacy. In this section, I will explore and analyze these conceptions. Although I am critical of most conceptions of privacy, I do not intend to imply that they are devoid of merit. In fact, many of the conceptions capture useful insights about privacy. Each of them, however, has significant limitations if it is to serve as a conceptual account of privacy.

The Right to Be Let Alone

In 1890, Samuel Warren and Louis Brandeis penned their famous article "The Right to Privacy," arguing for the legal recognition of a right to privacy, which they defined as a "right to be let alone."[3] Many scholars have proclaimed Warren and Brandeis's article the foundation of privacy law in the United States.[4] One has called it the "most influential law review article of all," and another has observed that it "has attained what some might call legendary status."[5] It has also been described as "one of the most brilliant excursions in the field of theoretical jurisprudence."[6] The influence of Warren and Brandeis's article cannot be questioned—the article brought significant attention to privacy, spawned at least four common-law tort actions to protect privacy, and framed the discussion of privacy in the United States throughout the twentieth century.[7]

Warren and Brandeis began by describing new technological developments that were posing a potential threat to privacy. They observed that "[i]nstantaneous photographs and newspaper enterprise have invaded the sacred precincts of private and domestic life; and numerous mechanical devices threaten to make good the prediction that 'what is whispered in the closet shall be proclaimed from the house-tops.' "[8] By "instantaneous photographs," they were referring to the new snap cameras invented by Eastman Kodak Company in 1884. Before this invention, photography was largely practiced by professionals, since cameras were large, expensive, and time consuming to set up. Kodak's new cameras were small and cheap, allowing anybody to become a photographer. In 1889, a year before Warren and Brandeis published their article, photography was so popular that it was referred to in newspapers as a "craze."[9]

Warren and Brandeis were concerned not only with new technology but with how it would intersect with the media. The press was highly sensationalistic at the time. "The press is overstepping in every direction the obvious bounds of propriety and of decency," Warren and Brandeis wrote. "Gossip is no longer the resource of the idle and of the vicious, but has become a trade."[10] Indeed, the press was quite piquant. The advent of "yellow journalism" and cheap papers brimming with lurid human-interest stories fueled a dramatic increase in newspaper circulation. In 1850, only about 100 papers were read by 800,000 readers; by 1890, the numbers had swelled to 900 papers being read by 8 million readers.[11]

"It is our purpose," Warren and Brandeis declared, "to consider whether the existing law affords a principle which can properly be invoked to protect the privacy of the individual; and, if it does, what the nature and extent of such protection is." The authors argued that a right to privacy could be derived from the common law. Warren and Brandeis defined privacy as the "right to be let alone," a phrase adopted from Judge Thomas Cooley's famous treatise on torts in 1880.[12] Cooley's right to be let alone was, in fact, a way of explaining that attempted physical touching was a tort injury; he was not defining a right to privacy. Warren and Brandeis used the phrase to demonstrate that many of the elements of a right to privacy existed implicitly within the common law.

The authors declared that the underlying principle of privacy was "that of inviolate personality." They noted that the value of privacy "is found not in the right to take the profits arising from publication, but in the peace of mind or the relief afforded by the ability to prevent any publication at all." While the law of defamation protected injuries to reputations, privacy involved "injury to the feelings." Warren and Brandeis argued that the "common law secures to each individual the right of determining, ordinarily, to what extent his thoughts, sentiments, and emotions shall be communicated to others." This right— the "right to be let alone"—was a "general right to the immunity of the person, the right to one's personality."[13]

Warren and Brandeis's article, and their conception of privacy as the right to be let alone, profoundly influenced privacy law in the United States. Soon after the article's publication, courts and legislatures began to recognize the right to privacy. Today, nearly all states in America recognize a number of privacy torts that trace their inspiration back to Warren and Brandeis.[14] The authors' conception of privacy influenced not only tort actions but constitutional and statutory law as well. Indeed, Warren and Brandeis spoke of privacy as a "right," not merely a ground for a tort lawsuit.[15] In 1891, just a year after the article was published, the Supreme Court referred to the right to be let alone in holding that a court could not force a plaintiff in a civil case to submit to a surgical examination: "As well said by Judge Cooley: 'The right to one's person may be said to be a right of complete immunity; to be let alone.' "[16]

Nearly forty years later, when he was a justice on the U.S. Supreme Court, Brandeis wrote his famous dissent in *Olmstead v. United States*. In *Olmstead*, the Court held that wiretapping was not a violation under the Fourth Amendment of the U.S. Constitution because it was not a physical trespass into the home.[17] Brandeis fired off a prescient dissent, declaring that the framers of the Constitution "conferred, as against the government, the right to be let alone—the most comprehensive of rights and the right most valued by civilized men."[18]

Warren and Brandeis's article and Brandeis's dissent in *Olmstead* shaped constitutional law significantly in the decades to come. In 1967, the Supreme Court adopted Brandeis's view of the Fourth Amendment, overruling *Olmstead* in *Katz v. United States*.[19] In its Fourth Amendment jurisprudence, as well as its protection of the right to privacy, the Supreme Court frequently has invoked Brandeis's formulation of privacy as "the right to be let alone."[20] "[The right to privacy] is, simply stated, the right to be let alone," Justice Abe Fortas observed, "to live one's life as one chooses, free from assault, intrusion or invasion except as they can be justified by the clear needs of community living under a government of law."[21] According to Justice William O. Douglas:

> [The] right of privacy was called by Mr. Justice Brandeis the right "to be let alone." That right includes the privilege of an individual to plan his own affairs, for "outside areas of plainly harmful conduct, every American is left to shape his own life as he thinks best, do what he pleases, go where he pleases."[22]

The conception of privacy as the right to be let alone, however, fails to provide much guidance about what privacy entails. Understanding privacy as being let alone does not inform us about the matters in which we should be let alone. Warren and Brandeis did speak of "inviolate personality," which could be viewed as describing the content of the private sphere, but this phrase is vague, and the authors failed to elaborate. To the extent that being let alone refers to "noninterference by the state," legal scholar Ruth Gavison argues, it often neglects to understand that "the typical privacy claim is not a claim for noninterference by the state at all. It is a claim *for* state interference in the form of legal protection against other individuals."[23]

The right to be let alone views privacy as a type of immunity or seclusion. As many commentators lament, defining privacy as the right to be let alone is too broad.[24] For example, legal scholar Anita Allen explains, "If privacy simply meant 'being let alone,' any form of offensive or harmful conduct directed toward another person could be characterized as a violation of personal privacy. A punch in the nose would be a privacy invasion as much as a peep in the bedroom."[25] According to philosopher Ferdinand Schoeman, Warren and Brandeis "never define what privacy is."[26] Edward Bloustein, a legal theorist of privacy, observed that instead of developing a conception of privacy, Warren and Brandeis's article focused mostly on the gaps in existing common-law torts.[27]

To its credit, the article was far ahead of its time, and it contained flashes of insight into a more robust theory of privacy. And to be fair, Warren and Brandeis's aim was not to provide a comprehensive conception of privacy but instead to explore the roots of the right to privacy in the common law and explain how it could develop. The article was certainly a profound beginning toward developing a conception of privacy. However, although the right to be let alone has often been invoked by judges and commentators, it still remains a rather broad and vague conception of privacy.

Limited Access to the Self

A number of theorists conceptualize privacy as "limited access" to the self. This conception recognizes the individual's desire for concealment and for being apart from others. In this way, it is closely related to the right-to-be-let-alone conception and is perhaps even a more sophisticated formulation of it.

The limited-access conception is not equivalent to solitude. Solitude is a form of seclusion, of withdrawal from other individuals, of being alone. Solitude is a component of limited-access conceptions, as well as of the right-to-be-let-alone conception, but these theories extend far more broadly than solitude, embracing freedom from government interference, as well as from intrusions by the press and others. Limited-access conceptions recognize that privacy extends beyond merely being apart from others.

E. L. Godkin, a well-known writer of the late nineteenth century, advanced an early version of the limited-access theory when he observed that "nothing is better worthy of legal protection than private life, or, in other words, the right of every man to keep his affairs to himself, and to decide for himself to what extent they shall be the subject of public observation and discussion."[28] Around the same time as the publication of Warren and Brandeis's article in 1890, Godkin published an article in which he noted that privacy constituted the "right to decide how much knowledge of [a person's] personal thought and feeling . . . private doings and affairs . . . the public at large shall have."[29]

Several contemporary theorists also have advanced limited-access conceptions. For philosopher Sissela Bok, privacy is "the condition of being protected from unwanted access by others—either physical access, personal information, or attention."[30] Hyman Gross, a legal theorist of privacy, conceives of privacy as "the condition of human life in which acquaintance with a person or with affairs of his life which are personal to him is limited."[31] According to Ernest Van Den Haag, "Privacy is the exclusive access of a person (or other legal entity) to a realm of his own. The right to privacy entitles one to exclude others from (a) watching, (b) utilizing, (c) invading (intruding upon, or in other ways affecting) his private realm."[32] Legal theorist Anita Allen asserts that "a degree of inaccessibility is an important necessary condition for the apt application of privacy."[33]

Legal scholar David O'Brien argues that there is an important distinction among theorists who propound privacy as limited-access formulations. Some view limited access as a choice, a form of individual control over who has access to the self. Others view limited access as a state of existence. Arguing for the latter view, O'Brien claims that privacy "may be understood as fundamentally denoting an existential condition of limited access to an individual's life experiences and engagements." "Privacy is not identical with control over access to oneself, because not all privacy is chosen. Some privacy is accidental, compulsory, or even involuntary."[34] For O'Brien, privacy boils down to the condition of being alone. O'Brien's conception, however, omits any notion of the individual's power to make certain choices about revealing aspects of herself to others. For example, O'Brien would claim that a person stranded on a deserted island has complete privacy, but this is probably better described as a state of isolation. Privacy involves one's relationship to society; in a world without others, claiming that one has privacy does not make much sense.

Without a notion of what matters are private, limited-access conceptions do not tell us the substantive matters for which access would implicate privacy. Certainly not all access to the self infringes upon privacy, only access relating to specific dimensions of the self or to particular matters and information. The theory provides no understanding as to the degree of access necessary to constitute a privacy violation. In the continuum between absolutely no access to the self and total access, the important question is where the lines should be drawn—that is, what degree of access should we recognize as reasonable? Like the right-to-be-let-alone conception, the limited-access conception suffers from being too broad and too vague.

In an attempt to address these shortcomings, legal theorist Ruth Gavison develops the most compelling limited-access conception. Her aim is to define "a neutral concept of privacy" that is "distinct and coherent" because "the reasons for which we claim privacy in different situations are similar." For Gavison, limited access is the common denominator of privacy: "Our interest in privacy . . . is related to our concern over our accessibility to others: the extent to which we are known to others, the extent to which others have physical access to us, and the extent to which we are the subject of others' attention." According to Gavison, privacy cannot be understood "as a claim, a psychological state, or an area that should not be invaded . . . [or] as a form of control." Unlike many limited-access theorists who neglect to elaborate on the value of privacy, Gavison argues that privacy as limited access to the self is valuable in furthering liberty, autonomy, and freedom.[35]

Further, Gavison explains what constitutes limited access, which consists of "three independent and irreducible elements: secrecy, anonymity, and solitude."[36] The way that Gavison defines access, however, restricts privacy to matters of withdrawal (solitude) and concealment (secrecy, anonymity). Excluded from this definition are invasions into one's private life by harassment and nuisance and the government's involvement in decisions regarding one's body, health, sexual conduct, and family life.[37] Although Gavison contends that "the collection, storage, and computerization of information" falls within her conception, these activities often do not reveal secrets, destroy anonymity, or thwart solitude.[38] Therefore, although Gavison avoids the broadness and vagueness of most limited-access conceptions, her attempt to define what "access" entails winds up being too narrow.

Secrecy

One of the most common understandings of privacy is that it constitutes the secrecy of certain matters. Under this view, privacy is violated by the public disclosure of previously concealed information. According to Judge Richard Posner:

> [T]he word "privacy" seems to embrace at least two distinct interests. One is the interest in being left alone—the interest that is invaded by the unwanted telephone solicitation, the noisy sound truck, the music in elevators, being jostled in the street, or even an obscene theater billboard or shouted obscenity. . . . The other privacy interest, concealment of information, is invaded whenever private information is obtained against the wishes of the person to whom the information pertains.[39]

The latter privacy interest, "concealment of information," involves secrecy, and Posner defines it as an individual's "right to conceal discreditable facts about himself."[40] Posner sees privacy as a form of self-interested economic behavior, concealing true but harmful facts about oneself for one's own gain. People "want to manipulate the world around them by selective disclosure of facts about themselves."[41] "[W]hen people today decry lack of privacy," Posner argues, "what they want, I think, is mainly something quite different from seclusion; they want more power to conceal information about themselves that others might use to their disadvantage."[42] In a less normatively charged manner, psychologist Sidney Jourard emphasizes secrecy in his definition of privacy: "Privacy is an outcome of a person's wish to withhold from others certain knowledge as to his past and present experience and action and his intentions for the future."[43]

The privacy-as-secrecy conception can be understood as a subset of limited access to the self. Secrecy of personal information is a way to limit access to the self. This conception is narrower than limited-access conceptions because secrecy involves only one dimension of access to the self—the concealment of personal facts.

The conception of privacy as concealing information about the self underpins the constitutional right to information privacy, an offshoot of the U.S. Supreme Court's "right-to-privacy" cases such as *Griswold v. Connecticut* and *Roe v. Wade*.[44] In *Whalen v. Roe*, the Court held that the constitutionally protected "zone of privacy" not only protects an individual's "independence in making certain kinds of important decisions" but also encompasses the "individual interest in avoiding disclosure of personal matters."[45] Consonant with the notion of privacy as secrecy, this formulation views privacy as limiting disclosure of concealed information.

In a variety of legal contexts, the view of privacy as secrecy often leads to the conclusion that once a fact is publicly divulged—no matter how limited or narrow the disclosure—it can no longer remain private. Privacy is thus viewed as coextensive with the total secrecy of information. For example, the Supreme Court's Fourth Amendment jurisprudence holds that matters that lack complete secrecy are not private. William Stuntz observes that according to the Supreme Court, Fourth Amendment privacy "flows out of the interest in keeping secrets, not out of the interest in being free from unreasonable police coercion or from other kinds of dignitary harms that search targets may suffer."[46] In a series of cases, the Supreme Court has held that there can be no "reasonable expectation of privacy" in things exposed to the public, even if it is highly unlikely that anybody will see or discover them. The Supreme Court observed in *Katz*: "What a person knowingly exposes to the public, even in his own home or office, is not a subject of Fourth Amendment protection."[47] Later, in *California v. Greenwood*, the Supreme Court held that there is no reasonable expectation of privacy in garbage because it is knowingly exposed to the public: "It is common knowledge that plastic garbage bags left on or at the side of a public street are readily accessible to animals, children, scavengers, snoops, and other members of the public."[48] Similarly, in *Florida v. Riley*, the

Supreme Court held that the Fourth Amendment did not apply to surveillance of a person's property from an aircraft flying in navigable airspace because the surveillance was conducted from a public vantage point.[49]

Several theorists have claimed that understanding privacy as secrecy conceptualizes privacy too narrowly. Legal theorist Edward Bloustein has criticized the theory of privacy as secrecy as failing to recognize group privacy.[50] Likewise, sociologist Arnold Simmel observes:

> We become what we are not only by establishing boundaries around ourselves but also by a periodic opening of these boundaries to nourishment, to learning, and to intimacy. But the opening of a boundary of the self may require a boundary farther out, a boundary around the group to which we are opening ourselves.[51]

The privacy-as-secrecy conception fails to recognize that individuals want to keep things private from some people but not others. Criticizing a boss to a coworker does not mean that the employee desires that her boss know her comments. Being a member of an organization, especially an unpopular one, is also regarded by many as a private matter. Further, the conception of privacy as secrecy maintained by many courts views secrecy as tantamount to total secrecy rather than selective secrecy. As sociologist Edward Shils notes, contrary to privacy as secrecy, the individual does not intend an act of disclosure to be limitless.[52] "Meaningful discussion of privacy," legal scholar Kenneth Karst states, "requires the recognition that ordinarily we deal not with an interest in total nondisclosure but with an interest in selective disclosure."[53] In other words, sometimes people do not want complete secrecy; rather, they desire confidentiality, which consists of sharing the information with a select group of trusted people.

Some theorists attempt to avoid these problems by focusing on selective secrecy. For example, sociologist Amitai Etzioni defines privacy as "the realm in which an actor (either a person or a group, such as a couple) can legitimately act without disclosure and accountability to others."[54] Nevertheless, even under the selective-secrecy conception, the harm caused by an invasion of privacy is understood as the disclosure of previously concealed information. Privacy, however, involves more than avoiding disclosure; it also involves the individual's ability to ensure that personal information is used for the purposes she desires. According to philosopher Judith Wagner DeCew, secrecy is certainly not coextensive with privacy; secret information is often not private (for example, secret military plans), and private matters are not always secret (for example, one's debts).[55]

We often expect privacy even in public. Not all activities we deem private occur behind the curtain. The books we read, the products we buy, and the people we associate with are often not secrets, but we nonetheless view them as private matters. Philosopher Julie Inness observes that privacy as secrecy omits the element of control: "[P]rivacy might not necessarily be opposed to publicity; its function might be to provide the individual with control over certain aspects of her life."[56] Likewise, Stanley Benn argues that matters are private not because they "are kept out of sight or from the knowledge of others" but because they "are matters that it would be inappropriate for others to try to find out about, much less report on, without one's consent."[57]

Therefore, although most theorists would recognize the disclosure of certain secrets to be a violation of privacy, many commonly recognized privacy invasions do not involve the loss of secrecy. Secrecy as the common denominator of privacy makes the conception of privacy too narrow.

Control over Personal Information

One of the most predominant theories of privacy is that of control over personal information. According to Alan Westin, "Privacy is the claim of individuals, groups, or institutions to determine for themselves when, how, and to what extent information about them is communicated to others."[58] Numerous other scholars have articulated similar theories.[59] Arthur Miller declares that "the basic attribute of an effective right of privacy is the individual's ability to control the circulation of information relating to him."[60] According to Charles Fried, "Privacy is not simply an absence of information about us in the minds of others; rather it is the *control* we have over information about ourselves."[61] President Bill Clinton's Information Infrastructure Task Force defined privacy as "an individual's claim to control the terms under which personal information—information identifiable to the individual—is acquired, disclosed, and used."[62] The Supreme Court has even stated that privacy constitutes the individual's "control over information concerning his or her person."[63]

The control-over-information conception can be viewed as a subset of the limited-access conception. The theory's focus on information, however, makes it too narrow, for it excludes those aspects of privacy that are not informational, such as the right to make certain fundamental decisions about one's body, reproduction, or rearing of one's children. Additionally, the theory is too vague because it fails to define the types of information over which individuals should have control. Philosopher Ferdinand Schoeman, for example, observes that "regarding privacy as a claim or entitlement to determine what information about oneself is to be available to others . . . [wrongly] presumes privacy is something to be protected at the discretion of the individual to whom the information relates."[64] In other words, the control-over-information conception focuses on all information over which individuals want to retain control, but privacy is not simply a subjective matter of individual prerogative; it is also an issue of what society deems appropriate to protect.

Some theorists attempt to define the scope of what constitutes personal information over which individuals should exercise control, but their attempts run into significant difficulties. For example, legal scholar Richard Parker's theory defines the scope of personal information extremely broadly: "Control over who can see us, hear us, touch us, smell us, and taste us, in sum, control over who can sense us, is the core of privacy."[65] Parker's definition would make most interpersonal contact in society a privacy invasion. We are frequently seen and heard by others without perceiving this as even the slightest invasion of privacy.

Other scholars limit the scope of personal information to that which relates to the individual. Richard Murphy, a law and economics scholar, defines the scope of personal information as consisting of "any data about an individual that is identifiable to that individual."[66] Murphy's definition is too broad because there is a significant amount of information identifiable to us that we do not deem as private. For example, the fact that a person is a well-known politician is identifiable to her, but is not private. Murphy's definition thus provides no reasonable limitation in scope.

In addition to failing to adequately define the scope of information, control-over-information conceptions fail to define what is meant by "control." Theorists provide little elaboration on what control really entails, and it is often defined too narrowly or too broadly. Frequently, control is understood as a form of ownership of information. For example, Westin concludes that "personal information, thought of as the right of decision over one's private personality, should be defined as a property right."[67] This notion is partially embodied in the tort of appropriation, which protects people against others' using their image or likeness for commercial gain.[68]

The notion that individuals have a property right in information about themselves can be traced to John Locke, who asserted that individuals have property rights in their person and the fruits of their labor. According to Locke, property flows naturally from selfhood: "[E]very man has a *property* in his own *person*." From this principle, Locke deduced that property extends to the products of one's labor: "Whatsoever then he removes out of the state that nature hath provided, and left it in, he hath mixed his *labor* with, and joined it to something that is his own, and thereby makes it his *property*."[69]

Locke's conception of property as the fruit of labor and as an extension of the self has formed the backbone of intellectual-property law, which, as legal theorist James Boyle has observed, has developed around the notion of the "romantic author," the individual who mixes her unique personality with ideas, who most displays originality and novelty in her creations.[70] Unlike physical property, intellectual property protects the expression of ideas. Copyright law, for example, protects "original works of authorship fixed in any tangible medium of expression."[71] Copyright law provides control not over the underlying ideas and facts but over the particular manner in which they are expressed. The "romantic-author" notion of intellectual property embodies Locke's idea that one gains a property right in something when it emanates from one's self.

Conceiving of personal information as property is justified by viewing it as an extension of personality. As the authors of our own lives, we generate information as we develop our personalities. The growth of individualism spawned the "belief that one's actions and their history 'belonged' to the self which generated them and were to be shared only with those with whom one wished to share them."[72] "One's self—for other people—is one's expression of one's self," observes Madame Merle in Henry James's *The Portrait of a Lady*, "and one's house, one's furniture, one's garments, the books one reads, the company one keeps—these things are all expressive."[73]

Extending property concepts to personal information, however, has difficulties. Information can be easily transmitted and, once known by others, cannot be eradicated from their minds. Unlike physical objects, information can be possessed simultaneously within the minds of millions. This is why intellectual-property law protects particular tangible expressions of ideas rather than the underlying ideas themselves. The complexity of personal information is that it is both an expression of the self and a set of facts—a historical record of one's behavior.

Further, there are problems with viewing personal information as equivalent to any other commodity. Personal information is often formed in relationships with others. All parties to that relationship have some claim to the information. For example, individuals are not the lone creators of their web-browsing information, for most of that information is created from the interaction between the user and websites.[74] Often, the market value of information is not created exclusively by the labor of the individual to whom it relates but in part by the third party that compiles the information.[75] For instance, the value of personal information for advertisers and marketers emerges in part from their consolidation and categorization of that information.

An example of the difficulty in assigning ownership to information is illustrated by *Haynes v. Alfred A. Knopf, Inc.*[76] This case involved Nicholas Lemann's highly praised book about the social and political history of African Americans who migrated from the South to northern cities. The book chronicled the life of Ruby Lee Daniels, who suffered greatly from her former husband Luther Haynes's alcoholism, selfishness, and irresponsible conduct. Haynes sued the author and the publisher under the public-disclosure-of-private-facts tort, claiming that he had long since turned his life around and that the disclosure of his past destroyed the new life he had worked so hard to construct. Judge Posner, writing for the panel, concluded that there could be no liability for invasion of privacy because "[a] person does not have a legally protected right to a reputation based on the concealment of the truth"[77] and because the book narrated "a story not only of legitimate but of transcendent public interest."[78]

Although this case did not hinge on the shared nature of the information, it illustrates that personal information rarely belongs to just one individual; it is often formed in relationships with others. Ruby Daniels's story was deeply interwoven with Haynes's story. Daniels had a right to speak about her own past, to have her story told. This was her life story, not just Luther Haynes's. In sum, understanding control as ownership presents difficulties in grappling with the unique shared nature of much private information. A claim of privacy is not the same as a claim of ownership.

Not only does defining control prove difficult, but also control over information is too broad a conception. Professor Tom Gerety claims that control-over-information conceptions include "*all* control over *all* information about oneself, one's group, one's institutions. Surely privacy should come, in law as in life, to much less than this."[79] According to Inness, not all personal information is private; she contends that "it is the *intimacy* of this information that identifies a loss of privacy."[80] Thus one possibility is that the control-over-information conception could be limited in scope by including only intimate information. Charles Fried seeks to limit his control-over-information conception in this manner, defining privacy as "control over knowledge about oneself" that is necessary to protect "fundamental relations" of "respect, love, friendship and trust."[81] His theory speaks about the value of privacy (promoting respect, love, friendship, and trust) and presumably would define the scope of information as "intimate" information (information necessary to form and foster relationships involving respect, love, friendship, and trust).

Even if the conception is narrowed to include only intimate information, however, it is still too broad. According to DeCew, we often lose control over information in ways that do not involve an invasion of our privacy.[82] To illustrate this point, Daniel Farber invokes the example of the flasher. A flasher is controlling visual access to his body by allowing it, but preventing flashing is not a violation of the flasher's privacy; rather, flashing is seen as a violation of the privacy of others.[83]

David O'Brien also criticizes the conception of privacy as the control of information for being too narrow.[84] Many privacy interests involve an individual's "freedom to engage in private activities" rather than the disclosure or nondisclosure of information.[85] O'Brien correctly recognizes that privacy is invaded not just by the loss of control over information but also by nuisances such as noises, smells, and other noxious disruptions of one's peace of mind.[86] DeCew points out that the control-over-information conception is too narrow because privacy does not involve only personal information. Privacy, contends DeCew, can be invaded even if nobody else knows something new about a person. Examples include being forced to hear propaganda, being manipulated by subliminal advertisements, or being disrupted in a manner that thwarts one's ability to think or read.[87] Anita Allen critiques the control-over-information conception for omitting issues such as abortion and sexual freedom.[88] The theory of privacy as control over information thus excludes many aspects of life that we commonly assume to be private.

Additionally, some theorists critique the control-over-information conception as being too narrow because it focuses too heavily on individual choice. Paul Schwartz argues that it wrongly assumes that individuals have autonomy to exercise control over their personal data in all situations. This assumption fails to recognize "that individual self-determination is itself shaped by the processing of personal data."[89] Schwartz also questions the assumption that individuals are able to exercise meaningful choices with regard to their information, given disparities in knowledge and power in bargaining over the transfer of their information.[90] The implication is that privacy involves not only individual control, but also the social regulation of information.[91] In other words, privacy is an aspect of social structure, an architecture of information regulation, not just a matter for the exercise of individual control.

To summarize, conceptualizing privacy as control over personal information can be too vague, too broad, or too narrow. Conceptions of information control are too vague or too broad when theorists fail to define what "control" entails. Attempts to define control often delineate it as a form of ownership, making the conception falter in a number of respects. Finally, conceptions of information control are too narrow because they reduce privacy to informational concerns, omit decisional freedom from the realm of privacy, and focus too exclusively on individual choice.

Personhood

Another theory of privacy views it as a form of protecting personhood. Building upon Warren and Brandeis's notion of "inviolate personality,"

Paul Freund coined the term "personhood" to refer to "those attributes of an individual which are irreducible in his selfhood."[92]

The theory of privacy as personhood differs from the theories discussed earlier because it is constructed around a normative end of privacy, namely, the protection of the integrity of personality. This theory is not independent of the other theories, and it often is used in conjunction with them to explain why privacy is important, what aspects of the self should be limited, or what information we should have control over.

What is personhood? What aspects of the self does privacy protect? According to Edward Bloustein, privacy protects individuality.[93] Privacy is a unified and coherent concept protecting against conduct that is "demeaning to individuality," "an affront to personal dignity," or an "assault on human personality."[94] Philosopher Jeffrey Reiman also recognizes a personhood component to privacy: "The right to privacy . . . protects the individual's interest in becoming, being, and remaining a person."[95]

Philosopher Stanley Benn also develops a personhood conception of privacy, noting that privacy amounts to respect for individuals as choosers: "[R]espect for someone as a person, as a chooser, implie[s] respect for him as one engaged in a kind of self-creative enterprise, which could be disrupted, distorted, or frustrated even by so limited an intrusion as watching." Drawing from Jean-Paul Sartre's *Being and Nothingness*, Benn explains that being "an object of scrutiny, as the focus of another's attention, brings one to a new consciousness of oneself, as something seen through another's eyes." The observed "becomes aware of himself as an object, knowable, having a determinate character." According to Benn, the result is that the observed person "is fixed as *something*—with limited probabilities rather than infinite, indeterminate possibilities."[96] In other words, Benn contends that surveillance restricts an individual's range of choices and thus limits her freedom. Accordingly, privacy is about respect for personhood, with personhood defined in terms of the individual's capacity to choose.

The U.S. Supreme Court has espoused a personhood theory of privacy in its right to privacy decisions, such as *Griswold v. Connecticut*, *Eisenstadt v. Baird*, and *Roe v. Wade*.[97] The Court characterized privacy as an "interest in independence in making certain kinds of important decisions."[98] Specifically, these cases involved decisions relating to marriage, procreation, contraception, family relationships, and child rearing.[99] In *Planned Parenthood v. Casey*, the Supreme Court provided its most elaborate explanation of what the constitutional right to privacy encompasses:

> These matters, involving the most intimate and personal choices a person may make in a lifetime, choices central to personal dignity and autonomy, are central to the liberty protected by the Fourteenth Amendment. At the heart of liberty is the right to define one's own concept of existence, of meaning, of the universe, and of the mystery of human life. Beliefs about these matters could not define the attributes of personhood were they formed under compulsion of the State.[100]

In other words, the Court has conceptualized the protection of privacy as the state's noninterference in certain decisions that are essential to defining personhood.

Some critics complain that personhood theories and the Court's privacy cases are really about liberty and autonomy, not about privacy. In *Democracy's Discontent*, Michael Sandel argues that the Court's privacy cases conflate privacy and autonomy.[101] Louis Henkin contends that *Griswold*, *Roe*, and *Baird* establish "not a right to freedom from official intrusion, but to freedom from official regulation."[102] But DeCew counters that there is an "intuitive notion of privacy invoked in the constitutional privacy cases." She argues that there is no need to view privacy as totally exclusive from autonomy and liberty, for conceptions can overlap.[103]

Theories of privacy as personhood, however, fail to elucidate what privacy is because they often do not articulate an adequate definition of personhood. Freund's notion of attributes irreducible in one's selfhood is far too vague and merely substitutes "selfhood" for "personhood." Bloustein's discussion of personhood as "individuality" fails to define the scope or nature of individuality. Other commentators define personhood as a type of autonomy,[104] but as legal scholar Jed Rubenfeld observes, "to call an individual 'autonomous' is simply another way of saying that he is morally free, and to say that the right to privacy protects freedom adds little to our understanding of the doctrine."[105]

Personhood theories are often too broad. Our personalities are not purely private; indeed, we readily express in public much that is unique to the self. An artistic work is frequently an expression of the deepest recesses of an artist's existence, yet it is often put on public display. Gavison, for example, criticizes Bloustein's dignity conception because "there are ways to offend dignity and personality that have nothing to do with privacy." She elaborates: "Having to beg or sell one's body in order to survive are serious affronts to dignity, but do not appear to involve loss of privacy."[106]

In his influential article "The Right of Privacy," Jed Rubenfeld has provided a sophisticated account of the problems of the personhood theory of privacy. According to Rubenfeld, the "personhood thesis is this: where our identity or self-definition is at stake, there the state may not interfere." Rubenfeld correctly observes that the law cannot protect all forms of self-definition, for some forms conflict with others, and very few meaningful acts of self-definition have no effects on others. "Personhood cannot exclude 'intolerant' identities without abandoning its value-neutrality as between identities." This fact leads Rubenfeld to conclude that personhood's "final defense" rests on a view of what is fundamentally important to individual identity.[107] Rubenfeld then critiques the personhood conception: "By conceiving of the conduct that it purports to protect as 'essential to the individual's identity,' personhood inadvertently reintroduces into privacy analysis the very premise of the invidious uses of state power it seeks to overcome."[108] When the state endeavors to protect personhood, it must adopt and enforce its own conception of individual identity, impinging upon the freedom of individuals to define for themselves what is central to their identities.

Rubenfeld offers an alternative conception that defines the right to privacy as "the fundamental freedom not to have one's life too totally determined by a progressively more normalizing state." Rubenfeld claims that privacy protects against a "creeping totalitarianism, an unarmed occupation of individuals' lives." Privacy "is to be invoked only where the government threatens to take over or occupy our lives—to exert its power in some way over the totality of our lives." Rubenfeld elaborates: "The anti-totalitarian right to privacy . . . prevents the state from imposing on individuals a defined identity."[109]

Although Rubenfeld's critique of the personhood conception is certainly warranted, he fails in his attempt to abandon a personhood conception. If privacy concerns only those exercises of state power that threaten the "totality of our lives," then it is difficult to conceive of anything that would be protected. Indeed, as Rubenfeld himself notes, infringements on privacy are "creeping"; that is, they often occur in small encroachments into our private lives. Privacy can be threatened by an aggregation of these minor encroachments, not always by a potent exercise of state or corporate power. For example, as I explain in greater depth in my book *The Digital Person*, one isolated piece of data about an individual is often not very revealing. Combining many pieces of information, however, begins to paint a portrait of our identities.[110] To use another example, being investigated and photographed by a single reporter can be a minor intrusion compared with being inundated by swarms of reporters in a media frenzy.

Rubenfeld's critique of personhood forbids him from sketching any conception of identity that the law should protect, for to do so would be to seize from individuals their right to define themselves. By abandoning any attempt to define a conception of identity, Rubenfeld's conception of privacy collapses into a vague right to be let alone. For it to tell us anything meaningful about which exercises of state power must be curtailed, a theory of privacy must have an affirmative conception of personhood. For example, Rubenfeld states, "[C]hildbearing, marriage, and the assumption of a specific sexual identity are undertakings that go on for years, define roles, direct activities, operate on or even create intense emotional relations, enlist the body, inform values, and in sum substantially shape the totality of a person's daily life and consciousness."[111] Rubenfeld defines these aspects of life as existing at the heart of identity because of their pervasiveness and longevity. Thus he is creating a conception of personhood that focuses on pervasiveness and longevity as the defining factors.

Rubenfeld is correct that laws purporting to protect personhood can impose a view of what aspects of life are essential to the individual and hence supplant the individual's own self-definition. However, Rubenfeld is too quick to condemn as "invidious" all state power that shapes identities.[112] Not all such exercises of state power are pernicious. In fact, privacy is both a positive and a negative right; it is not just a freedom from the state, but also a duty of the state to protect certain matters via property rights, tort law, criminal law, and other legal devices. Without protection against rape, assault, trespass, and the collection of personal information, we would have little privacy and scant space or security to engage in self-definition. To preserve people's ability to engage in self-definition, the state must actively intervene. Therefore, although Rubenfeld is correct that the state cannot be neutral when it becomes involved in one's self-definition, he errs in assuming that he can develop his theory of antitotalitarianism without an account of personhood.

Intimacy

An increasingly popular theory understands privacy as a form of intimacy. This theory appropriately recognizes that privacy is essential not just for individual self-creation, but also for human relationships. Daniel Farber notes that one virtue of privacy as intimacy is that it "expand[s] moral personhood beyond simple rational autonomy."[113] The theory views privacy as consisting of some form of limited access or control, and it locates the value of privacy in the development of personal relationships.

We form relationships with differing degrees of intimacy and self-revelation, and we value privacy so that we can maintain the desired levels of intimacy for each of our varied relationships. For example, political scientist Robert Gerstein claims that "intimate relationships simply could not exist if we did not continue to insist on privacy for them."[114] By focusing on the relationship-oriented value of privacy, the theory of privacy as intimacy attempts to define what aspects of life we should be able to restrict access to, or what information we should be able to control or keep secret.

In *Privacy, Intimacy, and Isolation*, Julie Inness advances an intimacy conception of privacy:

> [T]he content of privacy cannot be captured if we focus exclusively on either information, access, or intimate decisions because privacy involves all three areas. . . . I suggest that these apparently disparate areas are linked by the common denominator of intimacy—privacy's content covers intimate information, access, and decisions.

In contrast to many proponents of privacy as intimacy, Inness recognizes the need to define intimacy. She notes that there are two ways to do this: by looking at behavior or by looking at motivations. She rejects an empirical examination of particular instances of human behavior as inadequate to define intimacy because these behaviors "lack an intimate essence," and a theory that looks to behaviors could not account for the fact that intimacy "is not static across time or culture." According to Inness, "[I]ntimacy stems from something prior to behavior." It is an individual's motives that matter. Intimate matters or acts draw "their value and meaning from the agent's love, care, or liking." This, she claims, defines the scope of intimacy. Privacy is "the state of the agent having control over decisions concerning matters that draw their meaning and value from the agent's love, caring, or liking. These decisions cover choices on the agent's part about access to herself, the dissemination of information about herself, and her actions."[115]

Charles Fried, who understands privacy as control over information, advances an intimacy conception to locate the value of privacy and circumscribe the scope of information over which we should have control. For Fried, "Intimacy is the sharing of information about one's actions, beliefs or emotions which one does not share with all, and which one has the right not to share with anyone. By conferring this right, privacy creates the moral capital which we spend in friendship and love."[116] Similarly, James Rachels contends that privacy is valuable because "there is a close connection between our ability to control who has access to us and to information about us, and our ability to create and maintain different sorts of social relationships with different people."[117]

How is "intimate" information to be defined? For Fried and Rachels, intimate information is that which individuals want to reveal only to a few other people. Jeffrey Reiman argues that Fried and Rachels's view of intimacy "overlooks the fact that what constitutes intimacy is not merely the sharing of otherwise withheld information, but the context of caring which makes the sharing of personal information significant." The ability to love and care for others transcends the mere sharing of secrets. For example, Reiman states that "[o]ne ordinarily reveals information to one's psychoanalyst that one might hesitate to reveal to a friend or lover. That hardly means one has an intimate relationship with the analyst." "What is missing," Reiman declares, "is that particular kind of caring that makes a relationship not just personal but intimate." To illustrate his point, Reiman points out that merely providing special access to our bodies does not define sexual intimacy. If this were the case, a doctor's examination of our genitals would be intimate.[118]

Tom Gerety also bases his formulation of privacy on intimacy. Beginning with the criticism that existing theories of privacy are far too broad because they lack any meaningful limitation in scope, he goes on to claim that "[i]ntimacy is the chief restricting concept in the definition of privacy." Intimacy is "the consciousness of the mind in its access to its own and other bodies and minds, insofar, at least, as these are generally or specifically secluded from the access of the uninvited." In other words, his definition of intimacy is a form of limited access to the self. Gerety develops his definition of intimacy a bit further in terms of its expressiveness of individual identity and autonomy. He thus claims that abortion is a private decision because it is "an intimate one, expressive of both [a woman's] identity and her autonomy."[119]

But Gerety's intimacy theory of privacy, like the theories he critiques, is too broad. Gerety attempts to limit privacy by the terms "identity" and "autonomy," but these very broad terms could apply to almost every action or decision an individual undertakes. While Gerety complains about overbroad conceptions of privacy that have no meaningful limitation, his conception suffers from the same defect. Without limitations in scope, the word "intimacy" is merely a different word for "privacy" and is certainly not sufficient to determine which matters are private.

On the other hand, privacy-as-intimacy theories are too narrow because they focus too exclusively on interpersonal relationships and the particular feelings engendered by them. Although trust, love, and intimacy are facilitated by privacy, these are not the sole ends of privacy. As DeCew points out, information about our finances is private but not intimate.[120] Trust, love, and caring are not broad enough to constitute a conception of privacy. Although privacy helps us achieve these ends, these ends do not compose a complete conception of privacy. As Farber notes, there are many sexual relationships devoid of love, liking, or caring, and there are many acts expressive of love, liking, or caring (such as buying gifts) that are not considered intimate.[121]

Furthermore, privacy's value does not lie exclusively in the development of intimate human relationships. Intimacy captures the dimension of private life that consists of close relationships with others, but it does not capture the dimension of private life that is devoted to the self alone. W. L. Weinstein observes:

> [T]here is a wide range of instances where to speak of something as private is not to imply intimacy. Individuals not intimately related may nevertheless assert that their relation or activity is a private one in the sense that it is not the proper concern of the community or some institution, such as the state, a church, or a business firm.[122]

For example, as political scientist Priscilla Regan notes, computer databases pose a significant threat to privacy but "do not primarily affect . . . relationships of friendship, love, and trust. Instead, these threats come from private and governmental organizations—the police, welfare agencies, credit agencies, banks, and employers."[123]

In sum, privacy-as-intimacy conceptions can be too broad if they do not adequately define the scope of "intimacy." Most often, however, these conceptions are too narrow because they exclude many matters that do not involve the characteristics of intimate relationships.

Can Privacy Be Conceptualized?

Although each of the conceptions of privacy described in this chapter elaborates upon certain dimensions of privacy and contains many insights, settling upon any one of the conceptions results in either a reductive or an overly broad account of privacy. Any attempt to locate a common denominator for all the manifold things that fall under the rubric of "privacy" faces an onerous choice. A common denominator broad enough to encompass nearly everything involving privacy risks being overinclusive or too vague. A narrower common denominator risks being too restrictive.

Because of these difficulties, some theorists, referred to as "reductionists," argue that privacy is reducible to other conceptions and rights. The most prominent proponent of this view is philosopher Judith Thomson, who claims that the right to privacy is "overlapped by other rights." According to Thomson, the "right to privacy . . . is not a distinct cluster of rights but itself intersects with the cluster of rights which the right over the person consists in and also with the cluster of rights which owning property consists in."[124] In a similar vein, H. J. McCloskey claims that "any right to privacy will be a derivative one from other rights and other goods."[125] Likewise, legal scholar Harry Kalven observes that "privacy seems a less precise way of approaching more specific values, as, for example, in the case of freedom of speech, association, and religion."[126]

Reductionists, however, assume without sufficient justification that privacy derives from other, more primary conceptions rather than vice versa.[127] They attempt to carve up the conceptual landscape as colonists divide conquered territory on a map. Although privacy overlaps with other conceptions, it reveals certain dimensions of experience that are not captured in the same way by other conceptions. There is a rich tapestry of discussion around the concept of privacy, and we should be cautious about abandoning it.

Moreover, privacy issues are far too multifarious to be reduced to rights over the person and property. Thomas Scanlon argues that not "much insight into the problems raised by electronic surveillance or by conflicts between considerations of privacy and the requirements of a free press is to be gained by consulting rights of ownership or even rights of the person in the form in which Thomson presents them."[128]

I contend that the problem with the current theories of privacy is the method of conceptualizing. The theories fail on their own terms—they never achieve the goal of finding the common denominator, and thus commentators remain unsatisfied. But perhaps the quest for a common denominator is a search for the holy grail. What if there is no essence or core dimension of privacy? Can privacy be conceptualized?

~ 3

Reconstructing Privacy

In this chapter, I aim to develop a new way to understand privacy. In dealing with a social issue as vital as privacy, which is fraught with a litany of pressing problems, a central purpose of theory is to guide us in crafting legal and policy solutions. As demonstrated in the previous chapter, current attempts to conceptualize privacy have not adequately achieved this purpose. Although many ideas in the philosophical literature of privacy are insightful, the discourse has not led to increased clarity and direction but to more confusion and disarray.

If we persist in the existing discourse, we will continue down a road that leads nowhere. The problem runs deeper than the particular deficiencies of each conception. The problem is the very method most theorists employ when conceptualizing privacy. Using the traditional method—seeking to define privacy's essence or core characteristics—has inhibited the discourse. The current theoretical debate over privacy consists of endless disputes over what falls inside or outside the domain of privacy. Falling within privacy's boundaries is essential for an issue to be addressed because many laws provide protection only if a privacy interest exists. When a conception of privacy is too narrow, it ignores important privacy problems, often resulting in the law's failure to address them. On the other hand, privacy conceptions that are too broad fail to provide much guidance; they are often empty of meaning and have little to contribute to the resolution of concrete problems.

Existing attempts to conceptualize privacy struggle to create a conception that is inclusive, since the term "privacy" is extremely varied in meaning in popular usage and practice. Yet the quest for inclusiveness leads to conceptions that are so vague that they are unhelpful in shaping law and policy. Attempts to conceptualize privacy with the traditional method cannot escape this intractable dilemma.

We need a new approach to conceptualizing privacy. In the remainder of this book, I propose a theory of privacy that understands it in a pluralistic manner from the bottom up, as a set of protections against a related cluster of problems. My theory of privacy aims to conceptualize it in a way that will help us resolve a wide array of privacy problems. It endeavors to look at privacy from a different perspective, ask different questions, and build an understanding of privacy from the ground up that will avoid the continual pitfalls that plague most theories of privacy. My theory of privacy has four principal dimensions: a method, a degree of generality, a structure that accommodates variability, and a focus. In this chapter, I discuss each of these dimensions in depth.

Method. As demonstrated in the previous chapter, countless attempts at conceptualizing privacy have been unable to locate a common denominator to unify all instances of privacy. I propose that we abandon the traditional method of conceptualizing privacy in favor of an alternative method that draws from Ludwig Wittgenstein's idea of family resemblances. Under a family-resemblances approach, privacy is not defined by looking for a common denominator in all things we view under the rubric of privacy. Instead, we should understand privacy in a pluralistic manner. Privacy is not one thing, but a cluster of many distinct yet related things.

Generality. A theory of privacy, like all theories, must exist at some level of generality. The appropriate degree of generality depends upon the purposes the theory aims to serve. My theory of privacy aspires to aid the crafting of law and policy. Many existing theories of privacy are too general to provide much guidance for resolving concrete legal and policy issues. On the surface, they appear to provide answers to the questions of what privacy is and why it is important, but in practice, they are too vague to be of much use. Drawing from pragmatic philosophy, I argue that privacy issues should be worked out contextually rather than in the abstract. If a theory of privacy is too contextual, however, it has limited usefulness because not much can be said about privacy beyond each specific situation. The theory will struggle to guide the resolution of privacy issues in a principled and consistent manner. Therefore, a theory of privacy must establish a balance between generality and particularity. Although my theory of privacy is contextual, it also generalizes to provide a framework for understanding a broad range of privacy problems.

Variability. One of the key issues in developing a theory of privacy is how to deal with the variability of attitudes and beliefs about privacy. Privacy is a product of norms, activities, and legal protections, and as a result, it is culturally and historically contingent. A theory of privacy must therefore work from within history and culture, not from a position outside. This means that a theory should leave room for significant variability in norms and attitudes about privacy. It should be flexible enough to adapt to privacy's dynamic and evolving character. One of the criticisms of embracing such variability, however, is that the theory will become nothing more than a discordant collection of localized practices and cease to tell us much that is useful. I contend that there is indeed a way to develop an understanding of privacy with widespread applicability. Although such an understanding does not stand upon permanent and fixed foundations, it can still have sufficient stability while accommodating variability.

Focus. An approach to conceptualizing privacy must have a focus. Privacy issues are immensely complex and can be viewed from many different angles and perspectives. My theory of privacy focuses on privacy problems. Instead of pondering the nature of privacy in the abstract, we should begin with concrete problems and then use theory as a way to better understand and resolve these problems.

In this chapter, I discuss each of these dimensions in depth. I seek to develop a theory of privacy that is pluralistic and cognizant of context and contingency, but also general and stable enough to be useful in addressing legal and policy issues.

Method

The conceptions of privacy discussed in the previous chapter are deficient because they are based on the traditional method of conceptualizing. Focusing on necessary and sufficient conditions creates a game of inclusion and exclusion and fails to comprehend privacy problems in their various forms. I propose to conceptualize privacy by a different method that draws from Ludwig Wittgenstein's insight about family resemblances.

Wittgensteinian Family Resemblances

Ludwig Wittgenstein was an Austrian philosopher who focused extensively on problems in language and logic. In a posthumous work, *Philosophical Investigations*, written during the later part of his career, Wittgenstein critiques the traditional understanding of language. According to the traditional view, we should endeavor to locate the essence of a word or expression, to strive toward "making our expressions more exact." In contrast, Wittgenstein suggests that meaning is not an objectively true link between a word and the things to which it refers. Rather, the meaning of a word comes from the way a word is used in language, not from any inherent connection between the word and what it signifies.[1]

Wittgenstein demonstrates a way to conceptualize language apart from the traditional method of conceptualizing. Specifically, he explains that language does not have a single essence but involves a horde of different activities that have "no one thing in common," but "are *related* to one another in many different ways." Thus, in examining the concept of language, Wittgenstein suggests that certain concepts might not share one common characteristic; rather, they draw from a common pool of similar characteristics—"a complicated network of similarities overlapping and criss-crossing: sometimes overall similarities, sometimes similarities of detail." In various games, for example, such as "board-games, card-games, ball-games, Olympic games, and so on," there is not "something that is common to *all*, but similarities, relationships, and a whole series of them at that." There are "many correspondences" between board games and card games, "but many common features drop out, and others appear." Wittgenstein uses the term "family resemblances," analogizing to the overlapping and criss-crossing characteristics that exist between members of a family, such as "build, features, colour of eyes, gait, temperament, etc."[2] For example, in a family, each child may have certain features similar to each parent, and the children may share similar features with each other, but they may not all resemble each other in the same way. Nevertheless, they all bear a resemblance to each other.

In contrast, the traditional method of conceptualizing views things as related in the way that spokes are linked by the hub of a wheel, all connected by a common point. This common point, where all spokes converge, defines the way in which the spokes are related to each other. Wittgenstein suggests, however, that sometimes there is no hub, only a web of connected parts that lack a single center point.[3]

One might object that a conception consisting of a web of connected parts without a common denominator is deficient because it has no boundaries and thus is endless. Although Wittgenstein suggests that not all conceptions are "closed by a frontier," this does not mean that conceptions are endless. Rather, it means that not all conceptions have fixed and sharp boundaries that separate them from other conceptions. Boundaries can be fuzzy or can be in a state of constant flux. We can draw immutable boundaries, but we do so for special purposes, not because the boundary is a necessary part of a conception. As Wittgenstein asserts, conceptions can still be useful without having to be circumscribed by rigid boundaries.[4]

The ramification of Wittgenstein's insight is not that all attempts to conceptualize by locating a common denominator are doomed; rather, as he suggests, there are other ways to approach the conceptualization of certain things. Philosopher Judith Genova characterizes Wittgenstein's view: "Once one sees the variety of cases and the family resemblances between them, the attempt to establish an *a priori* generalization is thwarted. There is no one answer, but a variety of answers depending on a variety of factors. The moral is: Look to the circumstances!"[5] Shifting the focus away from finding a common denominator may prove immensely fruitful. The top-down approach of beginning with an overarching conception of privacy designed to apply in all contexts often results in a conception that does not fit well when it is applied to the multitude of situations and problems involving privacy. As philosopher Stanley Cavell observes, Wittgenstein's notion of family resemblances demonstrates that "universals are neither necessary nor even useful in explaining how words and concepts apply to different things." Cavell notes that "a new application of a word or concept will still have to be *made out, explained,* in the particular case, and then the explanations themselves will be sufficient."[6] In contrast to the view of the traditional method, where the quest for a common denominator leads to greater clarity, Wittgenstein shows us that such a quest can sometimes lead to confusion. This explains the problems currently experienced in the privacy discourse.

Wittgenstein's notion of family resemblances frees us from engaging in the debate over necessary and sufficient conditions for privacy, from searching for rigid conceptual boundaries and common denominators. If we no longer look for the essence of privacy, then to understand the "complicated network of similarities overlapping and criss-crossing," we should focus more concretely on the various forms of privacy and recognize their similarities and differences. We should act as cartographers, mapping the terrain of privacy by examining specific problematic situations rather than trying to fit each situation into a rigid predefined category. As Judith Genova explains Wittgenstein's views, "Knowledge is not a matter of guessing meanings, offering explanations, or other kinds of summaries that take law-like form, but of listening to and observing the connections that obtain without interfering."[7]

Adherents of the traditional method of conceptualizing might object that a pluralistic concept is too amorphous and lacks the rigor and specificity needed to resolve privacy issues. For example, legal scholar Richard Bruyer contends, "Unless a common denominator is articulated, combining conceptions simply perpetrates the piecemeal, haphazard approach to privacy that has marked the privacy landscape so far. Nor will it provide a satisfactory answer for the hard privacy cases as they occur."[8] But thus far, the traditional method has failed to provide a satisfactory conception of privacy. Existing conceptions of privacy have proved to be too narrow or broad. Under the traditional method, a theory of privacy faces a difficult trade-off—be narrow and underinclusive or be broad, overinclusive, and vague. A Wittgensteinian family-resemblances method of conceptualizing moves beyond the dilemma. If we no longer must search for one unifying common trait in all privacy violations, we can identify many specific elements of privacy without sacrificing inclusiveness. This approach will assist in the hard cases more than overly restrictive conceptions of privacy that fail to recognize many instances of privacy or overly broad conceptions that are so vague that they offer little guidance.

"Privacy"—An Umbrella Term for a Plurality of Things

One might ask why we should even retain the term "privacy" if it is merely a broader way to describe a group of different types of things. Why not simply refer to the particular things themselves and jettison the term "privacy" altogether? For example, legal theorist Raymond Wacks argues that the concept of privacy is too "large and unwieldy" to be of much use:

> In this attenuated, confused and overworked condition, "privacy" seems beyond redemption. . . . "Privacy" has become as nebulous a concept as "happiness" or "security." Except as a general abstraction of an underlying value, it should not be used as a means to describe a legal right or cause of action.[9]

Wacks correctly observes that we need a more precise way to describe privacy rights and legal protections than with the vague label "privacy." But although various privacy issues are different from one another and do not have a core characteristic in common, they still share many important similarities. The word "privacy" remains useful as shorthand, a way to talk collectively about a web of interconnected yet distinct things.

In contrast to attempts to develop a unified conception of privacy, I contend that privacy should be conceived in a more pluralistic way. "Privacy" is an umbrella term that refers to a wide and disparate group of related things. The use of such a broad term is helpful in some contexts, but quite unhelpful in others. Consider, for example, the term "animal." "Animal" refers to a large group of organisms—mammals, birds, reptiles, fish, and others—and within each of these groups are subgroups. For some purposes, using the term "animal" will suffice. Suppose Sue asks Bob, "How many animals are in the zoo?" Bob does not need to know anything more specific in order to answer this question. The use of the term "animal" in this sentence will be perfectly clear in most contexts. Now suppose Sue wants Bob to bring her a dog. She will not get very far by saying, "Bring me an animal." Rather, she will specify the kind of animal she wants. Even saying "dog" probably will not be adequate, since Sue probably wants a specific kind of dog. As with the term "animal," there are many times when using the general term "privacy" will work well, but there are times when more specificity is required. Using the general term "privacy" can result in the conflation of different kinds of problems and can lead to understandings of the meaning of "privacy" that distract courts and policymakers from addressing the issues before them.

Nevertheless, it is no accident that various things are referred to under the rubric of "privacy." They bear substantial similarities to each other. The analogies between different things can be useful and instructive, for we might seek to create similar laws and policies to regulate them. We should classify something as involving "privacy" when it bears resemblance to other things we classify in the same way. This is a form of analogical reasoning. "The key task for analogical reasoners," law professor Cass Sunstein observes, "is to decide when there are relevant similarities and differences."[10] Similarity, however, is not sameness, and we must also recognize where the many related things we call "privacy" diverge.

Generality

When we define privacy, we must do so at a certain level of generality. Framing a concept with a degree of generality allows it to transcend the particularities of specific contexts and thus gives it wide-ranging applicability. Many of the conceptions discussed in the previous chapter are framed at a very general level, such as control over information, limited access, and the right to be let alone. Their generality, however, often makes them so broad and vague that they frequently do not help us in identifying and addressing specific privacy issues.

The philosophy of pragmatism provides fruitful guidance about how to conceptualize in a more contextual way. Pragmatism was originally developed by Charles Sanders Peirce, William James, John Dewey, Josiah Royce, George Herbert Mead, and others.[11] A number of prominent contemporary scholars identify themselves as pragmatists, such as Richard Rorty, Richard Posner, and Cornell West.[12] Although many pragmatists share certain ideas and assumptions, they also have profound differences—sometimes more differences than similarities. The pragmatic ideas I draw from are generally those of the classical pragmatists, and they are ones that most classical pragmatists held in common. Primarily, I look to John Dewey and William James.

Pragmatism resists universals and embraces specific situations. According to William James, the pragmatist "turns away from abstraction and insufficiency, from verbal solutions, from bad *a priori* reasons, from fixed principles, closed systems, and pretended absolutes and origins. He turns towards concreteness and adequacy, towards facts, towards action and towards power." As James observed, one of the more common ideas of pragmatism is a focus away from the notion of a priori knowledge—the view that there are objective and universal truths that exist prior to, and independently of, experience.[13] According to the pragmatists, knowledge originates through experience.

Because it eschews broad abstractions and embraces a more pluralistic context-specific way of understanding concepts, pragmatism has many affinities with Wittgenstein's notion of family resemblances.[14] Therefore, the task of conceptualizing privacy should not begin by seeking to illuminate an abstract conception of privacy, but should focus instead on understanding privacy in specific contextual situations. "[W]e never experience nor form judgments about objects and events in isolation," observes Dewey, "but only in connection with a contextual whole."[15] Knowledge without its context loses much of its meaning, and we cannot ignore the "contextual situation in which thinking occurs."[16]

I join several theorists of privacy who recognize the importance of context in understanding privacy. Law professor Robert Post astutely points out that we cannot determine whether information is private "simply by examining the content of the information; we must instead have some notion of the circumstances surrounding the revelation of that information." It may be "deeply inappropriate" for information to be revealed in a particular manner and time and to a particular audience.[17] Theorist Serge Gutwirth observes, "Privacy . . . is defined by its context and only obtains its true meaning within social relationships."[18] Sociologist Gary Marx notes that public and private are "fluid and situational or contextual [conceptions], whose meaning lies in how they are interpreted and framed."[19] Likewise, information-law scholar Helen Nissenbaum develops a theory of "privacy as contextual integrity." According to Nissenbaum, privacy should be understood in terms of "contextual norms" that regulate information, in particular, "norms of appropriateness, and norms of flow or distribution." "Contextual integrity," she argues, "is maintained when both types of norms are upheld, and it is violated when either of the norms is violated." "According to the theory of contextual integrity," Nissenbaum contends, "it is crucial to know the context—who is gathering the information, who is analyzing it, who is disseminating it and to whom, the nature of the information, the relationships among the various parties, and even larger institutional and social circumstances."[20]

In any given case, we need to resolve privacy issues by looking to the specific context. How we value privacy and the countervailing interests depends upon the circumstances of each situation. For example, not all disclosures of information are the same. We must focus on the relationships in which information is transferred and the uses to which information is put. Relationships differ in their level of intimacy, expectations of confidentiality, and power dynamics. Certain relationships have strong expectations of confidentiality, while others have weaker ones. For instance, what people reveal to employers differs from what they tell doctors, lawyers, religious leaders, and family members. Even within families, people may reveal different things to spouses, children, and parents. Certain relationships involve ethical obligations to maintain the confidentiality of information, and the parties generally know these obligations. By contrast, a person's obligations to maintain a friend's secrets are less clearly defined, even though many people would condemn disclosure. Other relationships do not involve any normative expectations of nondisclosure. Few would contend that when a crime victim tells the police about the perpetrator, it violates the criminal's privacy.

As legal scholar Anita Allen observes, people are accountable to others even in their private lives—rarely do people's actions "concern only themselves." This fact, however, does not mean that one is accountable to everyone: "Accountability demands concerning private life may come from one's government, one's political community, one's employer, one's family, and even one's ethnic, racial, or religious group. Thus, sometimes people are held accountable, or feel accountable, because of who and what they are."[21] In other words, people are accountable for aspects of their private lives within certain *relationships*, but rarely across the board.

Looking at the context is necessary to weigh contrasting values, but a theory of privacy must do more than appeal to context to guide the analysis. Viewing privacy more contextually alone often fails to provide sufficient direction for making policymaking or legal decisions, which depend upon making generalizations. To have a useful theory of privacy, we must generalize. Too general a theory, however, will prove vague, simplistic, and reductive. Therefore, we must navigate the tension between generality and particularity, between abstraction and concreteness. To do this, we need a general framework to identify privacy harms or problems and to understand why they are problematic. Such a framework is essential if we are to make progress in understanding privacy.

Understanding the nature of a problem, what is at stake, and what important values are in conflict is necessary to guide the crafting of a solution. According to Dewey, defining a problem involves careful observation along with an attempt to conceptualize by making generalizations. Merely collecting facts will "lead nowhere." "On the other hand," observes Dewey, "it is possible to have the work of observation so controlled by a conceptual framework fixed in advance that the very things which are genuinely decisive in the problem in hand and its solution are completely overlooked. Everything is forced into the predetermined conceptual and theoretical scheme."[22]

Although Dewey emphasizes that we must be careful not to allow conceptual frameworks to impede our ability to assess concrete situations, he recognizes the importance of conceptualizing and formulating generalizations based on experience. For Dewey, the only way to "control and enrich concrete experience" is by making generalizations.[23] As William James put it, "The pragmatist clings to facts and concreteness, observes truth at its work in particular cases, and generalizes."[24] According to Dewey, the best way to avoid the problem of observation without direction, on the one hand, and observation overly distorted by one's theoretical framework, on the other hand, is to maintain "sensitivity to the quality of the situation as a whole."[25] Thus the pragmatist has a unique attitude toward theories. Theories are "working hypotheses," not fixed entities, and must be created from within concrete situations and constantly tested and shaped through an interaction with concrete situations.[26]

Therefore, I aim to conceptualize privacy from the bottom up and also to generalize by developing a framework for understanding and recognizing privacy interests. The framework need not be rigid and controlling; it can be flexible and open ended, much like Wittgenstein's notion of family resemblances.

Variability

Without an a priori conception of privacy, we must determine what is private at least in part by looking at social practices. Privacy is dependent on society and culture, and thus it is contingent. "The realm of the practical is the region of change," John Dewey observed, "and change is always contingent." Dewey also noted, "Experience cannot deliver to us necessary truths; truths completely demonstrated by reason. Its conclusions are particular, not universal."[27] We need not demand that a theory of privacy be impervious to history or culture. A theory can still be useful without being the immutable final answer. It might not work as effectively hundreds of years in the future, nor might it work in every society. But still it can help us advance in addressing problems, it can remain useful over a long period of time, and it can be applicable in many cultures.

The matters we consider private change over time. Although some form of dichotomy between public and private has been maintained throughout the history of Western civilization,[28] the matters that have been considered public and private have evolved because of changing attitudes, institutions, living conditions, and technology. The matters we consider private are shaped by culture and time and have differed across societies and epochs.

To say simply that something is private is to make a rather general claim; what it means for something to be private is the central question. Particular matters have long remained private, though in different ways. We consider our Social Security number, our sexual behavior, our diary, and our home private, but we do not consider them private in the same way.

A number of aspects of life have commonly been viewed as private: family, body, sex, home, and communications, to name a few. There appears to be broad consensus about the importance of protecting the privacy of these matters. For example, the right to privacy in the United Nations Universal Declaration of Human Rights of 1948 specifically mentions the family, home, and communications.[29]

Yet to say simply that these things are private is imprecise because what it means for them to be private is different today than it was in the past and different in each subject matter. I will sketch a brief genealogy of the privacy of the family, body, sex, home, and communications.

Examining the distinct, interconnected, and changing ways in which each of these matters has been private reveals several important insights for the understanding of privacy more generally.

Family

The family, viewed as the heart of the private sphere, was not always a sanctuary for privacy. Today, we often view the family as an institution of intimacy, where a nuclear family lives together in the home and has (or strives toward) a loving relationship. We consider the family as generally enhancing individual self-realization.

For much of Western history (and still today in some cultures), however, entry into marriage was not an individual autonomous choice based on selfhood-enhancing criteria. For many, marriages did not occur out of love or free choice, but were primarily controlled by parents and governed by economic and strategic concerns.[30] Marriage was not an institution to develop the self through an intimate relationship with one's family, but a set of social responsibilities and impediments to individual self-realization. In the world of the family, the individual was not free but regulated by different forms of authority, particularly for women, for whom marriage was often a life of submission.[31] Indeed, the family was viewed as the locus of social control, a miniature monarchy ruled by the patriarch.[32] For the expanding bourgeoisie, family life was inextricably linked to professional life. The family was a business asset used in public commerce, a network of connections and interdependent reputations built upon conformity to social norms.[33] The family existed for "sociability rather than privacy."[34]

Of course, many families were not devoid of love, many marriages were initiated through individual choice, and many women were not completely subservient to the men in the household. My point is that in earlier times, certain attitudes and practices regarding the nature of the family were more prevalent and widely accepted than they are today.

Beginning in the nineteenth century, the family increasingly developed into an institution that promoted the private lives of its members, transforming from an economic enterprise to an association of intimacy and self-fulfillment.[35] Work and home began to be physically separated, creating a public professional world of business and a more private intimate world of the family. The growth of individualism—the "concept of the self as unique, and free to pursue his or her own goals; and a related decline in the idea that the overriding obligation was to the kin, the society, or the state"—led to a rebellion against arranged marriages, transforming marriage into a venture based on personal choice.[36] Gradually, the family began to evolve into a "private entity focused into itself."[37]

Still, for women, the family was for a long time not associated with self-development. According to Anita Allen, throughout much of history, "[m]arriage has been described as a woman's greatest obstacle to privacy."[38] Reva Siegel explains that a "wife was obliged to obey and serve her husband, and the husband was subject to a reciprocal duty to support his wife and represent her within the legal system." Husbands could also physically punish their wives (known as "chastisement") so long as no permanent injury was inflicted. Chastisement was justified by courts not wanting to interfere with marital privacy.[39] As one court explained, although wife beating would typically be classified as an assault, doing so would "throw open the bedroom to the gaze of the public; and spread discord and misery, contention and strife, where peace and concord ought to reign."[40] Thus, "privacy" of the family consisted of an association of noninterference of the state in domestic affairs that served, as Siegel explains, "to enforce and preserve authority relations between man and wife."[41] This association has led a number of feminist scholars to attack privacy in the domestic context.[42]

That privacy of the family once meant noninterference of the state in domestic affairs does not mean that this is inherently what privacy of the family means. In contemporary American society, we accept greater government intervention in spousal relationships, as well as in child rearing. To argue that there is less privacy of the family today because of this development is too broad a claim. To the extent that family privacy consists of attributes such as independence, freedom of thought, freedom from coercion, self-development, and pursuing activities of personal interest, government intervention actually can enhance privacy.

Body

The evolution of attitudes toward the body is also instructive. For quite some time, theorists have viewed the body as being at the core of privacy.[43] The U.S. Supreme Court declared, "No right is held more sacred, or is more carefully guarded by the common law, than the right of every individual to the possession and control of his own person."[44] Another court declared: "One's naked body is a very private part of one's person and generally known to others only by choice."[45]

The claim that the body is "private" is really a claim about certain practices regarding the body, such as concealment of certain bodily parts, secrecy about specific diseases and physical conditions, norms of touching and interpersonal contact, and individual control and dominion over decisions regarding one's body. As legal scholar Radhika Rao explains, the constitutional right to privacy is often characterized by self-ownership of the body, the notion that a person belongs to herself.[46] These attributes were certainly not always associated with the body. Although we currently associate the body with concealment (we hide our bodies under layers of clothes), the naked body was far from private in ancient Greece and Rome.[47] Sociologist Richard Sennett observes that in ancient Athens, the public display of the naked body "marked the presence of a strong rather than vulnerable person—and more, someone who was civilized." Public nudity "affirmed one's dignity as a citizen."[48] At the gymnasium in ancient Greece, people exercised in the nude. In ancient Rome, men and women bathed naked together.[49] In the Middle Ages, it was also not uncommon for people to bathe in front of others, and bathing was often part of celebrations and social congregation.[50]

Norms of interpersonal contact and nudity gradually shifted toward today's norms of greater concealment and distancing from others. Christian beliefs about the body contrasted sharply with those of the ancient Greeks and Romans. To the Greeks and Romans, the body was an object of pride and beauty, something to be put on display. To the Christians, it was dirty and shameful, something to be hidden.[51] In the Renaissance, among the wealthy (and spreading to the middle class), people tried to distance themselves from their body and others' bodies: "[M]en and women became more secretive and modest about bodily functions; they ceased to share beds with strangers at home, at school, or in inns. They ceased to eat and drink out of communal dishes and cups, which might contain traces of saliva of others."[52] After the sixteenth century, people became quite guarded about their bodies and reserved about touching others.[53] This new modesty was so extreme at times that it even made it difficult for doctors to be at the bedside of women in labor.[54]

Another contemporary aspect of privacy of the body is the conceal-ment of certain bodily functions, such as urination, defecation, and copulation. In the seventeenth century, however, it was not anomalous for people to chat with friends while sitting above a chamber pot.[55] Be-fore the late nineteenth century, poor families (close to half the popu-lation of England) lived in one room and had to urinate, defecate, and copulate in view of others.[56] This practice varied depending upon the wealth of families and where they lived. Families in urban areas often did not have a privy in the rear of their homes. Historian Lawrence Stone observes, "Up to the end of the eighteenth century, close-stools and chamber pots had been scattered randomly about the house in the public rooms, a system which afforded little or no privacy."[57] Private houses rarely had bathrooms, and people would excrete waste in the corner and dump it into the street.[58]

We also currently associate the body with individual control and do-minion, and many agree with John Stuart Mill's observation that the individual is "sovereign" over his body.[59] For a long time, however, people viewed their body (in particular, their blood) as belonging in part to the family and their ancestors. As attitudes toward the family changed and new conceptions of individual identity developed, people began to view the body as their own possession.[60]

Sex

Sexual activity has long been considered private. In the United States, for example, the Restatement of Torts declares, "Sexual relations . . . are normally entirely private matters."[61] The European Court of Human Rights has held that "sexual orientation and sexual life are important elements of the personal sphere."[62] But even in this general notion of sex as private, there are several different meanings of "private." First is the ability of people to have sex in seclusion. Second, sex can be private in the sense that information about people's sexual activity is viewed as their personal business and not something spoken about in the com-munity. A third meaning of sex as being private is that it should remain free from regulation by the community and the law. As with privacy of the family and the body, these different dimensions of privacy regarding sex varied throughout history.

With regard to the seclusion of sexual activities, in countless societies, people have sought to conceal sexual activity. For example, in ancient Greece, "[p]rivacy was the norm governing both marital and extramarital intercourse, including homosexual affairs." In ancient China, "the sexual act was sacred like other ritual practices such as prayers and worship of the ancestors. Therefore one should not engage in it or talk about it before strangers."[63]

But for much of history, concealing sex was difficult to achieve. In medieval Europe, for example, couples faced numerous obstacles to copulating in private. Many families lacked a separate bedroom, and beds used to be part of the living room.[64] In urban areas, because houses were packed together, people had little privacy from inquisitive neighbors.[65] Having sex in seclusion was also quite difficult in colonial America. Because houses were tiny, and family members generally slept in the same room, a couple's sexual activities would often be overheard by their children.[66] In many instances, couples would share the same bed with children and guests.[67]

Today, modern architecture and the lessening of crowded living conditions in many societies enable people to have sex in seclusion. The fact that for much of history, people found it difficult to have sex in seclusion does not mean that they did not desire to do so. Philosopher Thomas Nagel points out, "Humans are the only animals that don't as a rule copulate in public."[68] Anthropologist Barrington Moore notes, "[S]ome quite good evidence exists that does demonstrate quite clearly a widespread desire for seclusion during sexual intercourse."[69]

Another sense in which sex can be private is the extent to which it is viewed as a personal versus a public matter. In medieval England, sexual transgression was seen as the community's business. People would frequently launch public accusations about others engaging in forbidden sex. When individuals were caught in sexual iniquity, the church courts demanded a public confession.[70] These practices carried over to colonial America, where nosy neighbors would freely scold others for illicit sex.[71] Ministers urged people to watch over their fellow citizens and admonish them when they lapsed into sin.[72] The punishment for sexual transgressions involved public confession.[73] Legal punishments, such as the wearing of letters (as depicted in Nathaniel Hawthorne's *The Scarlet Letter*), public whipping, or other forms of public humiliation, openly revealed the person as a trans-gressor.[74]

In eighteenth-century America, the publicizing of sexual transgres-sions waned. Urbanization made sexual surveillance more difficult. In the late eighteenth century, Philadelphia teemed with brothels, and people could "enjoy remarkably uninhibited sex."[75] The shift away from close-knit communities resulted in much less community in-volvement in people's sexual affairs.

A third sense in which sex can be private is the extent to which it is controlled by law. Sex has often been highly regulated by many soci-eties.[76] In colonial New England, nearly every form of nontraditional and extramarital sex was considered a transgression, such as masturba-tion, fornication, sodomy, and adultery. Adultery and sodomy were punished by death.[77] An orgy of sex cases populated seventeenth-century New England court records.[78]

In eighteenth-century America, and continuing into the nineteenth century, the law became less obsessed with sexual dereliction.[79] In-creasingly, adultery was no longer castigated by the community; as long as adulterous couples "expressed their love in coded, private let-ters, and behind locked doors, they could maintain a public façade of respectability."[80] Although adultery used to be policed by the commu-nity, it became a private affair in at least two ways. First, it was easier for people to commit adultery outside the watchful gaze of neighbors and others in the community. Second, society and the state became less obsessed with punishing adultery. Adultery became a private matter in the sense that the community no longer considered regulating adul-terous sex as its business. At the same time, sex became more public in the sense that nonmarital sex was carried out in the brothels, an open symbol of the sexual activity.[81]

This publicity of sexual practices created a backlash. In the late nine-teenth century, Victorian-age norms tightened on sexuality, and the antivice crusader Anthony Comstock led a charge to pass laws regu-lating sexual conduct and contraception in the United States. Open prostitution was gradually eliminated, and the red-light districts went dim by the first two decades of the twentieth century.[82] In what legal historian Lawrence Friedman calls the "Victorian compromise," disfa-vored sex was not prohibited, but was driven underground. Although the law still outlawed adultery during the late nineteenth century, "what was outlawed now was not simple adultery, but 'open and noto-rious' adultery."[83] As professors John D'Emilio and Estelle Freedman observe, "[S]exuality had to be restored to the private sphere; there-fore, any public expression of sexuality was considered, by definition, obscene."[84]

The Victorian reticence did not last long. In the early twentieth cen-tury, social reformers lambasted Victorian morality as prudish and suc-ceeded in reshaping attitudes about sex toward greater openness. Sig-mund Freud, for example, demonstrated an "unblinking candor about sex."[85] Throughout the twentieth century, regulation of sex diminished considerably.[86] In America, by the late 1960s, most of the legal hin-drances to contraception had vanished.[87] The Supreme Court issued a series of decisions that held that the Constitution protected a "right to privacy" preventing the state from becoming involved in people's inti-mate affairs. For example, in 1965, in *Griswold v. Connecticut*, the Supreme Court proclaimed that government invasion into "the precincts of marital bedrooms" is "repulsive to the notions of privacy surrounding the marriage relationship."[88] Although sodomy was a crime in every state in the United States in 1960, by the twilight of the twentieth century, antisodomy laws had been eliminated in many states.[89] In 2003, the Supreme Court held that laws prohibiting homo-sexual sodomy were an unconstitutional infringement of "the personal and private life."[90] "In the contemporary Western world," Friedman observes, "there is an extraordinary amount of sexual freedom. Almost all forms of sexual behavior between consenting adults are legal, in-cluding same-sex behavior. The laws against adultery and fornication have either disappeared or are moribund."[91] Nevertheless, certain forms of sex still remain outlawed in nearly every society, such as incest and bestiality. Simon Goldhill notes, "All societies find some form of sexual activity unacceptable or disgusting."[92]

The story of the privacy of sex illustrates that "privacy" means sev-eral different things. Privacy in each sense—seclusion, freedom from community meddling, and freedom from state regulation—has gener-ally increased in Western societies. Moreover, it is not happenstance that these forms of privacy increased together. Although they are dis-tinct, these forms of privacy are related. When sex between consenting adults was seen as the community's business, it is not surprising that the state heavily regulated sexual activity. The increased ability to have sex free from the watchful gaze of others is deeply connected to the extent to which society involves itself in matters of sex. Privacy thus includes many distinct but intertwined dimensions.

Home

The home has often been viewed as the quintessential place of privacy. Countless constitutions around the world safeguard privacy of the home; for example, Argentina proclaims that the "home is inviolable," Finland guarantees the "sanctity of the home," Greece declares that "[e]very person's home is a sanctuary," and South Korea declares that "[a]ll citizens are free from intrusion into their place of residence."[93]

For a long time, the home has been regarded as one's "castle," where the individual enjoyed freedom from government intrusion.[94] The "immunity" of the home originates in "ancient times, biblical literature, and Roman law."[95] Barrington Moore observes, "According to what appears to be an ancient tradition, the citizen's home was inviolable. . . . Thus the tradition that a man's home is his castle harks back not to English tradition but to classical Athens."[96] In England, the maxim that the home is one's castle found its way into law when it appeared in 1604 in *Semayne's Case:* "[T]he house of every one is to him as his castle and fortress."[97] William Pitt once remarked, "The poorest man may in his cottage bid defiance to the Crown. It may be frail—its roof may shake—the wind may enter—the rain may enter—but the King of England cannot enter—all his force dares not cross the threshold of the ruined tenement!"[98]

In 1886, in *Boyd v. United States,* the U.S. Supreme Court vigorously protected "the sanctity of a man's home."[99] The Court's preservation of the home has not wavered, and almost a century later, the Court reiterated its staunch protection of the home: "In none is the zone of privacy more clearly defined than when bounded by the unambiguous physical dimensions of an individual's home."[100] Privacy in people's houses is safeguarded by the Third Amendment's prohibition of the quartering of troops in homes during peacetime and the Fourth Amendment's prohibition of unreasonable searches and seizures.[101] The Court declared, "The Fourth Amendment, and the personal rights which it secures, have a long history. At the very core stands the

right of a man to retreat into his own home and there be free from unreasonable governmental intrusion."[102]

Beyond being a haven from the government, the home is currently
understood as a place where individuals retreat to find peace of mind,
cultivate intimate relationships, and engage in personal activities of
self-development. According to Justice Douglas, "The home of course
is the essence of privacy, in no way dedicated to public use, in no way
extending an invitation to the public."[103] Legal scholar Michelle Adams
aptly describes the contemporary view of the home in Western societies as "a place of retreat to the (not always) protective sphere of
family life, and it is reflective of, and a conduit for, familial and emotional intimacy."[104]

Although the home has long been viewed as a private space, in the
past it was private in a different way than it is now. For much of history,
many did not view the home as "the family's haven and domestic retreat." In Western societies, this concept became more widely held in
the nineteenth century and was at first limited to the urban middle
classes. Prior to this time, many people unrelated to the family would
be present in the home, such as apprentices, servants, and lodgers.
Tamara Hareven explains, "[B]y contrast to the conception of the
home in contemporary society as a private retreat from the outside
world, to preindustrial society the family conducted its work and public
affairs *inside* the household." This, of course, is a generalization about
the practices of particular families, mainly the families of shopkeepers
in urban centers. For these families, business was conducted in the
house, and the house was a crowded, bustling place with little opportunity for the family to retreat into isolation.[105]

Until the seventeenth century, many homes merely consisted of a
large, multipurpose space.[106] Among the rising bourgeoisie, homes
were primarily devoted to work—a shop, with a place in the back or
above to eat and sleep.[107] Houses were hectic, crowded places, often
crammed with one or more large families.[108] Dwelling places were
noisy; they were built of creaky wood with cracks and peepholes and
were equipped with no soundproofing to stop noise from echoing
throughout the home. One historian observes about living quarters in
Renaissance Europe: "An apartment building was a public theater.
Some held forth, others squabbled, but no one had any privacy. Marital
disputes, illicit love affairs, noisy tenants, restless children—nothing

could be concealed and everything could be heard."[109] In colonial New England, most houses were built entirely of wood. Spying on others was easy, and sound carried readily throughout the house. Moreover, people rarely locked their doors, and visitors simply entered without knocking.[110]

Throughout much of Western history, beds were large, scarce, and crammed with many people.[111] For example, Michelangelo sometimes slept in the same bed with several of his workmen.[112] In colonial New England, not only did a couple sleep with their children, but even guests shared the bed. Even among the Puritans of colonial New England, a couple thought nothing of sleeping in the same bed with another adult. Before the development of specialized rooms, beds were placed in public areas, and "family members slept behind curtains while social activities including outsiders were going on in other parts of the same room."[113]

In the seventeenth century, homes began to be partitioned into rooms, each assigned a distinct purpose and some even becoming personalized according to their occupants.[114] Historian Lewis Mumford notes, "The first radical change, which was to alter the form of the medieval house, was the development of a sense of privacy. This meant, in effect, withdrawal at will from the common life and the common interests of one's fellows."[115] As specialized rooms became more prevalent, "bedrooms were no longer mixed up with public rooms, and began to be concentrated upstairs."[116] Even with rooms, solitude was often disrupted because there were no corridors, and people shuffled through rooms to move about the house.[117]

Although solitude within the home developed first among the wealthy,[118] there were special impediments to making the home a place of solitude even among the affluent. According to Lawrence Stone, the wealthy owners of stately homes in England were "torn between the conflicting needs of their private selves and their public personae" because they wanted to maintain their houses to display their riches and status but also wanted privacy. The houses of the wealthy were continually on show. Further, servants, prone to gossip and even blackmail, prevented solitude in the home. Even in the eighteenth century, very wealthy families were unable to function without servants "even to the point of being unable to dress or undress without assistance."[119] Servants often slept in a bed in the same room as their masters. Eventually, innovations such as plumbing, central heating, and gas and electric lighting limited the need for servants to be ever-present.[120]

The expansion of living space also contributed to the growing association of solitude with the home. Among larger homes in the eighteenth century, hallways emerged, permitting an unprecedented ability to be alone and undisturbed.[121] Privacy began to be possible within certain special rooms. The study, for example, was a place where the master of the house could withdraw for quiet reading or for confidential conversations.[122] It was a private place for men only; women had no comparable private room of their own.[123] The study became so private that it was used to store the master's secret letters of extramarital affairs.[124]

When employment shifted from agriculture to factories and offices in the late nineteenth century, the homes of many began to be physically separated from the place of work.[125] One's professional life began to be viewed as a realm of existence separate from one's life at home.[126] The gradual severing of work from home helped alter the nature of the domestic life. Hareven notes, "Following the removal of the workplace from the home as a result of urbanization and industrialization, the household was recast as the family's private retreat, and home emerged as a new concept and existence."[127]

Communications

The privacy of communications—in a variety of forms—has long been protected in many societies. Numerous constitutions from around the world protect the privacy of communications. For example, Mexico provides that "[p]rivate communications are inviolable," Chile protects "the inviolability . . . of all forms of private communications," Germany ensures that the "[p]rivacy of letters, posts, and telecommunications shall be inviolable," Belgium guarantees that the "confidentiality of letters is inviolable," and the Czech Republic protects the "secrecy of letters," as well as "messages communicated by telephone, telegraph or other such facilities."[128]

The history of communications privacy indicates that it was more the product of social desires than existing realities. In other words, communications privacy was not a natural state the law preserved, but a form of protection the law created. For example, in America, the privacy of letters was formed in significant part by a legal architecture that protected the confidentiality of letters from other people and government officials. In colonial America, mail was often insecure; it was difficult to seal letters; and the wax often used to keep letters sealed was not very effective.[129] Before the post office was established, mail was deposited in taverns for travelers to deliver. Privacy of letters was precarious, but protected to some degree by the fact that many people were illiterate.[130]

The privacy of letters improved somewhat after the English Post Office Act of 1710 created the American colonial postal system. Many people, however, doubted that the colonial postal service would respect their privacy, and there was widespread suspicion that postal clerks read letters. A number of prominent individuals, such as Thomas Jefferson, Alexander Hamilton, and George Washington, decried the lack of privacy in their correspondence and sometimes even wrote in code.[131] Washington expressed concern that "by passing [letters] through the post-office, they should become known to all the world."[132] Jefferson complained in 1789, "The infidelities of the post office and the circumstances of the times are against my writing fully and freely."[133] Since letters could fall into the wrong hands and be gazed upon by the wrong eyes, people were guarded about revealing private information.[134]

Despite these realities and people's expectation that letters would not be confidential, the law evolved to provide strong protection of the privacy of letters. Early on, the 1710 English Post Office Act declared, "No Person or Persons shall presume wittingly, willingly, or knowingly, to open, detain, or delay, or cause, procure, permit, or suffer to be opened, detained, or delayed, any Letter or Letters, Packet or Packets." To address persisting privacy concerns, Benjamin Franklin, who served as the colonial postmaster general from 1753 until the Revolution, required his employees to swear an oath not to open mail.[135] In the late eighteenth and early nineteenth centuries, the U.S. Congress passed several laws prohibiting the improper opening of mail.[136] The U.S. Supreme Court held in 1877 that despite the fact that people turned letters over to the government for delivery in the postal system, sealed parcels were protected from inspection by the Fourth Amendment.[137]

The extensive protection of the privacy of letters stemmed from a public desire to treat them as "sacred." According to historian David

Seipp, "Nineteenth century public opinion regarded the 'sanctity of the mails' as absolute in the same way it esteemed the inviolability of the home."[138] One court declared in 1811 that the law must respect "the sacredness of a man's correspondence."[139] Many state laws protected against "the violation of epistolary correspondence."[140] According to Joseph Story, one of the most famous American jurists of the nineteenth century, the unwarranted disclosure of personal letters "is perhaps one of the most odious breaches of private confidence, of social duty, and of honorable feelings, which can well be imagined." For Story, letters contained "inviolable secrets" that were "reposed in the bosoms of others under the deepest and most affecting confidence." He noted that the law would prevent the publication of letters that "would be a violation of a trust or confidence."[141]

The story of the privacy of telegraph communications resembles that of letters. After the telegraph was invented in 1844, concerns about the privacy of telegraph communications soon arose. Western Union demanded that its employees keep all messages "strictly private and confidential."[142] Western Union's own rules were buttressed by laws in almost every state in America that restricted telegraph employees from improperly disclosing telegrams.[143] When Congress began seeking telegraph messages for investigations, a public outcry ensued. The *New York Times* proclaimed the practice "an outrage upon the liberties of the citizen which no plea of public necessity can justify" and asserted that "every person using the telegraph to communicate about his private affairs assumes that a telegram is as free from exposure as a letter."[144] Other newspapers chimed in with similar sentiments. A bill to protect the privacy of telegraph communications was proposed and ultimately rejected in Congress, which instead resolved to refrain from inquiring into telegraph communications except in compelling circumstances.[145] States further protected telegraph messages by prohibiting their interception. California, for example, outlawed intercepting telegraph communications as early as 1862.[146]

As with the telegraph, privacy concerns emerged shortly after the invention of the telephone in 1876. In the telephone's early days, calls were far from private. Until the middle of the twentieth century, many people used party lines—shared telephone service with several other households. Eavesdropping was a constant worry. In chronicling the history of the telephone, sociologist Claude Fischer notes, "From the beginning of telephony, people expressed concern that they were being overheard, at first simply by others in the same room—one had to speak loudly—and then by operators or fellow subscribers on a party line."[147]

These realities, however, did not lead to less privacy on the telephone. Instead, in America and elsewhere, laws protecting the privacy of telephone communications were passed. In particular, the practice of wiretapping stirred strong condemnation and a potent legal response. Soon after telephone wiretapping began in the 1890s, several states prohibited it, such as California in 1905.[148] In the first few decades of the twentieth century, over half the states had made wiretapping a crime.[149] In 1928, however, the Supreme Court held in *Olmstead v. United States* that the Fourth Amendment did not protect against wiretapping.[150] The Court's decision in this widely known case, nicknamed "the case of the whispering wires," received considerable public criticism.[151] In dissent, Justice Oliver Wendell Holmes went so far as to refer to wiretapping as a "dirty business."[152] A year later, bills were introduced in Congress to protect against wiretapping, and in 1934, Congress passed a law making wiretapping a federal crime.[153] In 1967, the Supreme Court changed its position on wiretapping, overruling *Olmstead* in *Katz v. United States*.[154] One year later, Congress passed Title III of the Omnibus Crime Control and Safe Streets Act of 1968, which required law-enforcement officials to obtain a special warrant before wiretapping and criminalized wiretaps by private parties.[155] Due to these developments, U.S. law strongly protects against wiretapping telephone communications. Today, countless countries around the world restrict wiretapping in their constitutions and laws.[156] Thus the law responded to the uncertain degree of privacy in telephone communications by imposing robust wiretapping regulations.

In discussing privacy of a particular matter, it is important to distinguish between its current status and society's aspirations. For a long time, communications were quite insecure, and their status could hardly be labeled "private." The social desire, however, was for communications to be private even when they were not. We make things private with the tools of law and technology. Communications became private because people wanted them to be private. Therefore, to assess whether a particular practice is private, we must look not only to the past and present, but also to our future aspirations. Privacy is a condition we create, and as such, it is dynamic and changing.

Privacy in a Dynamic World

The preceding discussion illustrates that technological and social change alters the extent to which privacy is a dimension of certain activities, as well as what we mean when we speak about certain activities as involving privacy. The history I related is told at a high level of generality; when historical practices regarding the family, body, sex, home, and communications are examined in more detail, there is a wide variation among such practices based on such factors as urbanization, class and social status, and ethnic and religious subgroups. Nonetheless, these brief historical sketches demonstrate that certain attitudes and practices are not universal, but are shaped by the realities of particular historical periods. The shrinking of the size of the family, the emergence of new social places, transformations in the nature of the family, the changing architecture of the home, new attitudes toward the body, increasing wealth and space, the separation of home from work, decreased crowding, and numerous other changes in the quality and nature of life had profound effects on the perception of what the private life entailed. What it currently means to call something "private" differs from what was meant in other times.

To be clear, although what is public and what is private are shaped by culture and history, I am not claiming that the privacy of the family, body, sex, home, and communications is entirely historical accident. They are private in part because people wanted them to be private. Moreover, certain desires for privacy may be rooted in our biological nature. In his analysis of privacy in primitive cultures, anthropologist Barrington Moore observed a general preference for seclusion during sexual intercourse (although this did not always occur in practice). Moore notes, "For defecation, urination, and sexual intercourse human beings tend to draw social boundary lines in a different way from that used for eating and drinking."[157] "The fact that human beings can control certain impulses does not mean they lack these impulses," Moore observes. "The human psyche is no blank slate upon which social training can write any message."[158] Thus, even though certain matters and activities were not private in the way we understand them today, one could claim that some desires for privacy stem from biological instinct. Further study is necessary to understand the origin of the desire for privacy in particular situations. Even if the desire for privacy in certain matters stems in part from biological nature, we control our desires, and a mere desire for privacy in a certain activity does not necessarily make that activity private.

Alan Westin aptly states, "[T]here are no universal needs for privacy and no universal processes for adjusting the values of privacy, disclosure, and surveillance within each society."[159] Nevertheless, although privacy is not universal, it should not be viewed as too radically contingent. There are remarkable similarities in attitudes toward privacy around the world. Professor Adam Moore notes that some cultures "appear to contain no privacy. The Tikopia of Polynesia, Thlinget Indians of North America, Java of Indonesia, as well as a few others, have cultural systems that appear to leave everything open for public consumption." The Tikopia have hardly any moments of solitude; they are rarely alone. The Thlinget Indians walk into each other's houses unannounced. Likewise, the Java wander into each other's homes; in fact, their houses have no doors. Upon closer examination, however, even these societies have dimensions of privacy. Moore observes, "The Java still have bathing enclosures, while the Thlingets and Tikopia hide behind psychological walls to ensure private domains. Like viewing a stripper, we may see everything and nothing at all of the real person. Moreover, in each of these cultures there are time restrictions on access—for example, visiting someone in the middle of the night would typically be prohibited." Moore astutely concludes, "While privacy may be a cultural universal necessary for the proper functioning of human beings, its form—the actual rules of association and disengagement—is culturally dependent."[160]

There is a tendency to create too strong a dichotomy between universality and contingency, with something being either universal or hopelessly variable. Instead, many things are somewhere in between. They are not universal, but there are many shared attitudes toward them. A theory of privacy should leave room for cultural and historical variation, but not err by becoming too variable. A theory should strive for enough generality so that it has stability and broad applicability. Otherwise, it becomes nothing but a catalog of activities specific to one culture at one particular time in history. There is indeed a wide array of different cultural norms regarding privacy, and the meanings of privacy have evolved historically. The breadth and dynamism of privacy, however, are not an insurmountable difficulty to theorizing about privacy if we can find the right focus. With the proper focus, we can concentrate on the dimensions of privacy that are the most stable and common. I now turn to this important issue.

Focus

I have argued thus far that a theory of privacy should be pluralistic, should be general but not too vague, and should accommodate the dynamic nature of privacy while maintaining widespread applicability. A theory of privacy, therefore, should consist of a framework for identifying the plurality of things that fall under the rubric of privacy. The framework must be concrete enough to be useful, but not so overly contextual as to fail to provide guidance across a multitude of situations. To develop a framework, however, one critical issue remains. The framework needs a particular focal point—a lens through which to view the territory. Privacy issues are remarkably complex because they are highly contextual and contingent. In order to generalize in a useful way about privacy, we must focus on a dimension of privacy that is stable enough to discuss generally but flexible enough to account for privacy's dynamism. Ultimately, I focus on problems, but to justify why this focal point is preferred, I will first explore some other potential ways to focus a conceptual analysis of privacy and why each has severe shortcomings.

The Nature of the Information or Matter

One focal point is the nature of the information or matter involved. We could identify various types of information and matters that are private. If we were to focus on the nature of the information, one possible way to identify private information would be to look at its intimacy or sensitivity. Data about health and sex are private because these matters are deeply personal, whereas more innocuous information, such as names and addresses, is not. Embodying this view, the Restatement of Torts notes that generally, celebrities must accept reduced levels of privacy, but that "[t]here may be some intimate details of [a

famous person's] life, such as sexual relations, which even [she] is entitled to keep to herself."[161]

Around the world, some courts approach privacy by focusing on the
nature of the information. The Constitutional Court of South Africa
has noted that there is "a continuum of privacy rights which may be regarded as starting with a wholly inviolable inner self, moving to a relatively impervious sanctum of the home and personal life and ending in
a public realm where privacy would only remotely be implicated."[162]
One Canadian court held that there is no reasonable expectation of
privacy in information gleaned from a dog sniff because the information "did not offer any insight into his private life or biographical core
of personal information, other than the fact that he was carrying prohibited drugs."[163]

U.S. law sometimes focuses heavily on the nature of the information.
In *Illinois v. Caballes*, the U.S. Supreme Court concluded that people
lack a reasonable expectation of privacy in the possession of drugs from
drug-sniffing dogs because "governmental conduct that *only* reveals
the possession of contraband compromises no legitimate privacy interest."[164] The Court's reasoning suggests that privacy is violated
only if information about legal activities is revealed. In *Smith v. Maryland*, the Supreme Court held that people lacked a reasonable expectation of privacy in the phone numbers they dialed because this information was not as sensitive as the "contents" of the communications.[165]
The Electronic Communications Privacy Act of 1986 makes a similar
distinction. It provides strict protections for the contents of communications but only limited protections for "envelope" data—information
used to deliver communications (such as names of senders and recipi-
ents, addresses, and phone numbers).[166] Law professor Orin Kerr de-
fends this distinction because "in the great majority of cases contents of
communications implicate privacy concerns on a higher order of mag-
nitude than non-content information, and it makes sense to give
greater privacy protections for the former and lesser to the latter."[167]
Envelope information, however, often exposes the identities of a
person's colleagues and friends, revealing a person's associational ties.
In many instances, people may care more about concealing with whom
they are talking than what they are saying.[168]

Thus far, the law has often viewed disclosure in black-and-white
fashion. Information is classified as public or private under the assump-

tion that these are qualities that inhere in the information. No particular kind of information or matter, however, is inherently private. The problem with focusing on the nature of the information or matter involved is that often there are strong privacy interests in relatively innocuous information or matters. For example, some people might not consider an address to be private because it is not an intimate secret. This view too rigidly focuses on the nature of the data. For many individuals, concealing their address is quite important. Celebrities want to keep their addresses private to prevent being hounded by obsessed fans, stalkers, and paparazzi. Domestic-violence victims strive to hide their whereabouts to seek refuge from their abusers. Witnesses, jurors, or judges in a criminal case may need to conceal where they live to prevent retaliation against themselves and their families.

Because of these concerns, the law in many instances recognizes addresses as private. In *Kallstrom v. City of Columbus*, for example, police officers successfully prevented the disclosure of their home addresses because it could enable the criminals whom they arrested to seek them out and threaten their families.[169] In another case, an antiabortion activist group published abortion doctors' names, photos, addresses, and other information on a website called the "Nuremberg Files." Names of doctors who were murdered were crossed out with a black line, and the names of wounded doctors were shaded in gray. The disclosure of this information, often relatively innocuous and not considered private, was quite an important matter for the doctors, who feared for their safety and that of their families. The doctors sued and won.[170] The Driver's Privacy Protection Act of 1994, which limits government disclosures of motor-vehicle record information, was inspired by an incident in which a deranged fan murdered actress Rebecca Shaeffer outside her home after acquiring Shaeffer's address from the Department of Motor Vehicles.[171] Therefore, although address information is not intimate, this does not automatically make it public. Information is public or private depending upon the purposes for which people want to conceal it and the uses that others might make of it.

In sum, a theory of privacy should not focus on the nature of the information or matters. The privacy of information or matters also involves the condition of the information or matter. By "condition," I am referring to a particular state of existence, such as being concealed, held in confidence, or kept secure. Something is private in part if certain conditions exist—it is not inherently private because of its subject matter. For example, even very sensitive or intimate information is not private if it is exposed widely to others. We generally consider a person's medical information private, but if that person has openly spoken about her disease on national television, then it is no longer private.

Furthermore, privacy may be implicated if one combines a variety of relatively innocuous bits of information. Businesses and governments often aggregate a wide array of information fragments, including pieces of information we would not view as private in isolation. Yet when combined, they paint a rather detailed portrait of our personalities and behavior, a problem I call "aggregation," which I will discuss in Chapter 5. Focusing on the nature of the information or matter neglects to account for this problem.

The Individual's Preferences

One could develop a theory of privacy that focuses on individual preferences. If we cannot simply look to the nature of the information or matters involved, we could look instead to what the individual desires to preserve as private. Many conceptions of privacy focus on the individual's desires. For example, access or control definitions are often tied to what the individual wants to control or limit access to. Philosopher Iris Young declares, "The Private [is] what the individual chooses to withdraw from public view."[172] Philosopher Beate Rössler also defines privacy in an individual-centered manner: "Something counts as private if one can oneself control the access to this 'something.' Conversely, the protection of privacy means protection against unwanted access by other people."[173]

Focusing on individual preferences accounts for the wide range of attitudes and beliefs people have about privacy. It is virtually impossible, however, to devise a workable set of legal protections around a conception of privacy that varies with each individual's idiosyncrasies. Theorist Luciano Floridi notes, "To one person, a neighbour capable of seeing one's garbage in the garden may seem an unbearable breach of their privacy, which it is worth any expenditure and effort to restore; to another person, living in the same room with several other family members may feel entirely unproblematic."[174] A theory of privacy based on individual preferences would be unstable and fickle. Individuals can have unreasonable demands for privacy. We could never know if we could look at other people or speak about other people without violating their privacy. If we focused on the individual's preferences, privacy would know no bounds.

Of course, we cannot completely divorce privacy from individual desire. Unless we adopt an a priori conception of privacy, we must determine what is private by looking to experience, and that depends upon how people behave and what they desire. It would be difficult to claim that something is a privacy violation if nobody viewed it as such. In short, although we cannot ignore people's attitudes, we should not use individual attitudes as the means by which to focus an approach to defining privacy.

The Reasonable Expectation of Privacy

Another potential focal point is the information or matters in which people have a reasonable expectation of privacy. Privacy does not turn solely on the individual's particular expectation but upon expectations that society considers reasonable. The rationale for recognizing only expectations of privacy that society deems reasonable is to address the problem of idiosyncratic individual preferences. Some individuals may have an unusually strong desire for privacy and may make impossible demands for privacy at great variance with social practice. The focus, therefore, should be on societal expectations.

The reasonable-expectation-of-privacy approach is the prevailing method that American courts use to identify privacy interests protected by the Fourth Amendment. Under the reasonable-expectation-of-privacy approach, which was set forth in Justice Harlan's concurrence to *Katz v. United States*, the Supreme Court first looks to whether "a person [has] exhibited an actual (subjective) expectation of privacy" and then to whether "the expectation [is] one that society is prepared to recognize as 'reasonable.'"[175] In addition to Fourth Amendment law, the reasonable-expectation-of-privacy approach has been used in many American privacy tort cases.[176] Several statutes also employ this approach, such as the federal Video Voyeurism Prevention Act of 2004 and California's Anti-Paparazzi Act of 1998.[177]

Courts outside the United States also use the reasonable-expectation-of-privacy approach. New Zealand, for example, adopted a public-disclosure tort, which depends on the "existence of facts in respect of which there is a reasonable expectation of privacy."[178] Since 1984, the Canadian Supreme Court has applied a "reasonable expectation of privacy" test in interpreting the protection against "unreasonable search and seizure" in the Canadian Charter of Rights and Freedoms.[179] The European Court of Human Rights has used a reasonable-expectation-of-privacy test in several cases.[180]

The central virtue of the reasonable-expectation-of-privacy approach is that it avoids pinning privacy to a particular set of matters. Legal scholar Lior Strahilevitz observes, "[T]he advantage of the reasonable expectations of privacy approach is its flexibility and responsiveness to technological and social changes that affect privacy norms."[181] Looking to reasonable expectations of privacy does not try to reduce privacy to an unchanging essence.

One unanswered question about the test, however, is how reasonable expectations of privacy are to be determined. Because this test purportedly focuses on what people and society treat as private, it appears to call for an empirical analysis. In practice, the Supreme Court has never engaged in an empirical study in applying the reasonable-expectation-of-privacy test. Justice Antonin Scalia once observed, "In my view, the only thing the past three decades have established about the *Katz* test . . . is that, unsurprisingly, [reasonable expectations of privacy] bear an uncanny resemblance to those expectations of privacy that this Court considers reasonable."[182] In one study, professors Christopher Slobogin and Joseph Schumacher examined whether the Supreme Court's decisions accurately reflected people's expectations of privacy. They found that people's expectations of privacy varied significantly from what the Supreme Court had determined. For example, despite the fact that people found a search of bank records to be highly intrusive, the Court has held that there is no reasonable expectation of privacy in such records. Slobogin and Schumacher concluded that the Court's determinations of whether a reasonable expectation of privacy exists often "do not reflect societal understandings."[183]

If a more empirical approach to determining reasonable expectations of privacy were employed, how should the analysis be carried out? Reasonable expectations could be established by taking a poll. But there are several difficulties with such an approach. First, should the poll be local or national or worldwide? Different communities will likely differ in their expectations of privacy. Second, people's stated preferences often differ from their actions. Economists Alessandro Acquisti and Jens Grossklags observe that "recent surveys, anecdotal evidence, and experiments have highlighted an apparent dichotomy between privacy attitudes and actual behavior." Although many people in surveys express strong desires for privacy, "individuals are willing to trade privacy for convenience or to bargain the release of personal information in exchange for relatively small rewards."[184] This disjunction leads Strahilevitz to argue that what people say means less than what they do. "Behavioral data," he contends, "is thus preferable to survey data in privacy."[185]

But care must be used in interpreting behavior because several factors can affect people's decisions about privacy. Acquisti and Grossklags point to the problem of information asymmetries, when people lack adequate knowledge of how their personal information will be used, and bounded rationality, when people have difficulty applying what they know to complex situations.[186] Some privacy problems shape behavior. People often surrender personal data to companies because they perceive that they do not have much choice. They might also do so because they lack knowledge about the potential future uses of the information. Part of the privacy problem in these cases involves people's limited bargaining power respecting privacy and inability to assess the privacy risks.[187] Thus looking at people's behavior might present a skewed picture of societal expectations of privacy.

Even with the appropriate empirical metric for current social expectations of privacy, a significant problem remains. Without a normative component to establish what society should recognize as private, the reasonable-expectations approach provides only a status report on existing privacy norms rather than guides us toward shaping privacy law and policy in the future. Indeed, if the government has a long-standing practice of infringing upon privacy, then a logical conclusion would be that people should reasonably expect that their privacy will be invaded in these ways.[188] Similarly, the government could gradually condition people to accept wiretapping or other privacy incursions, thus altering society's expectations of privacy.[189] Indeed, in George Orwell's *Nineteen Eighty-four*, Big Brother conditioned its citizens to have virtually no expectations of privacy:

How often, or on what system, the Thought Police plugged in on any individual wire was guesswork. It was even conceivable that they watched everybody all the time. But at any rate they could plug in your wire whenever they wanted to. You had to live—did live, from habit that became instinct—in the assumption that every sound you made was overheard, and, except in darkness, every movement scrutinized.[190]

The problem with examining when people can expect privacy is that it is becoming increasingly difficult to expect privacy in today's world. With so much data collection, so many cameras, and so many easy ways of spreading information, people are frequently lamenting the steady erosion of privacy. Thus we should look not just to what our expectations of privacy actually are (a purely descriptive test) but to what our expectations of privacy should be (a normative test). Societies protect privacy through law not just to preserve existing realities but to resolve problems and deficiencies and to improve the status quo. The brief history of communications privacy I discussed earlier in this chapter demonstrates this point. We want certain matters to be private, even if we need to create this privacy through the use of law.

Therefore, determining what the law should protect as private depends upon a normative analysis. Privacy is not just about what people expect but about what they desire. Privacy is not simply a resource existing in the state of nature that the law must act to conserve. Instead, privacy is something we construct through norms and the law. It is a set of boundaries we create between ourselves and others. Privacy is a need that arises from society's intrusiveness, and we employ the law as a tool to address the problems society creates. We construct laws to bring about a state of affairs we want, not just to preserve existing realities. Thus we call upon the law to protect privacy because we experience a lack of privacy and desire to rectify that situation, not because we already expect privacy. The law should thus be a tool used proactively to create the amount of privacy we desire.

Focusing on Problems

As I have demonstrated in the previous sections, we should not focus on the nature of the information or matter. Privacy is not an inherent property of things; it depends upon conditions that can attach to particular information or matters. Privacy is not an individual preference, yet it is shaped by people's attitudes. Nor is privacy merely a societal expectation; it is a normative desire. On what, then, should we focus when we seek to understand privacy?

I contend that the focal point for a theory of privacy should be the problems we want the law to address. According to John Dewey, philosophical inquiry begins with problems in experience, not with abstract universal principles.[191] Philosophical inquiry must be "experimental," making generalizations based on one's encounters with problems, and then testing these generalizations by examining their consequences in other contexts.[192] "Empirically, all reflection sets out from the problematic and confused. Its aim is to clarify and ascertain."[193] Specific problematic situations spur inquiry.[194] "[K]nowledge is an affair of *making* sure," Dewey observed, "not of grasping antecedently given sureties."[195] Pragmatism emphasizes that we begin philosophical inquiry with the problems we need to solve. In other words, pragmatism suggests a particular relationship between theory and practice—a view that theory should emerge from practical problems and help guide us in addressing them.

In a related manner, law professor Alan Dershowitz contends that we need not have a conception of the ideal society in order to define rights: "It is enough to have a conception—or a consensus—about the very bad society, and about the wrongs that made it so. Based on this experience with wrongs, rights can be designed to prevent (or at least slow down) the recurrence of such wrongs." He argues that "*rights* come from *wrongs*"—they "*come from human experience*, particularly experience with injustice."[196] Indeed, some of the most potent and enduring depictions of privacy problems emerge from literary dystopias—the oppressive surveillance and control of George Orwell's *Nineteen Eighty-four*, the stifling and clandestine bureaucratic uses of data in Franz Kafka's *The Trial*, the commercialization and diminution of people's faculties in Aldous Huxley's *Brave New World*, and the complete domination over women's lives and bodies in Margaret Atwood's *The Handmaid's Tale.*[197]

With its emphasis on concrete situations, pragmatism locates the starting point for theorizing in specific contexts. Conceptualizing privacy is about understanding and attempting to solve certain problems. A privacy interest exists whenever there is a problem from the related cluster of problems we view under the rubric of privacy. A privacy problem disrupts particular activities, and the value of protecting against the problem stems from the importance of safeguarding the activities that are disrupted. After identifying the privacy interest and its value, the next step is to weigh the privacy interest against the value of any countervailing interests. Practices that cause privacy problems often are not wholly negative—they have benefits. Once we weigh the privacy interest against the harm, we can determine how privacy should be protected in a particular case. In some instances, privacy might outweigh the countervailing interest or vice versa. In many cases, compromise solutions can be found to protect both privacy and the conflicting interest. But this balancing depends upon first identifying privacy interests, and it is here that law and policy often go astray.

A theory of privacy should focus on the problems that create a desire for privacy. Privacy concerns and protections do not exist for their own sake; they exist because they have been provoked by particular problems. Privacy protections are responses to problems caused by friction in society. Henry David Thoreau once wrote, "[W]e live thick and are in each other's way, and stumble over one another, and I think that we thus lose some respect for one another."[198] Society is fraught with conflict. Individuals, institutions, and governments can all engage in actions that have problematic effects on the lives of others. Privacy concerns and protections are a reaction to these problems. Barrington Moore aptly observes, "[T]he need for privacy is a socially created need. Without society there would be no need for privacy."[199] "Privacy," he declares, "appears as an escape from the demands and burdens of social interaction."[200] By addressing problems caused by social friction, privacy enables people to engage in worthwhile activities in ways that would otherwise be difficult or impossible. Of course, privacy is not freedom from all forms of social friction; rather, it is protection from a cluster of related problems that impinge upon our activities in related ways.

Privacy problems arise when the activities of governments, businesses, organizations, and people disrupt the activities of others. These problems are difficult because the conflicting activities are often both valuable. Privacy facilitates certain activities; it can even be an essential or constitutive part of some activities. For example, privacy is important for such activities as writing diaries or letters, talking to one's doctor or psychotherapist, or making certain decisions. We should conceptualize privacy by focusing on the specific types of disruption and the specific activities disrupted rather than looking for the common denominator that links all of them. Privacy protections address a web of interconnected problems that disrupt specific activities. The act of conceptualizing privacy should consist of mapping the topography of the web.

For too long, however, the quest for a traditional conception of privacy has led to a dead end. In the meantime, real problems exist, but they are often ignored because they do not fit into a particular conception of privacy. Instead of constructing an understanding of privacy from the top down by first seeking to elucidate an overarching conception of privacy, we should develop our understanding from a bottom-up examination of the problems based on analogical reasoning. These problems exist regardless of whether they are labeled "privacy" violations. The term "privacy" can be useful as a shorthand to refer to a related cluster of problems, but beyond this use, the term adds little.

I have discussed the method and parameters for conceptualizing privacy. Two tasks remain. First, I will discuss how we should assess the value of privacy. Second, I will set forth a taxonomy to help identify and understand the plurality of privacy problems that currently arise.

～ 4

The Value of Privacy

One of the most important dimensions of a theory of privacy is how to assess its value. The value of privacy involves the rationales why privacy is worth protecting. A theory of privacy should articulate why privacy is good or how it will further the good life. Privacy often clashes with important opposing interests, and it is thus critical that a theory of privacy provide guidance as to privacy's value. What, then, is the value of privacy? How ought we to assess and analyze it?

In this chapter, I begin by discussing existing accounts of the value of privacy. I explore some of the reasons commentators articulate regarding why privacy is beneficial or harmful. I then move beyond these specific arguments to develop a pragmatic approach to ascribing a value to privacy. In contrast to attempts to state the value of privacy in the abstract, I argue that privacy's value differs depending upon the type of problem it protects against. Privacy problems impede certain activities, and the value of privacy emerges from the value of preserving these activities. Privacy, therefore, does not have a uniform value. Its value must be worked out as we balance it against opposing interests.

There are difficulties, however, in balancing privacy against countervailing values that lead the balancing process astray. Privacy is often cast as an individual right and balanced against the greater social good, which results in privacy being frequently undervalued in relation to many conflicting interests. I contend that privacy has a social value and that its importance emerges from the benefits it confers upon society.

The Virtues and Vices of Privacy

Many commentators have offered compelling reasons why privacy is of significant value. Privacy, several have argued, promotes psychological well-being. According to an influential 1973 report by the U.S. Department of Health, Education, and Welfare, "There is widespread belief that personal privacy is essential to our well-being—physically, psychologically, socially, and morally."[1] Michael Weinstein asserts that "privacy is valuable because it is a means to lessening the personal tensions which are built into the conduct of social relations."[2] Privacy, Alan Westin contends, allows people "respite" from the "whirlpool of active life."[3]

Others have argued that privacy is vital to self-development. Paul Freund declares that "privacy offers a shelter for the loosening of inhibitions, for self-discovery and self-awareness, self-direction, innovation, groping, nourishment for a feeling of uniqueness and a release from the oppression of commonness."[4] Westin contends that privacy "is basically an instrument for achieving individual goals of self-realization."[5] Privacy enables people to create, explore, and experiment. It provides moments for intellectual and spiritual contemplation. By shielding people from social opprobrium for their activities, privacy enables expressions of selfhood that conflict with prevailing social norms. With privacy, people can be more eccentric and unique, more candid and uninhibited, and less guarded about their words and deeds. Joseph Bensman and Robert Lilienfeld observe, "Privacy is required simply because the expression of an inner self would place one at odds with one's cultural environment."[6] According to Arnold Simmel, "In privacy we can develop, over time, a firmer, better constructed, and more integrated position in opposition to the dominant social pressures."[7]

A number of commentators have located privacy's value in the space it creates for intimate relationships.[8] Robert Gerstein declares that "intimate relationships simply could not exist if we did not continue to insist on privacy for them."[9] Jeffrey Rosen observes, "In order to flourish, the intimate relationships on which true knowledge of another person depends need space as well as time: sanctuaries from the gaze of the crowd in which slow mutual self-disclosure is possible."[10]

Several others have pointed out privacy's importance for democracy. Ruth Gavison argues, "Privacy is also essential to democratic government because it fosters and encourages the moral autonomy of the citizen, a central requirement of a democracy."[11] Keith Boone observes that privacy is "vital to a democratic society in several specific ways as well. For example, it underwrites the freedom to vote, to hold political discussions, and to associate freely away from the glare of the public eye and without fear of reprisal."[12] For Paul Schwartz, privacy creates spaces for civic dialogue and democratic deliberation.[13] According to Anita Allen, "[P]rivacy make[s] persons more fit for social participation and contribution to the pool of resources and assets available to all."[14]

Privacy permits individuals to contemplate and discuss political change, create counterculture, or engage in a meaningful critique of society. Privacy also enables creative expression that is often not possible within the constraints of public life.[15] People have the opportunity to develop their views, political opinions, and artistic expressions without having them prematurely leaked to the world, where harsh judgments might crush them. Growth and development require experimentation and the opportunity to alter one's opinions before making them public.[16] Privacy allows people to speak anonymously, encouraging robust communication without fear of community reprisal.

But others see privacy as socially detrimental. Privacy has long been criticized as a form of retreat from society. According to Hannah Arendt, the ancient Greek conception of privacy "meant literally a state of being deprived of something." The public sphere was the truly important realm of existence; the private sphere was valuable solely to the extent that it nourished people for public participation. For the Greeks, Arendt writes, "an entirely private life means above all to be deprived of things essential to a truly human life: to be deprived of the reality that comes from being seen and heard by others, . . . to be deprived of the possibility of achieving something more permanent than life itself."[17]

Privacy has been viewed as a threat to community and solidarity. In more communal societies, a prevailing view is that privacy protects the individual to the detriment of the community. Professor Yao-Huai Lü observes that in "traditional Chinese society, the old collectivism that ignored individual interests certainly had no serious interest in protecting individual privacy." Although modern Chinese society recognizes a greater degree of individualism and allows for a limited degree of privacy, "the opinion that the collective is more important than the individual still makes it impossible to have a sense of privacy as strong as Western societies that, by contrast, begin with individualism as the foreground assumption undergirding privacy conceptions."[18] Utopian literature often envisions communal societies that provide little space for private life. Sir Thomas More's *Utopia* (1516), for example, depicts the idyllic society as one of communal life in which nothing is hidden and social order is paramount: "With the eyes of everyone upon them, [people] have no choice but to do their customary work or to enjoy pastimes which are not dishonorable."[19]

Privacy has been criticized for impeding social control because it can cloak illicit activities and reduce accountability. Joseph Pulitzer once famously declared, "There is not a crime, there is not a dodge, there is not a trick, there is not a swindle, there is not a vice which does not live by secrecy."[20] Psychologist Bruno Bettelheim observed that there is an "absence of crime, delinquency and other antisocial behavior in the Israeli agricultural communal settlements, the kibbutzim. They have no police because there is no need for policing." Although he "felt suffocated by the lack of privacy" when visiting a kibbutz, he noted, "I could not blind myself to the incredibly successful control of antisocial behavior in this society."[21] Privacy lessens a society's ability to detect and punish disobedience, which makes it harder to enforce laws and norms.[22]

Privacy can make it difficult to establish trust and judge people's reputations.[23] According to sociologist Francis Fukuyama, "Trust is the expectation that arises within a community of regular, honest, and cooperative behavior, based on commonly shared norms, on the part of members of that community."[24] Sociologist Steven Nock argues, "Trust and the ability to take others at their word are basic ingredients in social order." Privacy, he continues, "makes it difficult to know others' reputations," which in turn makes it difficult to determine whether to trust them.[25] Richard Posner and Richard Epstein contend that the law should not protect against disclosures of discreditable information, since this information is useful to others in judging people, and concealment is tantamount to fraud.[26]

A number of feminist scholars argue that privacy is problematic because it shrouds the abuse and oppression of women in the home.[27]

They claim that historically the public sphere has been the domain of men, with women, families, and the household composing the private sphere. By being relegated to the private sphere, women were excluded from public life, and many women's issues were banished from public discourse because they were considered private matters. Courts in the nineteenth century, for example, turned a blind eye to issues of domestic abuse in the name of family "privacy."[28] Therefore, some feminist scholars attack privacy as a shadowy realm that has impeded women's political power. According to legal scholar Catharine MacKinnon, the "right of privacy is a right of men 'to be let alone' to oppress women one at a time." Thus "feminism has seen the personal as the political. The private is public for those for whom the personal is political."[29] Carole Pateman contends that "the dichotomy between the private and the public obscures the subjection of women to men within an apparently universal, egalitarian and individualist order."[30]

Some commentators view privacy as a vestige of a genteel age that has long since passed away. Alan Westin, for example, argues that Warren and Brandeis's call for a right to privacy "was essentially a protest by spokesmen for patrician values against the rise of the political and cultural values of 'mass society.'"[31] Legal scholar Harry Kalven contends that "[t]here is a curious nineteenth-century quaintness about the grievance [of privacy], an air of injured gentility."[32] Cultural historian Rochelle Gurstein notes that during the twilight of the Victorian age, many critics of privacy championed the value of exposure and publicity. Calls for privacy were viewed as yearning for a return to Victorian prudishness.[33] In contemporary times, the criticism is made in terms of emerging generations growing accustomed to living in the open and not expecting privacy. One commentator writes that young people increasingly blog "about their personal lives [with details] their elders would have blushed to put in their diaries. Parents and teachers . . . chalk this up to naïvete, suggesting that, when these children grow up, they will be as concerned about privacy as past generations were. But maybe not."[34] Privacy, in other words, is a fading expectation and value that people increasingly find to be of little concern or consequence. It is the lingering reticence of a bygone era.

Privacy can impede commercial efficiency and profitability. Fred Cate contends, "Privacy interferes with the collection, organization, and storage of information on which businesses and others can draw to make rapid, informed decisions, such as whether to grant credit or accept a check." Privacy, he argues, "may reduce productivity and lead to higher prices for products and services."[35]

Privacy also conflicts with the free flow of information. It can impede transparency and openness. Libertarian writer Virginia Postrel observes that privacy restricts "the freedom to gather and disseminate truthful information—otherwise known as freedom of speech and the press."[36] Eugene Volokh contends that privacy interferes with people's right to speak about each other. Privacy impedes speech that is "of interest to people deciding how to behave in their daily lives, whether daily business or daily personal lives—whom to approach to do business, whom to trust with their money, and the like."[37] Commentator Solveig Singleton argues that "[t]hroughout history, people have generally been free to learn about one another in the course of business transactions and other day-to-day contracts. Restrictions that alter this default rule sweep a potentially enormous pool of facts and ideas out of the shared domain."[38] Legal scholar Diane Zimmerman contends that privacy is outweighed by the "powerful countervailing interest in exchanges of accurate information about the private lives and characters of its citizenry."[39]

Privacy also conflicts with other values, such as the detection and prevention of crime and national security. Law professor William Stuntz argues that "effective, active government—government that innovates, that protects people who need protecting, that acts aggressively when action is needed—is dying." Because it impedes swift government responses to security threats, privacy is one of the "diseases."[40] Judge Richard Posner points out the emerging dangers of terrorism: "In an era of global terrorism and proliferations of weapons of mass destruction, the government has a compelling need to gather, pool, sift, and search vast quantities of information, much of it personal."[41]

Thus there is a litany of reasons for and against protecting privacy. How do we make sense of the bewildering array of arguments about privacy's benefits and harms? A broader examination of the value of privacy is necessary because several critical issues must be resolved regarding the basic method and approach to understanding privacy's value.

Theories of the Valuation of Privacy

Intrinsic and Instrumental Value

What is the source of the value of privacy? Several theorists view privacy's value as originating from the very condition of privacy itself. Privacy, in other words, is understood as having an intrinsic value. According to Ronald Dworkin, certain things "are valuable in themselves and not just for their utility or for the pleasure or satisfaction they bring us."[42] When something has intrinsic value, we value it for itself. In contrast, when something has instrumental value, we value it because it furthers other important ends.

Intrinsic and instrumental value need not be mutually exclusive, and many things have both intrinsic and instrumental value. Being free from pain has intrinsic value because it is a state of existence that is good in and of itself. It also has instrumental value because it enables us to do many activities we otherwise would not be able to do.

One of the primary problems with theories of intrinsic value is that they often sidestep the difficult task of articulating why we value something. For example, legal scholar Anita Allen rejects intrinsic-value accounts because they view privacy as having an "unanalyzable value."[43] Philosopher Beate Rössler points out that even to the extent that privacy may have intrinsic value, there is a "deeper explanatory need" to examine "*why* we value privacy" and "what it is that would be lost if we were to lose our privacy."[44]

The difficulty with intrinsic value is that it is often hard to describe it beyond being a mere taste. Vanilla ice cream has intrinsic value for many people, but reasons cannot readily be given to explain why. Individuals like vanilla ice cream, and that is about all that can be said. Privacy's value is often more complex than a mere taste, and it can be explained and articulated. Although it is possible that some forms of privacy may have intrinsic value, many forms of privacy are valuable primarily because of the ends they further. As I have sought to define it, privacy involves protection against a plurality of kinds of problems. Articulating the value of privacy consists of describing the benefits of protecting against these problems. Protection against intrusion, for example, is valuable not in and of itself, but because it enables us to do things we ordinarily could not, have moments of respite from society's turmoil, and be free from being disturbed in our activities. The value of ameliorating privacy problems lies in the activities that privacy protections enable.

Nonconsequentialist Accounts of Privacy's Value

According to nonconsequentialist accounts, privacy's value consists of adhering to a moral duty to respect each individual's dignity and autonomy.[45] For example, philosopher Stanley Benn contends that "respect for someone as a person, as a chooser, implie[s] respect for him as one engaged on a kind of self-creative enterprise, which could be disrupted, distorted, or frustrated even by so limited an intrusion as watching."[46] "[P]rivacy is valuable," philosopher Julie Inness claims, "because it acknowledges our respect for persons as autonomous beings with the capacity to love, care and like—in other words, persons with the potential to freely develop close relationships."[47] Philosopher Beate Rössler argues that "we value privacy for the sake of autonomy. In liberal societies, privacy has the function of permitting and protecting an autonomous life." "Respect for a person's privacy," Rössler contends, "is respect for her as an autonomous subject."[48] Charles Fried observes that "a threat to privacy seems to threaten our very integrity as persons." He elaborates that privacy is one of the "basic rights in persons, rights to which all are entitled equally, by virtue of their status as persons. . . . In this sense, the view is Kantian; it requires recognition of persons as ends, and forbids the overriding of their most fundamental interests for the purpose of maximizing the happiness or welfare of all."[49]

One of the difficulties in determining privacy's value in terms of respecting individual autonomy and dignity is that conflicting interests often involve the same fundamental aspects of personhood. For example, in the case *Bonome v. Kaysen*, Susana Kaysen wrote an autobiographical book about her struggles with severe vaginal pain. She described in detail her sexual activities with her boyfriend, as well as other aspects of their relationship. The boyfriend, who was no longer in a relationship with Kaysen when the book was published, sued for public disclosure of private facts. The court concluded that Kaysen should prevail because she had "a right to disclose her own intimate affairs" and tell "*her own* personal story—which inextricably involves [the boyfriend] in an intimate way."[50] This case involved individual autonomy and dignity on both sides of the scale. Kaysen's interest in free speech, her autonomy to speak about her own life, was in conflict with her boyfriend's privacy, his autonomy to live his life without it being exposed to others. Respecting people as "choosers," as "autonomous beings," or as "ends" does not tell us whether to respect the boyfriend's desire to keep his private life concealed or Kaysen's right to speak about her own life.

Even in cases where individual rights do not appear to clash, the freedom and autonomy of individuals can still be intertwined with countervailing interests to privacy. For example, when the government invades privacy in the name of security, it is reductive to view it as merely a struggle between individual rights and state power. Security is a component of individual freedom. Author Thomas Powers argues, "In a liberal republic, liberty presupposes security; the point of security is liberty."[51] Individual dignity and autonomy are often on both sides of the conflict between privacy and its opposing interests.

Like scholars who view privacy's value as respect for individual autonomy and dignity, theorist Luciano Floridi argues that privacy is valuable because it protects "inalienable identity," and therefore "the presumption should always be in favour of its respect." Personal information is a "constitutive part of someone's personal identity and individuality." According to Floridi, "[V]iolations of information privacy are now more fruitfully compared to a digital kidnapping rather than trespassing." Floridi notes that although privacy has a very high value, "this is not to say that informational privacy is never negotiable in any degree."[52]

Floridi's account, however, fails to provide guidance about when conflicting interests should prevail in the balance. Identity and individuality are also involved in free speech, even when it conflicts with privacy. Floridi's metaphor of kidnapping is not particularly apt in capturing why privacy is valuable. We do not experience the collection of our personal information as akin to kidnapping, so the analogy works in rhetoric rather than in felt experience. Additionally, not all visual observation or collection of information violates privacy. Even when it does, not all information gathering creates severe harm. Suppose I peek through your window and see that you are reading a book by Rousseau. I learned information about your consumption of ideas, which ultimately involves information about your identity. Without more details, however, it is hard to see how my snooping rises to the level of kidnapping. I have gleaned knowledge about you that will shape my judgment of you, but my judgment of you is not equivalent to your identity. The harm does not stem from the fact that I have seized your identity but that I have used information you did not want to expose to me in forming my impression of you.

A Pragmatic Account of Privacy's Value

In contrast to nonconsequentialist approaches, I advance a pragmatic approach to ascribing a value to privacy. We should understand the value of privacy in terms of its practical consequences. Privacy should be weighed against contrasting values, and it should win when it produces the best outcome for society. A pragmatic approach to valuing privacy involves balancing it against opposing interests. In American constitutional law, for example, rights are balanced against government interests. We live in an "age of balancing," and the prevailing view is that most rights and liberties are not absolute.[53] Because privacy conflicts with other fundamental values, such as free speech, security, curiosity, and transparency, we should engage in a candid and direct analysis of why privacy interests are important and how they ought to be reconciled with other interests. We cannot ascribe a value to privacy in the abstract. The value of privacy is not uniform across all contexts. We determine the value of privacy when we seek to reconcile privacy with opposing interests in particular situations.

One objection to balancing is that it requires that all interests be converted into quantifiable terms, and a value as complex as privacy cannot be adequately translated in this manner. However, according to law professor James Nehf, although the benefits of privacy "are often personal, emotional, intangible, and not readily quantifiable," this does not mean that it is impossible to weigh privacy against opposing interests. "Despite the basic incomparability of competing values in everyday life," Nehf argues, "people have no trouble making decisions when it is clear, for whatever reason, which alternative is best."[54] We often make choices without converting everything into the same metric.[55] The value of privacy often emerges from the way it influences social structure, power, democracy, and freedom, and this kind of benefit is nearly impossible to translate into quantifiable terms. Pragmatism counsels that we articulate how we reach a particular balance between conflicting interests. This articulation requires us to consider our deeply held commitments, the ends furthered by privacy and countervailing interests, and our larger social vision and view of the good. Even if two interests are incommensurate, we can still evaluate which interest should prevail on the basis of the consequences for society. Among other things, privacy can be valuable to avoid chilling speech or association and to keep the government's power in check. These justifications for the value of privacy are not easy to quantify, but they are nevertheless compelling and important.

Balancing has come under strong criticism for being cursory and facile. Legal scholar Alexander Aleinikoff argues, "What is so surprising is how rudimentary the process appears. No system of identification, evaluation, and comparison of interests has been developed."[56] The criticisms indeed point to a shortcoming of balancing: it is often done in a perfunctory manner or in ways that skew the result in one way or another. But Judge Frank Coffin aptly observes that if "done well, [balancing] is a disciplined process, a process of demanding standards of specificity, sensitivity, and candor."[57] Balancing can be a meaningful way to reconcile conflicts between opposing interests if it is performed properly. The challenging task is ensuring that the balancing process be as rigorous and thoughtful as possible.

Balancing privacy against opposing interests has suffered from systemic difficulties that often result in the undervaluation of privacy interests. One difficulty stems from failure to recognize privacy problems, which results in the opposing interest prevailing without any balancing taking place. This difficulty emerges in the confusion about conceptualizing privacy, a complication that can be redressed by the pluralistic framework of privacy problems that I develop in the next chapter. Another difficulty in the balancing process emerges from the notion of privacy as an individual right. When weighed against countervailing interests, often cast in terms of their social value, privacy frequently is outweighed. As I contend later, this way of understanding privacy's value is misguided, and we thus must develop a better understanding of its value to appropriately balance privacy against conflicting interests.

The Social Value of Privacy

Privacy as an Individual Right

Traditional liberalism often views privacy as a right possessed by individuals and in tension with the larger community. According to First Amendment scholar Thomas Emerson, privacy "is based upon premises of individualism, that the society exists to promote the worth and dignity of the individual. . . . The right of privacy . . . is essentially the right not to participate in the collective life—the right to shut out the community."[58] Richard Hixson notes, "Generally speaking, the concept of privacy, as old as human history, tries to distinguish between the individual and the collective, between self and society. The concept is based upon respect for the individual, and has evolved into respect for individualism and individuality."[59]

Warren and Brandeis's influential 1890 article described privacy as "the right to be let alone," which focused on the individual.[60] Privacy, they contended, consisted of a "general right to the immunity of the person—the right to one's personality."[61] The torts inspired by their article have also been justified as protecting the individual. According to the Restatement of Torts, "The right protected by the action for invasion of privacy is a personal right, peculiar to the individual whose privacy is invaded."[62] In the words of one court: "Privacy is inherently personal. The right to privacy recognizes the sovereignty of the individual."[63]

The problem with framing privacy solely in individualistic terms is that privacy becomes undervalued. Often, privacy receives inadequate protection in the form of damages to compensate individual emotional or reputational harm; the effects of the loss of privacy on freedom, culture, creativity, innovation, and public life are not factored into the valuation. According to Priscilla Regan, the value of privacy is not well articulated in federal policymaking: "[I]n congressional attempts to protect privacy, defining privacy primarily in terms of its importance to the individual and in terms of an individual right has served as a weak basis for public policy."[64] The interests aligned against privacy—for example, efficient consumer transactions, free speech, or security—are often defined in terms of their larger social value. In this way, protecting the privacy of the individual seems extravagant when weighed against interests of society as a whole.

The Communitarian Critique

Communitarian scholars argue that privacy should not be understood as an individual right that trumps the community interest. Richard Hixson contends that privacy depends upon society for its existence: "[T]he right to privacy is a societal bequeathal, not an individual possession."[65] In *The Limits of Privacy*, Amitai Etzioni argues that privacy is "a *societal license* that exempts a category of acts (including thoughts and emotions) from communal, public, and governmental scrutiny."[66] Hixson and Etzioni emphasize that privacy cannot be viewed in purely individual terms, without due consideration for the common good.

Communitarians further claim that the existing theoretical discourse of privacy views it in absolutist terms and fails to provide guidance about how to balance it against the common good. According to Hixson, "[P]rivacy affords an escape from the obligations and burdens of public life and threatens collective survival. If the state is to survive, the individual must be more public than private."[67] Etzioni argues that existing accounts of privacy privilege privacy over the common good. He claims that the existing right to privacy in the law "treats privacy as an unbounded good." This view, Etzioni argues, is wrong because "privacy is not an absolute value and does not trump all other rights or concerns for the common good." Individualism has expanded at the cost of the common good, and "social formulations of the common good [are] values that need to be balanced with concerns for individual rights and subgroup autonomy."[68]

Although they recognize that the privacy discourse has neglected to account for the common good and has improperly seen privacy as an inherent right of the individual, communitarian critics such as Hixson and Etzioni still associate privacy with the individual. Privacy, although a social creation, is valued exclusively for the benefits it provides for the individual. The association of privacy with the individual and the assumed conflict between the individual and the common good lead communitarians to view the private sphere as antagonistic to the public sphere. Privacy is seen as an individual indulgence at the expense of society, a form of protection of the individual that conflicts with the greater needs of society.

While communitarians account for both the individual and the common good, they often do not integrate the two; rather, they see them in irreconcilable conflict. Etzioni views the task of communitarians as "balanc[ing] individual rights with social responsibilities, and individuality with community."[69] He assumes that individual and societal interests are in conflict. The problem with communitarianism is that it pits the individual against the common good. Individualism becomes not an element valued for its contributions to the common good, but a countervalue that stands in opposition to the common good.

The Pragmatic Approach

Although the communitarians are correct that viewing privacy as an individual right fails to justify why the needs of the individual should trump societal interests, they subscribe to the same dichotomy between individual and society that forms the backbone of the view they critique. In contrast, I take a pragmatic approach to the value of privacy. The value of privacy should be assessed on the basis of its contributions to society. Protecting individual privacy need not be at society's expense—in fact, the value of safeguarding people's privacy should be justified by its social benefits. We do not live in isolation, but among others, and social engagement is a necessary part of life. In direct contrast to John Locke and many modern liberals, who view the individual as preceding society, John Dewey noted that the individual is inextricably bound up in society: "We cannot think of ourselves save as to some extent *social* beings. Hence we cannot separate the idea of ourselves and our own good from our idea of others and of their good."[70] The individual is not born in a self-sufficient state; instead, the individual requires nurture and care. Society forms the individual, for it provides protection, education, food, and entertainment necessary for the individual's development.

Individualism should be incorporated into the conception of the common good, not viewed as outside it. As Dewey aptly argued, we must insist upon a "social basis and social justification" for civil liberties.[71] When individualism is severed from the common good, the weighing of values is often skewed toward those equated with the common good, since the interests of society often outweigh the interests of particular individuals. When individualism is not considered at odds with the common good, we can better assess its values, contributions, and limitations.

Although privacy certainly protects individuals, this does not mean that privacy is an individualistic right. Understanding privacy as having a social value—the benefits it confers on society by enhancing and protecting certain aspects of selfhood—does not oppose the individual to the community or value privacy solely in terms of its benefits to particular individuals. Dewey astutely argued that individual rights need not be justified as the immutable possessions of individuals; instead, they are instrumental in light of "the contribution they make to the welfare of the community."[72] Employing a similar insight, several scholars contend that privacy is "constitutive" of society. Constitutive privacy understands privacy harms as extending beyond the mental anguish caused to particular individuals; privacy harms affect the nature of society and impede individual activities that contribute to the greater social good. Spiros Simitis recognizes that "privacy considerations no longer arise out of particular individual problems; rather, they express conflicts affecting everyone."[73] Robert Post contends that the tort of invasion of privacy "safeguards rules of civility that in some significant measure constitute both individuals and community."[74] The theory of constitutive privacy has been further developed by Julie Cohen and Paul Schwartz, who both argue that privacy is a constitutive element of a civil society.[75]

A social value of privacy does not mean that people's injured feelings, reputations, or embarrassment are irrelevant to the value of privacy. Understanding the social value of privacy, however, requires that we demonstrate the benefits to society of remedying certain harms to individuals. Thus a theory of the value of privacy requires a theory of the relationship of the individual to the community. Privacy protects aspects of individuality that have a high social value; it protects individuals not merely for their sake but for the sake of society.[76] As John Dewey aptly observed:

Every invention, every improvement in art, technological, military and political, has its genesis in the observation and ingenuity of a particular innovator. All utensils, traps, tools, weapons, stories, prove that some one exercised at sometime initiative in deviating from customary models and standards. Accident played its part; but *some one* had to observe and utilize the accidental change before a new tool and custom emerged.[77]

Privacy is valuable not only for our personal lives, but for our lives as citizens—our participation in public and community life. It is hard to imagine how people could freely participate in public life without some degree of control over their reputation and private life. Thus privacy is more than a psychological need or desire; it is a profound dimension of social structure. In addition to protecting individuals, privacy safeguards relationships between individuals, which are essential for family life, social engagement, and political activities.

If privacy is understood from the individual's perspective, it will often fare poorly when balanced against societal interests. Individual needs or desires will rarely trump the welfare of an entire society. Privacy, however, has a social value—it shapes the communities in which we live, and it provides necessary protection of individuals against various types of harms and disruptions. Privacy is not something that atomistic individuals possess in the state of nature and sacrifice in order to join the social compact. We establish privacy protections because of their profound effects on the structure of power and freedom within society as a whole. The protection of privacy shields us from disruptions to activities important to both individuals and society.

Privacy, Society, and Norms

Life in society involves jostling and conflict. Unless we tuck ourselves away in a remote place without human contact, we are bound to interfere with each other. Our curiosity can be intrusive and prying. Our speech can reveal information about others that wounds or humiliates them. In providing services and marketing products, businesses can use people's information in ways that increase their vulnerability to fraud and identity theft. Our activities—and those of businesses and the government—do not occur in a vacuum; they have profound effects on the lives of many persons. Protecting privacy involves reducing the extent to which individuals, institutions, and the government can encroach on people's lives.

One of the primary ways that society intervenes in people's lives is through the enforcement of norms. According to legal scholar Robert Ellickson, a norm is "a rule governing an individual's behavior that is diffusely enforced by third parties other than state agents by means of social sanctions."[78] Norms involve widely shared social attitudes about what behavior is acceptable or unacceptable, and they shape social stigmas and attitudes.[79] Norms work externally on individuals through social rewards and sanctions, as well as internally within individuals through feelings of guilt and shame.

The harm caused by privacy problems often stems from the power of social norms, which can sometimes be excessive, misplaced, and unproductive. We have idealized norms and hence harbor a significant amount of ambivalence and hypocrisy about them. People are often condemned for being caught doing things commonly done by others in society.

Majoritarian norms can conflict with those of social subgroups, such as minority ethnic and religious groups. Richard McAdams argues that certain unnecessary and undesirable norms may exist, or norms may produce an excessive level of compliance. For example, "nosy" norms may arise, where "a majority turns its weak other-regarding preferences into social obligations." The majority does not gain much by altering minority behavior, and the majority's gain does not offset the loss to the minority. Privacy is a recognition that in certain circumstances, it is in society's best interest to curtail the power of its norms. Therefore, "privacy is a means of norm regulation. When privacy rights impede an undesirable norm, this effect can provide an economic justification for those rights."[80]

Sometimes, even protection against desirable norms can be socially beneficial. We may not want to change or abolish certain norms, but we may want them to be imperfectly enforced. Conformity is socially beneficial only to a point. We naturally judge and condemn even though our judgment can be stifling and counterproductive if not carefully controlled and restrained. Privacy enables people to escape from the relentless force of social judgment, which in too pervasive a dose can stunt self-development. Privacy protections emerge from society's recognition that without some limitations, the community can be suffocating to individuals. Privacy is thus a protection of the individual for the good of society.

Of course, a significant degree of social control is necessary for all societies. Social control keeps behavior in line, prevents disputes from erupting, and establishes order. Privacy makes it harder for society to enforce norms, which decreases the power of social control. If people cannot monitor and share information about each other's private lives, a zone opens up where people can act contrary to a society's norms without repercussion.

Although privacy can permit people to flout social norms, too much control by norms may lead to an authoritarian society. In *On Liberty*, John Stuart Mill observed that society can engage in "a social tyranny more formidable than many kinds of political oppression." Although violations of norms may not carry severe sanctions, social control by norms can penetrate "deeply into the details of life, enslaving the soul itself." Mill contended that there must be protection "against the tyranny of the prevailing opinion and feeling; against the tendency of society to impose, by other means than civil penalties, its own ideas and practices as rules of conduct on those who dissent from them; to fetter the development, and, if possible, prevent the formation of any individuality not in harmony with its ways."[81] Privacy is a recognition that in certain circumstances, it is in society's best interest to curtail the power of its norms.

The question of how much social control is optimal, of course, is far too complex and context-dependent to resolve in this discussion. Nevertheless, although many forms of deviance are harmful to society, some deviance is socially beneficial, for it is the engine of social change. Many of the most important rights and liberties were engendered by resistance to existing forms of social control.

Since privacy cloaks norm violations from society's view, privacy can serve to retard the process of changing norms. It can allow society to cling to norms that might otherwise be eliminated. In the late nineteenth century, for example, blackmail law served as a way for Victorian norms about sex to remain entrenched by pushing deviant sexual activity into the dark recesses of the private realm. Strict moral standards condemned homosexual sodomy and heterosexual adultery. In England, sodomy was illegal and carried harsh penalties. Historian Angus McLaren observes, "Modern blackmail first emerged when criminals in the eighteenth century recognized that the laws against sodomy provided them with the means by which they could extort money from those whom they could entrap." Elite gentlemen often had sex with servants, prostitutes, and other less well-off individuals who might stand to gain much from blackmailing them. When the rich and powerful realized that their reputations could be ruined by relatively powerless people in society, they sought the protection of the law—and they received it. The law of blackmail criminalized extorting money from people by threatening to reveal their secrets.

Instead of blaming the rise of blackmail on problematic moral laws and social norms, society condemned the blackmailer. McLaren observes, "Society preferred to blame the eruption of blackmail on certain 'dangerous' women and men rather than come to terms with the tension between the laws and the sexual practices that often provided temptation to unscrupulous individuals." Blackmail cases "put the courts in a potentially awkward position." In many instances, the evidence showed that the blackmail victims did indeed engage in deviant sexual conduct, and "the courts did not want to be seen as defending immoralists." Therefore, prosecutors and courts would avoid looking at whether the blackmailer's accusations were true. Although people knew that the victims were not always innocent, victims were portrayed as "foolish" and "gullible" rather than "perverse."[82] Thus the solution was to protect privacy—to push deviance into the dim corners of society, to keep sodomy and adultery secret. As legal historian Lawrence Friedman notes, Victorian society aimed to preserve outward "respectability" and keep people's skeletons in their closets.[83]

The story of blackmail law in Victorian times demonstrates a potential dark side to privacy. Privacy allows society to maintain norms on the surface while transgressions occur in secret. Society can maintain the fiction that its norms are being followed while deviant conduct is hidden behind the veneer. Without the privacy protection of blackmail laws, Victorian norms might have been challenged and altered sooner because very powerful people might not have tolerated their reputations being ruined.

Changing norms, however, can be a long, gradual, and difficult process. Disclosing people's secrets will often not lead to norm change. Instead, it often affects a few unfortunate individuals. The result is that these people's lives are ruined for very little corresponding change in social norms.[84] Moreover, as law professor Paul Schwartz contends, if such disclosures were condoned and even if norms changed, society might be worse off because it would foster an atmosphere of oppressiveness.[85]

Feminist scholars point to another way privacy can insulate outmoded norms from the engines of reform. As discussed earlier, according to several feminists, privacy has historically functioned to shut women out of the public sphere, silence discourse about women's issues, and ignore claims of spousal abuse. Despite its tainted history, however, privacy can still be of much value for women. Anita Allen observes, "Privacy can strengthen traits associated with moral personhood, individuality, and self-determination. It can render a woman more fit for contributions both in her own family and in outside endeavors."[86] Ruth Gavison argues that the real problem is not the "verbal distinction between public and private," but the "power structures which manipulate them in unjustifiable ways."[87] Judith DeCew contends that dissolving the distinction between public and private is fraught with peril since it may grant "excessive power to the state."[88] Indeed, since the late 1960s, in the United States, privacy has also encompassed protections of contraception and abortion, which many consider key rights that enhance women's liberty. Moreover, historically, the lack of privacy harmed women just as much as the imposition of privacy. For example, the lack of privacy of sex throughout much of Western history had disproportionate effects on women. Women's sexual transgressions were viewed as more subversive than men's, and women caught engaging in illicit sex were often punished more harshly than men.[89] The lack of privacy enabled extensive surveillance and control over women's lives. Thus whether privacy is good or bad for women depends upon which form of privacy is involved and its function. Although privacy can entrench norms and other forms of social control, it can liberate people from them as well.

Thus far, I have discussed the social value of privacy's restricting the reach of norms. As Robert Post aptly recognizes, privacy is not simply the protection of the individual against the norms of society but also involves the promotion of society's norms. Privacy protects "rules of civility" that shape life in the community.[90] Privacy does not merely inhibit the norms, for it emerges from norms as well. We respect the privacy of others on the basis of norms of appropriate behavior, which disfavor excessive nosiness and prying. An apt analogy can be made to Ulysses and the Sirens:

> [Sirens] weaving a haunting song over the sea
> we are to shun, she said, and their green shore
> all sweet with clover; yet she urged that I
> alone should listen to their song. Therefore

> you are to tie me up, tight as a splint,
> erect upon the mast, lashed to the mast,
> and if I shout and beg to be untied,
> take more turns of the rope to muffle me.[91]

Ulysses desires to be self-restrained; he wants to be tied up because he knows that he might not be able to control himself. Similarly, people may recognize the value of being restrained from learning certain details about others, even if they crave gossip and would gain much pleasure from hearing it. Privacy protections represent society tying itself to the mast. These are not paternalistic restrictions imposed on a society, but ones that are self-imposed. Privacy protections promote civility. Without privacy, the friction of society might increase, potentially igniting into strife and violence. By modulating disruptive invasions, privacy can promote social order.

By understanding privacy as shaped by the norms of society, we can better see why privacy should not be understood solely as an individual right. Privacy certainly protects the individual, but not because of some inherent value of respect for personhood. Instead, privacy protects the individual because of the benefits it confers on society.

Privacy's Pluralistic Value

In contrast to many conceptions of privacy that describe the value of privacy in the abstract, I contend that there is no overarching value of privacy. As discussed earlier, theorists have proclaimed the value of privacy to be protecting intimacy, friendship, dignity, individuality, human relationships, autonomy, freedom, self-development, creativity, independence, imagination, counterculture, eccentricity, freedom of thought, democracy, reputation, and psychological well-being.

None of these ends, however, is furthered by all types of privacy. The problem with discussing the value of privacy in the abstract is that privacy is a dimension of a wide variety of activities, each having a different value—and what privacy is differs in different contexts. Privacy does not possess a unitary value. Because privacy consists of a plurality of protections against different types of problems, its value is plural as well. The value of privacy emerges from the activities that it protects. Activities have purposes—they are performed for particular reasons and goals.[92]

Privacy problems are disruptive to certain activities, and the value of privacy depends upon the importance of the activities.

In assessing the value of protecting against a privacy problem in a particular circumstance, however, we cannot merely focus on the value of the specific activities compromised in that situation. Privacy facilitates many activities, from the worthy to the wicked. Alan Wolfe aptly notes, "Privacy in itself is morally ambiguous. Individuals can use private spaces to develop their character, demean others, plan rebellions, collect stamps, masturbate, read Tolstoy, watch television, or do nothing."[93] Since privacy nurtures both good and bad activities, its value would vary far too widely if it were merely based upon the particular activities involved in any given case.

Thus, in a particular case, we must value privacy on the basis of the range of activities it protects beyond the specific activities involved in the situation. For example, suppose the police randomly barge into a person's home and conduct an intrusive search. In the process, they discover that the person committed a heinous crime. One might argue that because the person engaged in a crime, the value of protecting his privacy should be minimal. After all, he was using privacy to conceal criminal activity that society denounces. Such an argument can be made for any privacy violation that impedes illegal activities or other socially disapproved activities. The law protects privacy in these circumstances not because the particular activities are valuable but to preserve the full range of activities that can be compromised by a particular type of privacy problem. We protect against random searches of the home because they pose a threat to us all. The value of protecting against such searches emerges from society's interest in avoiding such searches, not from any one particular individual's interest.

In assessing the value of privacy, we must generalize. Instead of focusing narrowly on the particular activities involved in a particular case, we should look more generally to the range of activities that each type of privacy problem will impede. If most or all of the activities that a privacy problem inhibits are socially detrimental, then this should definitely lower the value of privacy in that context. But if many of the activities that a privacy invasion interferes with are beneficial, then the fact that a particular case involves activities that are not beneficial should not control. In other words, although the value of privacy is pluralistic and context dependent, it cannot be too contextual. Privacy's value emerges from the activities it protects, but the value must be assessed more systemically, not merely by the happenstance of the specific activities involved in any one particular circumstance.

Privacy, therefore, is a set of protections from a plurality of problems that all resemble each other, yet not in the same way. The value of protecting against a particular problem emerges from the activities that are implicated. Privacy problems impede valuable activities, and ameliorating these problems is essential to protecting the activities. The value of privacy is not absolute; privacy should be balanced against conflicting interests that also have significant value. The value of privacy is not uniform, but varies depending upon the nature of the problems being protected against.

Thus far, I have spoken generally about my approach to conceptualizing privacy and its value. It is now time to set forth a framework for understanding privacy in a pluralistic way.

~ 5

A Taxonomy of Privacy

Although various attempts to explicate the meaning of "privacy" have been undertaken, few have tried to identify privacy problems in a comprehensive and concrete manner.[1] The legendary torts scholar William Prosser made the most famous attempt in 1960. He discerned four types of harmful activities redressed under the rubric of privacy:

1. Intrusion upon the plaintiff's seclusion or solitude, or into his private affairs.
2. Public disclosure of embarrassing private facts about the plaintiff.
3. Publicity that places the plaintiff in a false light in the public eye.
4. Appropriation, for the defendant's advantage, of the plaintiff's name or likeness.[2]

Prosser's great contribution was to synthesize the cases that emerged from Samuel Warren and Louis Brandeis's famous law review article "The Right to Privacy."[3] Prosser, however, focused only on tort law. Moreover, he wrote nearly a half century ago, before the breathtaking rise of the information age. New technologies have spawned a panoply of different privacy problems, and many of them do not readily fit into Prosser's four categories. Therefore, a new taxonomy to address privacy violations for contemporary times is sorely needed.

In this chapter, I develop a taxonomy of privacy problems to provide a more pluralistic understanding of privacy. The taxonomy accounts for privacy problems that have achieved a significant degree of social recognition. I identify these problems through a bottom-up cultural analysis, using historical, philosophical, political, sociological, and legal sources. My primary focus will be on the law because it provides concrete evidence of what problems societies have recognized as warranting attention. My examination of legal sources will extend to those of many countries, although I will discuss the law in the United States in the most depth. The purpose of this taxonomy, however, is not merely to take stock of where the law currently stands today, but to provide a useful framework for its future development. Therefore, when I examine the law, my purpose is to use it as evidence of the existence of particular privacy problems, not as an indication of what I deem to be the appropriate level of protection. My taxonomy focuses on activities that can and do create privacy problems. A privacy violation occurs when a certain activity causes problems that affect a private matter or activity. This taxonomy focuses on the problems rather than on what constitutes a private matter or activity. Because determining which matters and activities are private is too culturally variable, this taxonomy focuses on potentially problematic activities, about which meaningful generalizations can be made. The taxonomy aims to carve up the landscape in a way that the law can begin to comprehend and engage. All taxonomies are generalizations based upon a certain focus, and they are valuable only insofar as they are useful for a particular purpose. The purpose of this taxonomy is to aid the crafting of law and policy, and it is my hope that it succeeds in facilitating this end.

The activities that affect privacy often are not inherently problematic. When a person consents to most of these activities, there is no privacy violation.[4] Thus, if a couple invites another to watch them have sex, this observation would not constitute a privacy violation. Without consent, however, it most often would.

Of course, declaring that an activity is problematic does not automatically imply that there should be legal redress, because there may be valid reasons why the law should not get involved or why countervailing interests should prevail. As Anita Allen argues, there are certainly times when people should be held accountable for their private activities.[5] The purpose of this taxonomy is not to argue whether the law should protect against certain activities that affect privacy. Rather, the goal is simply to define these activities and explain why and how they can cause trouble. The question of when and how the law should regulate can be answered only in each specific context in which the question arises. But attempts to answer this question are increasingly suffering because of confusion about defining the troublesome activities that fall under the rubric of privacy. This taxonomy will aid us in analyzing various privacy problems so the law can better address them and balance them with opposing interests. Since the goal of the law is to have privacy protections that best prevent and redress particular problems, we first need to understand the problems in order to evaluate the effectiveness of the protections.

Therefore, my focus is on activities that create problems. I aim to show that these activities differ significantly, yet share many commonalities. Privacy is too complicated a concept to be boiled down to a single essence. Attempts to find such an essence often end up being too broad and vague, with little usefulness in addressing concrete issues. Therefore, my goal is to define more precisely what the problem is in each context—how it is unique, how it differs from other problems, and how it is related to other types of privacy problems.

In the taxonomy that follows, there are four basic groups of harmful activities: (1) information collection, (2) information processing, (3) information dissemination, and (4) invasion. Each of these groups consists of different related subgroups of harmful activities.

I have arranged these groups around a model that begins with the data subject—the individual whose life is most directly affected by the activities classified in the taxonomy. From that individual, various entities (other people, businesses, and the government) collect information. The collection of this information itself can constitute a harmful activity, though not all information collection is harmful. Those that collect the data (the "data holders") then process it—that is, they store, combine, manipulate, search, and use it. I label these activities "information processing." The next step is "information dissemination," in which the data holders transfer the information to others or release the information. The general progression from information collection to processing to dissemination is the data moving further away from the individual's control. The last grouping of activities is "invasions," which involve impingements directly on the individual. Instead of the progression away from the individual, invasions progress toward the

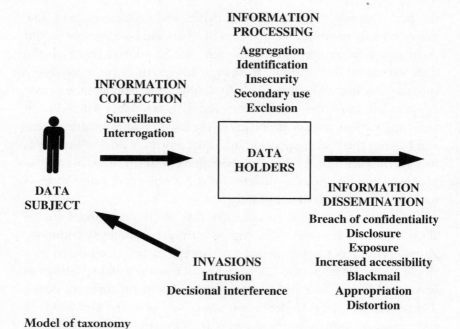

Model of taxonomy

individual and do not necessarily involve information. The relationship between these different groupings is depicted in the figure.[6]

The first group of activities that affect privacy is information collection. *Surveillance* is the watching, listening to, or recording of an individual's activities. *Interrogation* consists of various forms of questioning or probing for information.

A second group of activities involves the way information is stored, manipulated, and used—what I refer to collectively as "information processing." *Aggregation* involves the combination of various pieces of data about a person. *Identification* is linking information to particular individuals. *Insecurity* involves carelessness in protecting stored information from leaks and improper access. *Secondary use* is the use of collected information for a purpose different from the use for which it was collected without the data subject's consent. *Exclusion* concerns the failure to allow the data subject to know about the data that others have about her and participate in its handling and use. These activities do not involve the gathering of data, because it has already been collected. Instead, these activities involve the way data is maintained and used.

The third group of activities involves the dissemination of information. *Breach of confidentiality* is breaking a promise to keep a person's information confidential. *Disclosure* involves the revelation of truthful information about a person that affects the way others judge her reputation. *Exposure* involves revealing another's nudity, grief, or bodily functions. *Increased accessibility* is amplifying the accessibility of information. *Blackmail* is the threat to disclose personal information. *Appropriation* involves the use of the data subject's identity to serve another's aims and interests. *Distortion* consists of disseminating false or misleading information about individuals. Information-dissemination activities all involve the spreading or transfer of personal data or the threat to do so.

The fourth and final group of activities involves invasions into people's private affairs. Invasion, unlike the other groupings, need not involve personal information (although in numerous instances, it does). *Intrusion* concerns invasive acts that disturb one's tranquility or solitude. *Decisional interference* involves incursion into the data subject's decisions regarding her private affairs.

In each category, I discuss the problem, why it is harmful, and the value of protecting against it. My taxonomy is an attempt at categorization, and all attempts at categorization are artificial. One might claim that each situation is incomparable, and that my categorization of problems distorts contextually unique situations into a framework, albeit a more finely grained framework than the unitary conceptions of privacy currently developed in the discourse. As I explained in Chapter 3, however, a theory of privacy should not be too contextual, or else it has little to say beyond each specific situation.

My taxonomy's categories are not based upon any overarching principle. We do not need overarching principles to understand and recognize problems. Too often, attempts to identify such principles about privacy result in failing to address important problems. If we focus on the problems, we can better understand and address them. I aim to shift the approach to a bottom-up focus on problems that are all related to each other, yet not in exactly the same way. If we study the problems together, we can better understand the entire cluster.

One can certainly quarrel with my taxonomy's categories. Since they are not the product of any overarching notion of privacy, they are not final and immutable. I have formulated them from a bottom-up examination of the problems. The pragmatic method counsels that we begin by studying and understanding problems. We then generalize and theorize about them. Finally, we test our theories and continually tweak them so that they work effectively.

Although I have attempted to identify problems on the basis of a detached interpretation of law, policy, and culture, no such attempt can be completely neutral and free from value judgments. I am imposing a framework on a very complex landscape, and in doing so, my own normative views are inescapably bound up in this framework. Nevertheless, my intent is to locate problems based not on my own normative perspective but on broader cultural recognition. The taxonomy is an exercise in cultural interpretation, which occurs through observation and generalization.

Some readers may disagree with the specific problems I identify, a disagreement I expect and welcome. Debating the problems is a fruitful way to discuss privacy. In this book, my attempt is to shift the discussion from elucidating the inherent meaning of the term "privacy" to discussing the nature of certain problems. I aim to set forth the parameters of the kind of discussion that will be most helpful and propose a taxonomy of privacy problems as an example of a pluralistic problem-centered approach. This approach will better help us identify and solve problems than attempting to create a unified conception of privacy that seeks to identify essential elements or core characteristics.

Information Collection

Information collection creates disruption through the process of data gathering. Even if no information is revealed publicly, information collection can create harm. I will identify two forms of information collection: (1) surveillance and (2) interrogation.

Surveillance

The black-mustachio'd face gazed down from every commanding corner. . . . BIG BROTHER IS WATCHING YOU, the caption said, while the dark eyes looked deep into Winston's own. . . . In the far distance a helicopter skimmed down between the roofs, hovered for an instant like a blue-bottle, and darted away again with a curving flight. It was the Police Patrol, snooping into people's windows.

—*George Orwell*, Nineteen Eighty-four *(1949)*[7]

For a long time, surveillance has been viewed as problematic. Ancient Jewish law prohibited building windows that could "peer or look into" neighboring homes. The Jewish scholar Maimonides observed in the twelfth century, "[T]he harm of being seen in privacy is a legal wrong."[8] The term "Peeping Tom" originates from a legend dating back to 1050. When Lady Godiva rode naked on a horse in the city of Coventry to protest taxes, a young man named Tom gawked at her, and he was punished by being blinded.[9] Today, many states have Peeping Tom laws. South Carolina, for example, criminalizes "peep[ing] through windows, doors, or other like places, on or about the premises of another, for the purpose of spying upon or invading the privacy of the persons spied upon."[10] Some states prohibit two-way mirrors in certain areas.[11]

As with visual surveillance, audio surveillance has long been viewed as troubling. William Blackstone noted that eavesdropping was a common-law crime and defined it as "listen[ing] under walls or windows, or the eaves of a house, to hearken after discourse, and thereupon to frame slanderous and mischievous tales."[12] These attitudes persisted after the emergence of electronic eavesdropping. In the early twentieth century, many states prohibited wiretapping of telephone conversations.[13] The U.S. Congress passed major laws regulating wiretapping in 1934, 1968, and 1986.[14] Numerous countries on all continents regulate wiretapping and electronic surveillance in their statutes and constitutions.[15] For example, the European Union Directive on Privacy and Electronic Communications mandates that all member states "shall ensure the confidentiality of communications" and "shall prohibit listening, tapping, storage or other kinds of interception or surveillance."[16]

What is the harm if the government or people watch or listen to us? Certainly, we all watch and listen, even when others may not want us to, and we often do not view this as problematic. However, when done in a certain manner, such as continuous monitoring, surveillance has problematic effects. For example, people expect to be looked at when they ride the bus or subway, but persistent gawking can create feelings of anxiety and discomfort.

Not only can direct awareness of surveillance make a person feel extremely uncomfortable, but it can also cause that person to alter her behavior. Surveillance can lead to self-censorship and inhibition.[17] Because of its inhibitory effects, surveillance is a tool of social control. It enhances the power of social norms, which work more effectively when people are being observed by others.[18] Political scientist John Gilliom observes, "Surveillance of human behavior is in place to control human behavior, whether by limiting access to programs or institutions, monitoring and affecting behavior within those arenas, or otherwise enforcing rules and norms by observing and recording acts of compliance and deviance."[19] This aspect of surveillance does not automatically make it harmful, though, because social control can be beneficial, and every society must exercise a sizeable degree of social control. For example, surveillance can serve as a deterrent to crime. Many people desire the discipline and control surveillance can bring. Jeffrey Rosen observes that Britain's closed-circuit television (CCTV)—a network of over four million public surveillance cameras—is widely perceived as "a friendly eye in the sky, not Big Brother but a kindly and watchful uncle or aunt."[20]

Too much social control, however, can adversely impact freedom, creativity, and self-development. According to Julie Cohen, "[P]ervasive monitoring of every first move or false start will, at the margin, incline choices toward the bland and the mainstream." Monitoring constrains the "acceptable spectrum of belief and behavior," and it results in "a subtle yet fundamental shift in the content of our character, a blunting and blurring of rough edges and sharp lines." Surveillance thus "threatens not only to chill the expression of eccentric individuality, but also, gradually, to dampen the force of our aspirations to it."[21] Similarly, Paul Schwartz argues that surveillance inhibits freedom of choice and impinges upon self-determination.[22]

In many instances, people are not directly aware that they are being observed. Does covert surveillance cause a problem? Under one view, surveillance is a prima facie wrong, whether overt or covert, because it demonstrates a lack of respect for its subject as an autonomous person. Philosopher Stanley Benn explains that overt surveillance threatens its target's "consciousness of pure freedom as subject, as originator and chooser." Benn contends, "Finding oneself an object of scrutiny, as the focus of another's attention, brings one to a new consciousness of oneself, as something seen through another's eyes." Turning to covert observation, Benn explains that it "is objectionable because it deliberately deceives a person about his world, thwarting, for reasons that *cannot* be his reasons, his attempts to make a rational choice."[23]

Although concealed spying is certainly deceptive, Benn's argument is unconvincing. It is the awareness that one is being watched that affects one's freedom, and Benn fails to explain why covert surveillance has any palpable effect on a person's welfare or activities. A more compelling reason why covert surveillance is problematic is that it can still have a chilling effect on behavior. In fact, there can be a more widespread chilling effect when people are generally aware of the possibility of surveillance but are never sure if they are being watched at any particular moment. This phenomenon is known as the Panoptic effect from Jeremy Bentham's 1791 architectural design for a prison called the Panopticon. The prison design arrayed the inmates' cells around a central observation tower. The guards could see each prisoner from the tower, but the prisoners could not see the guards from their cells.[24] In Michel Foucault's words, the cells were akin to "small theatres, in which each actor is alone, perfectly individualized and constantly visible."[25] The prisoner's "only rational option" was to conform with the prison's rules because, at any moment, it was possible that he was being watched.[26] Thus awareness of the possibility of surveillance can be just as inhibitory as actual surveillance.

One might imagine surveillance so covert that its subjects are completely unaware of even the possibility of being observed. Although such well-concealed surveillance might eliminate any discomfort or chilling effect, it would still enable the watchers to gather a substantial degree of information about people. Surveillance is a sweeping form of investigatory power. It extends beyond a search, for it records behavior, social interaction, and potentially everything that a person says and does. Rather than targeting specific information, surveillance can ensnare a significant amount of data beyond any originally sought. If watched long enough, a person might be caught in some form of illegal or immoral activity, and this information could then be used to discredit or blackmail her. A prime example is the FBI's extensive wiretapping of Martin Luther King, Jr., widely believed to have been initiated in order to expose King's alleged Communist ties. Though the surveillance failed to turn up any evidence of such ties, it did reveal King's extramarital affairs. The FBI then attempted to blackmail King with the information, and FBI officials leaked it in order to discredit him.[27]

American law addresses surveillance, but does so by focusing on where surveillance takes place rather than on its problematic effects. In the United States, the law often recognizes surveillance as a harm in private places but rarely in public places. In Fourth Amendment law, courts frequently conclude that surveillance in private places implicates a reasonable expectation of privacy, whereas surveillance in public places does not. In *Kyllo v. United States*, the U.S. Supreme Court concluded that the Fourth Amendment required a warrant in order to use a thermal-imaging device to detect heat patterns emanating from a person's home.[28] The Court's holding relied heavily on the fact that, though conducted outside the person's home, the surveillance was capturing information about activities within it: "We have said that the Fourth Amendment draws a firm line at the entrance of the house."[29]

When surveillance occurs in a public place, however, the Supreme Court has refused to recognize a reasonable expectation of privacy. In *Florida v. Riley*, the police flew over the defendant's greenhouse in a helicopter at 400 feet and peered down through a few missing roof panels to observe that he was growing marijuana. The Court concluded that the defendant lacked a reasonable expectation of privacy: "As a general proposition, the police may see what may be seen from a public vantage point where [they have] a right to be."[30] In *Dow Chemical Co. v. United States*, the Supreme Court held that the government not only could fly over the petitioner's property and observe it with the naked eye, but also could use a powerful aerial mapping camera that enabled the identification of objects as small as one-half inch in diameter.[31]

The contrast between the law's approach to surveillance in private and in public is most evident in a pair of Supreme Court cases involving location-tracking devices. In *United States v. Karo*, the Supreme Court concluded that a tracking device used to monitor a person's movements within his home implicated that person's reasonable expectation of privacy.[32] In contrast, in *United States v. Knotts*, the police used a tracking device to monitor the location of the defendant's vehicle. According to the Supreme Court, the surveillance "amounted principally to the following of an automobile on public streets and highways." The Fourth Amendment did not apply because a "person traveling in an automobile on public thoroughfares has no reasonable expectation of privacy in his movements from one place to another."[33] Thus the Supreme Court has concluded that although the Fourth Amendment protects against surveillance in private places such as one's home, it has little applicability to surveillance in public places.[34] This understanding of privacy stems from what I call the "secrecy paradigm."[35] Under the secrecy paradigm, privacy is tantamount to complete secrecy, and a privacy violation occurs when concealed data is revealed to others. If the information is not previously hidden, then no privacy interest is implicated by the collection or dissemination of the information. In many areas of law, this narrow view of privacy has limited the recognition of privacy violations.

American tort law is generally consistent with this approach. Courts have applied the tort of intrusion upon seclusion, which protects against intrusion "upon the solitude or seclusion of another or his private affairs or concerns,"[36] to surveillance of private places. In *Hamberger v. Eastman*, for example, the court concluded that a couple had a valid intrusion claim against their landlord for his installation of a hidden recording device in their bedroom.[37] In contrast, plaintiffs who have brought claims involving surveillance in public have generally not been successful.[38]

In some cases, however, courts in the United States have recognized a harm in public surveillance. For example, in *Nader v. General Motors Corp.*, Ralph Nader charged that General Motors' automobiles were unsafe. General Motors undertook a massive investigation seeking information that would discredit Nader. Among other things, General Motors wiretapped his telephone and placed him under extensive public surveillance. In a 1970 opinion, the court recognized that although observation in public places is generally not a privacy violation, sometimes "surveillance may be so 'overzealous' as to render it actionable." The court noted, "A person does not automatically make public everything he does merely by being in a public place, and the mere fact that Nader was in a bank did not give anyone the right to try to discover the amount of money he was withdrawing." The court, however, only recognized a harm when public surveillance could reveal hidden details that would ordinarily not be observed. The court did not recognize the surveillance as a harm itself—only surveillance that exposed secrets represented an actionable harm.[39]

Although the law often focuses on whether surveillance occurs in a public or private place, surveillance is harmful in all settings, not just private ones.[40] Surveillance in public can certainly cause uneasiness, as illustrated by the example of being stared at continuously in public. Alan Westin observes, "Knowledge or fear that one is under systematic observation in public places destroys the sense of relaxation and freedom that men seek in open spaces and public arenas."[41] Moreover, public surveillance can have chilling effects that make people less likely to associate with certain groups, attend rallies, or speak at meetings.[42] Espousing radical beliefs and doing unconventional things take tremendous courage; the attentive gaze, especially the government's, can make these acts seem all the more daring and their potential risks all the more inhibitory. Thus surveillance can cause problems that occur both in public and private places. The law, however, tends to focus more on secrecy than on the particular problems and harms caused by surveillance.

Interrogation

I am not willing to answer you to any more of these questions, because I see you go about this Examination to ensnare me.

—*John Lilburne, in response to interrogation in
1637 for seditious libel in England*[43]

There are times when and persons for whom I am not obliged to tell what are my principles and opinions in politicks or religion.

—*John Adams (1770)*[44]

The Fifth Amendment to the U.S. Constitution provides that "[n]o person . . . shall be compelled in any criminal case to be a witness against himself."[45] It creates a "privilege against self-incrimination," and it prevents the government from forcing individuals to testify against themselves.[46] The privilege has been justified as protecting against "[t]he essential and inherent cruelty of compelling a man to expose his own guilt,"[47] as "a safeguard of conscience and human dignity,"[48] and as promoting "respect for personal integrity."[49] Many other countries protect against compelled self-incrimination in their constitutions.[50] The United Nations International Covenant on Civil and Political Rights contains a restriction on compelled self-incrimination.[51] The European Court of Human Rights declared that although not "specifically mentioned" in the Convention on Human Rights, "there can be no doubt that the right to remain silent under police questioning and the privilege against self-incrimination are generally recognized international standards which lie at the heart of the notion of a fair procedure."[52] What is so inhumane about having to answer the government's questions about one's criminal acts? Why protect a potentially guilty person from having to divulge her criminal activities?

A different, less coercive form of interrogation occurs when the government or others ask questions for purposes other than criminal prosecution. In the late nineteenth century, there was a loud public outcry when the U.S. census began including more questions relating to personal affairs, such as marital status, literacy, property ownership, health, and finances.[53] In the 1870s, an editorial in the *New York Times*, as well as editorials in other papers, decried the "inquisitorial" nature of the census. A poem in the *New York Sun* in 1890 humorously criticized the census:

> I am a census inquisitor.
> I travel about from door to door,
> From house to house, from store to store,
> With pencil and paper and power galore.
> I do as I like and ask what I please.
> Down before me you must get on your knees;
> So open your books, hand over your keys,
> And tell me about your chronic disease.[54]

Why was there such an outcry? When asked probing questions, many people respond with the snippy reply, "None of your business!" Why do such questions evoke this response? Why do people take offense even at being asked certain questions—let alone being compelled to answer them?

Understood broadly, these examples all involve a similar practice that I call "interrogation." Interrogation is the pressuring of individuals to divulge information. Interrogation has many benefits; it is useful for ferreting out information that others want to know. However, interrogation can create harm. Part of this harm arises from the degree of coerciveness involved. The Fifth Amendment privilege protects against highly coercive interrogation about matters with enormous personal stakes for the examined subject.[55] For interrogation generally, however, the compulsion need not be direct, nor must it rise to the level of outright coercion. Compulsion can consist of the fear of not getting a job or of social opprobrium. People take offense when others ask an unduly probing question even if there is no compulsion to answer. One explanation may be that people still feel some degree of compulsion because not answering might create the impression that they have something to hide. This is why, I believe, there are social norms against asking excessively prying questions: they make the person being questioned feel uncomfortable. Interrogation makes people concerned about how they will explain themselves or how their refusal to answer will appear to others.

Interrogation resembles intrusion in its invasiveness because interrogation is a probing, a form of searching. Like disclosure, interrogation often involves the divulgence of concealed information; unlike disclosure, interrogation can create discomfort even if the information is barely disseminated. To some degree, surveillance resembles interrogation because both involve the involuntary gathering of information. Interrogation, however, occurs with the conscious awareness of the subject; surveillance can be clandestine.

Historically, interrogation has been employed to impinge upon freedom of association and belief. One of the most extreme examples, the Spanish Inquisition, persisted for centuries and left behind a trail of pain and blood. In England during the Middle Ages, people who diverged from church teachings were forced to submit to the ex officio oath—to "answer upon their oath in causes against themselves—and also to answer interrogations touching their own contempts and crimes objected against them."[56] Public outrage over the ex officio oath erupted in the mid-seventeenth century when John Lilburne refused to submit to the oath after being accused of seditious libel. The oath was abolished in 1641.[57] In the United States, during the McCarthy era in the 1950s, the House Un-American Activities Committee (HUAC) employed interrogation to attack Communists and inhibit their association and expression of political beliefs.[58] Dissenting in *Barenblatt v. United States*, in which the Supreme Court upheld the committee's power to force a witness to answer questions about Communist ties, Justices Hugo Black, Earl Warren, and William O. Douglas argued that the interrogation's harm did not affect the witness alone. They spoke of interrogation impeding "the interest of *the people as a whole* in being able to join organizations, advocate causes and make political 'mistakes' without later being subjected to governmental penalties for having dared to think for themselves."[59]

Another aspect of the power of interrogation is its potential for resulting in distortion. The interrogator possesses extraordinary control over what information is elicited, how it is interpreted, and the impressions created by its revelations. A skillful interrogator can orchestrate a dialogue that creates impressions and inferences that she wants to elicit. In cross-examination, an attorney can carefully manipulate what a witness says and can intimidate a witness into coming across less favorably. Thus one of the rationales justifying the privilege against self-incrimination is that it protects accuracy.[60] Even in the absence of deliberate manipulation, the interrogation process can distort. "The interrogat[ion]," observes Peter Brooks, "seeks to pattern the unfolding narrative according to a preconceived story."[61] Interrogation can distort because information is elicited by another, often without an interest in learning the whole story. In questionnaires and standardized forms, for example, distortion creeps in because the questions often do not ask for the entire story or are phrased in certain ways that yield deceptive results.

Beyond the Fifth Amendment, there are numerous legal protections against interrogation. The First Amendment prevents government questioning about one's political associations. In *Shelton v. Tucker*, the Supreme Court struck down a law requiring public school teachers to list all organizations to which they belonged or contributed.[62] Later, in *Baird v. State Bar of Arizona*, the Court held that a state may not ask questions solely to gain information about a person's political views or associations.[63] According to the Court, "[W]hen a State attempts to make inquiries about a person's beliefs or associations, its power is limited by the First Amendment. Broad and sweeping state inquiries into these protected areas, as Arizona has engaged in here, discourage citizens from exercising rights protected by the Constitution."[64]

Rape shield laws restrict the questioning of rape victims in court.[65] The Americans with Disabilities Act of 1990 limits certain employer inquiries about employee disabilities.[66] Many states prohibit employers from questioning employees or applicants about certain matters. For example, Wisconsin forbids employers from requiring employees or applicants to undergo HIV testing.[67] Massachusetts prohibits employers from asking about arrests not leading to conviction, misdemeanor convictions, or any prior commitment to mental health treatment facilities.[68] Several states restrict employers from requiring employees or applicants to undergo genetic testing.[69] Evidentiary privileges protect against interrogation about communications between attorneys and clients, priests and penitents, and doctors and patients.[70]

Although the law protects against interrogation, it does so in a complicated and unsystematic way. The Fifth Amendment's protection against interrogation is very limited. The Fifth Amendment certainly does not protect the information itself; if the same facts can be produced at trial via other witnesses or evidence, they are not prohibited. The Fifth Amendment is therefore concerned only partly with the type of information involved—its applicability turns on compelled self-disclosure. However, as William Stuntz observes, under current Fifth Amendment law,

> As long as use immunity is granted, the government is free to compel even the most damning and private disclosures. . . . If the privilege were sensibly designed to protect privacy, . . . its application would turn on the *nature* of the disclosure the government wished to require, and yet settled fifth amendment law focuses on the criminal *consequences* of disclosure.[71]

Incriminating information may thus be compelled even under the Fifth Amendment if there are no criminal consequences—even if the disclosure would cause a person great disrepute.[72] In *Ullmann v. United States*, for example, a witness granted immunity to testify about his activities in the Communist Party contended that he would suffer disgrace and severe social sanctions by testifying. He claimed that he might lose his job and friends, as well as be blacklisted from future employment. The Court rejected the witness's argument because no criminal sanctions would be imposed as a result of his testifying.[73] In dissent, Justice

Douglas argued that the "curse of infamy" could be as damaging as criminal punishment, but his view has not been accepted in Fifth Amendment doctrine.[74] It remains unclear what interests the Fifth Amendment protects. Stuntz observes, "It is probably fair to say that most people familiar with the doctrine surrounding the privilege against self-incrimination believe that it cannot be squared with any rational theory."[75]

Evidentiary privileges, like the Fifth Amendment, are also quite narrow in scope. Despite strong public disapproval of forcing parents and children to testify against each other, the majority of courts have rejected a parent-child privilege.[76] Still, in the words of one court, "[F]orcing a mother and father to reveal their child's alleged misdeeds . . . is shocking to our sense of decency, fairness and propriety."[77]

Privacy law's theory of interrogation is incoherent. Despite recognizing the harms and problems of interrogation—compulsion, divulgence of private information, and forced betrayal—the law only addresses them in limited situations.

Information Processing

Information processing is the use, storage, and manipulation of data that has been collected. Information processing does not involve the collection of data; rather, it concerns how already-collected data is handled. I will discuss five forms of information processing: (1) aggregation, (2) identification, (3) insecurity, (4) secondary use, and (5) exclusion.

Processing involves various ways of connecting data and linking it to the people to whom it pertains. Even though processing can involve the transmission of data, it diverges from dissemination because the data transfer does not involve the disclosure of the information to the public—or even to another person. Rather, data is often transferred between various record systems and consolidated with other data. Processing diverges from information collection because processing creates problems through the consolidation and use of information, not through the means by which it is gathered.

Aggregation

The whole is greater than the sum of its parts.

—Anonymous aphorism[78]

The rising use of computers in the 1960s raised public concern about privacy in both the United States and Europe. In the United States, commentators devoted significant attention to the issue, and privacy became an important topic on Congress's agenda.[79] Much concern was focused on the data maintained by the federal government. In 1965, the Bureau of the Budget (now called the Office of Management and Budget) developed a plan to create a Federal Data Center to consolidate the government's decentralized data systems. The plan was quickly attacked in Congress and scrapped.[80]

In France in 1974, an article in *Le Monde* with the headline "Safari, or the Hunt for Frenchmen" reported on a project called Safari, which involved a plan to link various government databases of personal information. After a public outcry, the minister of justice appointed a commission led by Bernard Tricot to examine the threats to privacy posed by computer databases. In 1978, France passed a broad privacy law based on the Tricot Commission's recommendations.[81]

What was the concern with the Federal Data Center and with Safari? The data was already in the record systems of government agencies. Why was it a problem for the government to combine it into one gigantic database?

The problem is one that I have called "aggregation."[82] Aggregation is the gathering of information about a person. A piece of information here or there is not very telling, but when combined, bits and pieces of data begin to form a portrait of a person. The whole becomes greater than the parts.[83] This occurs because combining information creates synergies. When analyzed, aggregated information can reveal new facts about a person that she did not expect would be known about her when the original, isolated data was collected.

Aggregating information is certainly not a new activity. It was always possible to combine various pieces of personal information, to put two and two together to learn something new about a person. But aggregation's power and scope are different in the information age; the data gathered about people is significantly more extensive, the process of combining it is much easier, and the technologies to analyze it are more sophisticated and powerful.

Combining data and analyzing it certainly can have beneficial uses. Amazon.com, for example, uses aggregated data about a person's book-buying history to recommend other books that the person might find of interest. Credit reporting allows creditors to assess people's financial reputations in a world where firsthand experience of their financial condition and trustworthiness is often lacking.[84] These developments make sense in a world where there are billions of people and word of mouth is insufficient to assess reputation.

Alongside these benefits, however, aggregation can cause harm because of how it unsettles expectations. People expect certain limits on what is known about them and on what others will find out. Aggregation upsets these expectations because it involves the combination of data in unanticipated ways to reveal facts about a person that are not readily known. People give out bits of information in different settings, revealing only a small part of themselves in each context. Indeed, people selectively spread around small pieces of data throughout most of their daily activities, and they have the expectation that in each disclosure, they are revealing relatively little about themselves. When these pieces are consolidated, however, the aggregator acquires much greater knowledge about the person's life.

Like surveillance, aggregation is a way to acquire information about people. It reveals facts about data subjects in ways far beyond anything they expected when they gave out the data. However, aggregation is a less direct form of data acquisition than surveillance because it occurs through processing data already gathered from individuals.

Aggregation can also increase the power that others have over individuals. The dossier created by aggregating a person's data is often used as a way to judge her. Aggregations of data, such as credit reports, are used to evaluate people's financial reputations and then make decisions that profoundly affect their lives, such as whether they receive a loan, lease, or mortgage. In many other ways, personal information is being used to make important decisions about individuals. The government and businesses are combining repositories of personal information into what I call "digital dossiers"—extensive records pertaining to people. Increasingly, each individual is living alongside a counterpart who exists in the world of computer databases, a digital person constructed not of flesh and blood but of bits and bytes of data.[85]

Although making decisions based on aggregated data is efficient, it also creates problems. Data compilations are often both telling and incomplete. They reveal facets of our lives, but the data is often reductive and disconnected from the original context in which it was gathered. This leads to distortion. H. Jeff Smith observes:

> [D]ecisions that were formerly based on judgment and human factors are instead often decided according to prescribed formulas. In today's world, this response is often characterized by reliance on a rigid, unyielding process in which computerized information is given great weight. Facts that actually require substantial evaluation could instead be reduced to discrete entries in preassigned categories.[86]

Some courts have recognized aggregation as violating a privacy interest. In *United States Department of Justice v. Reporters Committee for Freedom of the Press*, the Supreme Court concluded that the disclosure of FBI "rap sheets" was an invasion of privacy. Under the Freedom of Information Act (FOIA), "any person" may request "records" maintained by an executive agency. The rap sheets contained extensive information about individuals compiled from a variety of criminal records. FOIA exempts law-enforcement records that "could reasonably be expected to constitute an unwarranted invasion of personal privacy." Although the reporters argued that the rap sheets were not private because all the information in them had already been disclosed, the Court disagreed, noting that in "an organized society, there are few facts that are not at one time or another divulged to another." Thus, the Court observed, there is a "distinction, in terms of personal privacy, between scattered disclosure of the bits of information contained in a rap sheet and revelation of the rap sheet as a whole."[87]

Reporters Committee is one of the rare instances where American law has recognized that aggregation can make a material difference in what is known about an individual. Most courts adhere to the secrecy paradigm, which fails to recognize any privacy interest in information publicly available or already disseminated to others.[88] The Restatement of Torts declares that for the tort of publicity given to private life, "[t]here is no liability when the defendant merely gives further publicity to information about the plaintiff that is already public. Thus there is no liability for giving publicity to facts about the plaintiff's life that are matters of public record."[89] Similarly, the Restatement provides that for the tort of intrusion upon seclusion, "there is no liability for the examination of a public record concerning the plaintiff."[90] In contrast, aggregation violates a privacy interest when the aggregation significantly increases what others know about a person, even if the information originates from public sources.

Differing from *Reporters Committee*, courts have refused to find privacy interests in compilations of information disclosed in Megan's Laws, which involve the dissemination of personal data about convicted sex offenders.[91] In *Russell v. Gregoire*, the court rejected a constitutional challenge to Washington's Megan's Law because the information was not private since it was "already fully available to the public."[92] Similarly, in *Paul P. v. Verniero*, the court declined to follow *Reporters Committee* in concluding that New Jersey's Megan's Law was constitutional.[93] One court observed, "Both the Third Circuit and this Court have repeatedly stressed that *Reporters Committee* is inapposite on the issue of those privacy interests entitled to protection under the United States Constitution."[94] These cases limited *Reporters Committee* to the FOIA context, but they did not supply a reason why recognizing a privacy interest in aggregated data is necessarily linked only to FOIA and does not apply to other areas of law. Legally, the cases have drawn a line, but conceptually, no justification has been offered for the limitation.

Of course, there are many reasons why Megan's Laws might outweigh privacy interests—for example, as a means to promote safety of children, to keep parents informed of which neighbors to avoid, and to help parents make sure that the babysitter they hired is not a prior child molester. However, *Russell* and *Paul P.* did not recognize a privacy interest in the aggregated data, and thus no balancing took place between this privacy interest and the safety interest.

Identification

Every human being carries with him from his cradle to his grave certain physical marks which do not change their character, and by which he can always be identified—and that without shade or doubt or question. These marks are his signature, his physiological autograph.

—*Wilson's address to the jury in Mark Twain,*
Pudd'nhead Wilson *(1894)*[95]

Although a national identification card has been proposed many times in the United States, it has been rejected on each occasion. When the Social Security system was first developed, "President Roosevelt and members of Congress promised that the Social Security card would be kept confidential and would not be used for identification purposes."[96] The cards even stated that they were "not for identification."[97] In 1973, the influential report *Records, Computers, and the Rights of Citizens* concluded:

> We take the position that a standard universal identifier (SUI) should not be established in the United States now or in the foreseeable future. By our definition, the Social Security Number (SSN) cannot fully qualify as an SUI; it only approximates one. However, there is an increasing tendency for the Social Security number to be used as if it were an SUI.[98]

When Congress passed the Privacy Act in 1974, it included a provision to regulate the use of SSNs in order to "eliminate the threat to individual privacy and confidentiality of information posed by common numerical identifiers."[99] But the act did not limit the use of SSNs by businesses, and today, SSNs are widely used for identification purposes.[100] SSNs, combined with increasing requirements to show drivers' licenses and passports, are creating a de facto national identification system in the United States.

In Sweden, plans to issue personal identification numbers led to the passage of one of the earliest comprehensive privacy protection laws, the Data Act of 1973.[101] In the 1980s, the Australian government proposed the "Australia Card," a national identification system. The proposal met with a public backlash that resulted in the passage of the Privacy Act of 1988. The Australia Card proposal was abandoned.[102] In contrast to Australia, the United States, and several other nations, many countries have adopted a national identification card.[103] Why have identification cards been such a contentious issue? What is the problem with identifying people?

"Identification" is connecting information to individuals. According to Roger Clarke, identification is "the association of data with a particular human being."[104] Identification enables us to attempt to verify identity—that the person accessing her records is indeed the owner of the account or the subject of the records. Identification enables us not only to confirm the identity of a person, but also to discover the perpetrator of a crime from traces left behind, such as fingerprints and genetic material.[105]

Identification is related to disclosure in that both involve revealing true information. Identification involves a particular form of true information (one's identity), which enables databases of information to be linked to people. Identification is similar to aggregation because both involve the combination of different pieces of information, one being the identity of a person. However, identification differs from aggregation in that it entails a link to the person in the flesh. For example, there can be extensive aggregations of data about a person in many databases, but these aggregations might be rarely connected to that person as she goes through her day-to-day activities. This situation involves high aggregation and low identification. On the flip side, one can have high identification and low aggregation, as in a world of checkpoints, where people constantly have to show identification but where there are few linkages to larger repositories of data about people.

Identification has many benefits.[106] In order for people to access various accounts, their identity must be verified, a step that can reduce fraud and enhance accountability. Identification can deter misleading political campaign ads. Under federal election law, television ads advocating the election or defeat of a candidate must identify the person or group placing the ad.[107] If an ad is not authorized by a candidate, it "shall clearly state the name and permanent street address, telephone number, or World Wide Web address of the person who paid for the communication."[108] Identification requirements such as this one can help prevent misinformation and enable people to better assess the ad.

Although identification of people or sources of particular messages can be beneficial, it also creates problems. Some argue that identification is demeaning to dignity because it reduces people to a number or to bodily characteristics.[109] But identification is a means to link people to data, not necessarily an indication that people are the equivalent of their identifying characteristics. Therefore, identification is not inherently demeaning to dignity.

There is, nonetheless, a more compelling argument why identification can negatively affect identity. The problem stems not from the identifier itself but from how it links data to individuals. Because it connects people to data, identification attaches informational baggage to people. This alters what others learn about people as they engage in various transactions and activities. An interesting example of this was a case before the European Court of Human Rights (ECHR), which enforces the Council of Europe's Convention for the Protection of Human Rights and Fundamental Freedoms.[110] In *B. v. France*, a French citizen who had surgically changed her sex from male to female sought to have her identification documents (birth certificate, identity card, passport, and voting card) changed from listing her former male name to a female one. Since gender was "indicated on all documents using the identification number issued to everyone" and since this "number was used as part of the system of dealings between social security institutions, employers and those insured," it prevented her from concealing the fact that she was a transsexual and effectively assuming a female identity. The court stated:

> A transsexual was consequently unable to hide his or her situation from a potential employer and the employer's administrative staff; the same applied to the many occasions in daily life where it was necessary to prove the existence and amount of one's income (taking a lease, opening a bank account, applying for credit, etc.). This led to difficulties for the social and professional integration of transsexuals.

The court concluded that the applicant, "as a result of the frequent necessity of disclosing information concerning her private life to third parties, suffered distress which was too serious to be justified on the ground of respect for the rights of others." This case illustrates how identification can inhibit people's ability to change and can prevent their self-development by tying them to a past from which they want to escape.[111]

In some ways, identification resembles interrogation because identification often involves the questioning of individuals to compel them to identify themselves. Identification is a component of certain forms of surveillance insofar as it facilitates the detection and monitoring of a person and enables surveillance data to be categorized according to the individuals to which they pertain.

Identification is thus interrelated with other privacy problems, and, like those problems, it reveals, distorts, and intrudes. Identification diverges, however, because it is primarily a form of connecting data to people. Aggregation creates what I have called a "digital person," a portrait composed of combined information fragments.[112] Identification goes a step further—it links the digital person directly to a person in realspace.

Some forms of identification can have effects similar to those of disclosure. For example, expressive methods of identification, such as branding, tattooing, or scarlet letters, have been used, "usually in the context of slavery, racial subjugation or harsh criminal systems."[113] The identification marker conveys certain information and often bears a particular stigma. In contrast, nonexpressive means of identification, such as fingerprints, identify people without signaling anything to the public.

Identification also affects social structure because it increases the government's power over individuals. Identification has been a critical tool for governments seeking to round up radicals or disfavored citizens.[114] It is also an efficient means for controlling people. In the United States, passports were used to stifle dissent. During the McCarthy era, the government prohibited Communists from using passports and thus prevented them from traveling outside the country.[115]

Identification can inhibit one's ability to be anonymous or pseudonymous. Anonymous speech has a long history as an important mode of expression. Between 1789 and 1809, numerous U.S. presidents and congressmen published anonymous political writings. Benjamin Franklin used more than forty pen names.[116] James Madison, Alexander Hamilton, and John Jay published *The Federalist Papers* using the pseudonym "Publius," and the Anti-Federalists also used pseudonyms.[117] Anonymity and pseudonymity protect people from bias based on their identities and enable people to vote, speak, and associate more freely by protecting them from the danger of reprisal.[118] Anonymity can enhance the persuasiveness of one's ideas because identification can shade the reception of ideas with readers' biases and prejudices. This is why, in many universities and schools, exams are graded anonymously. Anonymity provides people with the ability to criticize the companies for which they work and to blow the whistle on illegal activities.[119] Anonymity also protects people who read or listen to certain unpopular ideas.[120]

In a series of cases, the U.S. Supreme Court has recognized that "identification and fear of reprisal might deter perfectly peaceful discussions of public matters of importance."[121] Thus requiring the disclosure of identifying information would chill free speech, violating the First Amendment. However, in *Hiibel v. Sixth Judicial District Court*, the Supreme Court concluded that a law requiring people to identify themselves during a police stop did not violate the Fourth and Fifth Amendments. In particular, responding to the Fifth Amendment challenge, the Court concluded, "Answering a request to disclose a name is likely to be so insignificant in the scheme of things as to be incriminating only in unusual circumstances."[122] However, as Justice John Paul Stevens wrote in dissent:

> A name can provide the key to a broad array of information about the person, particularly in the hands of a police officer with access to a range of law enforcement databases. And that information, in turn, can be tremendously useful in a criminal prosecution. It is therefore quite wrong to suggest that a person's identity provides a link in the chain to incriminating evidence "only in unusual circumstances."[123]

Stevens's dissent recognizes that the harm of identification is often not in the disclosure of the identifying marker (such as name or fingerprint) itself, but in the ability to connect this marker to a stream of collected data. Being asked to identify oneself, therefore, is being asked to link oneself to data, not just to state a name.

Insecurity

> I live in peace in the innermost chamber of my house, and meanwhile the enemy may be burrowing his way slowly and stealthily straight toward me.
>
> —*Franz Kafka, "The Burrow" (1924)*[124]

Identity theft is the fastest-growing white-collar crime.[125] An identity thief opens accounts and conducts fraud in the victim's name. Identity theft is made possible because we all have digital dossiers—extensive collections of personal information about us—that are maintained by various companies and institutions.[126] The thief taps into a person's dossier, which becomes polluted with discrediting information when debts go unpaid, or when the thief uses the person's identity to commit a crime. Victims of identity theft are submerged into a bureaucratic hell where, according to one estimate, they must spend approximately two years and almost 200 hours to decontaminate their dossier.[127] While their dossier remains defiled, victims have difficulty getting jobs, loans, or mortgages.[128]

Identity theft is the result of a larger group of problems I call "insecurity." Glitches, security lapses, abuses, and illicit uses of personal information all fall into this category. Insecurity is a problem caused by the way our information is handled and protected. In 2005, for example, a litany of companies in the United States revealed that they had leaked scores of records of personal information—over 100 million records in all.[129] These leaks generated considerable attention in the media and led to the passage of dozens of state laws to improve security, notify people of data leaks, and combat identity theft.

Insecurity is related to aggregation because it creates risks of downstream harm that can emerge from inadequate protection of compendiums of personal data. Insecurity is also related to identification—it often occurs because of difficulties in linking data to people. As Lynn LoPucki observes, identity theft occurs because "creditors and credit-reporting agencies often lack both the means and the incentives to correctly identify the persons who seek credit from them or on whom they report."[130] In this sense, insecurity can be a cost of lack of identification.[131]

Distortion—the dissemination of false information about a person—is related to insecurity because problems with security can result in one's records being polluted with false data. This can destroy a person's financial reputation, which today is based in large part on the records maintained by credit-reporting agencies.[132] Insecurity, therefore, can involve not only a threat of disclosure but also a threat of distortion.

Insecurity exposes people to potential future harm. Combating identity theft after it happens has proven immensely difficult. The careless use of data by businesses and the government makes the crime of identity theft incredibly easy. Companies use Social Security numbers (SSNs) as passwords for access to accounts, and since SSNs can be readily obtained by identity thieves from public records or from database companies, people's accounts and personal information are insecure.[133]

In cases involving the constitutional right to privacy, courts have sometimes recognized insecurity as a privacy harm. In *Whalen v. Roe*, the U.S. Supreme Court declared that the constitutional right to privacy also extended to the "individual interest in avoiding disclosure of personal matters." As the Court observed, the government's collection of personal data for its record systems "is typically accompanied by a concomitant statutory or regulatory duty to avoid unwarranted disclosures." The Court noted that "in some circumstances that duty arguably has its roots in the Constitution."[134] Applying *Whalen*, a federal circuit court in *Fraternal Order of Police, Lodge No. 5 v. City of Philadelphia* concluded that certain questions on a police department employee questionnaire were unconstitutional because no guidelines existed about maintaining the security of the information.[135]

Information security is protected around the world. One of the original Fair Information Practices of 1973 provides that organizations using records "must take reasonable precautions to prevent misuse of the data."[136] The APEC Privacy Framework, the OECD Privacy Guidelines, and the EU Data Protection Directive all require security safeguards.[137] The Council of Europe Convention for the Protection of Individuals with Regard to Automatic Processing of Personal Data mandates security measures for data stored electronically.[138]

In the United States, the Privacy Act of 1974 requires federal agencies maintaining personal data to "establish appropriate administrative, technical, and physical safeguards to ensure the security and confidentiality of records." The Children's Online Privacy Protection Act states that websites must protect the "confidentiality, security, and integrity of personal information collected from children." The Gramm-Leach-Bliley Act and the Health Insurance Portability and Accountability Act require security standards for personal information. The Computer Fraud and Abuse Act prohibits hacking into people's computers.[139]

Although the law recognizes injuries when a breach of security results in overt harm to an individual, courts are sometimes reluctant to find harm simply from the insecure storage of information.[140] Several privacy statutes attempt to avoid problems in measuring harm by providing for minimum liquidated damages.[141] In many instances, however, courts ignore insecurity as a problem. Although insecurity increases the possibility of disclosure, courts often do not recognize a problem unless there has been an actual disclosure or data leak. Even with a data leak, courts are reluctant to recognize a harm without a more concrete injury. In one case, for example, a bank failed to adequately secure people's personal information, and a hacker accessed the data of tens of thousands of individuals. A group of people sued, but the court dismissed the case because "[w]ithout more than allegations of increased risk of future identity theft, the plaintiffs have not suffered a harm that the law is prepared to remedy."[142]

In some recent cases, the U.S. Federal Trade Commission (FTC) has recognized insecurity as a problem. Since 1998, the FTC has viewed companies that violate their privacy policies as engaging in "unfair or deceptive acts or practices in or affecting commerce."[143] Equipped with the ability to bring civil actions and obtain injunctions, the FTC has brought several cases against companies for improperly disclosing or leaking data in violation of their privacy policies. In a handful of cases, the FTC has brought an action even before any data was improperly released. For example, the FTC contended that Microsoft's Passport, a system allowing people to use a single login password for a variety of websites, was not providing an adequate level of security despite Microsoft's promise to do so in its privacy policy. Microsoft settled with the FTC, agreeing to implement an improved level of security.[144] In another case, the FTC pursued Guess.com for providing inadequate security for customers' personal data.[145] Thus the law clearly recognizes insecurity as a problem, but although it sometimes comprehends the harm, in other instances, it fails to view insecurity alone as an injury.

Secondary Use

[An] individual who is asked to provide a simple item of information for what he believes to be a single purpose may omit explanatory details that become crucial when his file is surveyed for unrelated purposes.

—*Arthur Miller,* The Assault on Privacy *(1971)*[146]

In 1977, in an attempt to catch people engaging in fraud, the U.S. government began matching its employee records with the records of individuals receiving federal benefits.[147] These matchings were done electronically through the use of computers. Although the information was not originally collected for this purpose, it was readily used to conduct investigations of millions of people.[148] In 1988, Congress passed the Computer Matching and Privacy Protection Act to regulate computer matching. The act requires agencies to do a cost-benefit analysis on computer matching programs and to enable people who suffer an adverse decision based on data matching to have a hearing.[149]

In 1973, the U.S. Department of Health, Education, and Welfare (HEW), in its influential report on the harms caused by computer databases, set forth a series of Fair Information Practices, one of which provides that "[t]here must be a way for an individual to prevent information about him obtained for one purpose from being used or made available for other purposes without his consent."[150] This principle, which has become known as the purpose specification principle, has been embodied in various privacy principles and laws.

In the United States, a number of statutes restrict secondary use. The Privacy Act of 1974, for example, requires agencies to inform people of "the principal purpose or purposes for which the information is intended to be used" when their information is collected. Federal laws also limit secondary uses of credit reports, motor-vehicle records, cable records, financial records, and video records.[151] The Federal Election Campaign Act states that records of contributors to political committees are "available for public inspection . . . except that any information copied from such reports . . . may not be sold or used by any person for the purpose of soliciting contributions or for commercial purposes." The Health Insurance Portability and Accountability Act regulations restrict secondary uses of medical information beyond those necessary for treatment, payment, and health care operations.[152]

Around the world, the laws of many countries regulate the secondary use of personal information. The EU Data Protection Directive provides strong regulation of secondary use: Personal data must be "collected for specified, explicit and legitimate purposes and not further processed in a way incompatible with those purposes."[153] The Council of Europe Convention for the Protection of Individuals with Regard to Automatic Processing of Personal Data provides that personal data shall be "stored for specified and legitimate purposes and not used in a way incompatible with those purposes."[154] The OECD Privacy Guidelines and the APEC Privacy Framework also contain a restriction on secondary use.[155] In Australia, the Privacy Act "prohibits an organisation using or disclosing personal information about an individual for a purpose other than the primary purpose of collection (described as the 'secondary purpose'), unless an exception applies."[156] South Korea's Information Protection Act and Canada's Personal Information Protection and Electronic Documents Act (PIPEDA) protect against secondary uses.[157] According to the United Nations Guidelines Concerning Computerized Personal Data Files, "All the personal data collected and recorded [must] remain relevant and adequate to the purposes . . . specified [at the time the data was collected]."[158]

What is the concern over secondary uses of information beyond those purposes for which it is collected? Why are there so many legal attempts to limit secondary uses of data?

"Secondary use" is the use of data for purposes unrelated to the purposes for which the data was initially collected without the data subject's consent. There are certainly many desirable instances of secondary use. Information might be used to stop a crime or to save a life. The variety of possible secondary uses of data is virtually infinite, and they range from benign to malignant. Secondary use is often referred to as "mission creep" or "data creep," which describes the gradual expansion of uses of information over time.

Secondary use can cause problems. It involves using information in ways that a person does not consent to and that she might not find desirable. Secondary uses thwart people's expectations about how the data they give out will be used. People might not give out data if they know about a potential secondary use, such as telemarketing, spam, or other forms of intrusive advertising. For example, fingerprints of U.S. military recruits originally collected to screen their backgrounds were sent to the FBI and incorporated into the FBI's criminal fingerprint database.[159] These individuals may not have expected nor desired to have their fingerprints maintained in a law-enforcement database of convicts and criminals. Secondary use resembles breach of confidentiality in that there is a betrayal of the person's expectations when giving out information.

Perhaps people should simply expect that their data might be used in different ways when they relinquish it. Under this view, there is no harm to expectations. But even when privacy policies state that information might be used in secondary ways, people often do not read or understand these policies. Privacy policies rarely specify future secondary uses, so people cannot make an informed decision about their information because they have little idea about the range of potential uses. According to Paul Schwartz, this is an asymmetry-of-knowledge problem:

> [I]ndividuals are likely to know little or nothing about the circumstances under which their personal data are captured, sold, or processed. This widespread individual ignorance hinders development through the privacy marketplace of appropriate norms about personal data use. The result of this asymmetrical knowledge will be one-sided bargains that benefit data processors.[160]

The potential for secondary use generates fear and uncertainty over how one's information will be used in the future, creating a sense of powerlessness and vulnerability. In this respect, secondary use resembles the harm created by insecurity. The harm is a dignitary one that emerges from denying people control over the future use of their data, which can be used in ways that have significant effects on their lives.

The secondary use of information can create problems because the information may not fit as well with the new use. When data is removed from the original context in which it was collected, it can more readily be misunderstood.

Although the United States has many laws with secondary-use restrictions, its protections are less comprehensive than those of many other countries. The problem of secondary use is recognized inconsistently. In many instances, once a person relinquishes control over personal data to others, there are few, if any, limitations on its use. In *Dwyer v. American Express Co.*, for example, American Express sold the personal information of its cardholders to others without their consent. A group of cardholders sued, but their case was dismissed because they "voluntarily" turned over their information to American Express. The court did not recognize a problem in the fact that the cardholders gave their data for one purpose, but it was being used for an entirely different purpose.[161]

In other contexts, however, courts have recognized the problem of secondary use. In *Sheets v. Salt Lake County*, police investigating a bombing asked the husband of a woman killed in the incident for a copy of her diary. He provided the diary believing that it would remain confidential. However, the police allowed a writer to read the diary and quote from it in a book about the bombing. The court concluded that the police violated the constitutional right to information privacy. The police argued that the diary was not private "considering the many investigators who had access to the diary." However, the court concluded, "To turn a diary over to a limited group for what one perceived to be a limited and proper purpose is quite different than inviting publication of the material."[162] Similarly, in another case, the police disclosed a video of a rape to a television station. Although the video would eventually be played at trial, the court held that "[j]ust because disclosing private information at a possible criminal trial is justified by the evidentiary nature of that information, it does not follow that disclosing the same information on a television news broadcast is similarly justified."[163]

Exclusion

For in general the proceedings are kept secret not only from the public but from the accused as well.

—*Franz Kafka*, The Trial *(1925)*[164]

Nowadays, an individual must increasingly give information about himself to large and relatively faceless institutions, for handling and use by strangers—unknown, unseen, and, all too frequently, unresponsive.

—*U.S. Department of Health, Education, and Welfare*, Records, Computers, and the Rights of Citizens *(1973)*[165]

Among the Fair Information Practices are three related principles: (1) the existence of record systems cannot be kept secret; (2) an individual must be able to "find out what information about him is in a record and how it is used"; and (3) an individual must be able to "correct or amend a record of identifiable information about him."[166] Together these principles allow individuals to have some knowledge of the records about them maintained by government agencies and businesses. The principles require transparency in the record systems and provide individuals with a right to ensure that the information is accurate.

Around the world, countries provide various rights for people to access and correct their records. In Argentina, for example, a person has a constitutional right to "obtain information on the data about himself and their purpose, registered in public records . . . or in private ones."[167] Brazil's constitution gives individuals a right to find out what information the government keeps about them in its record systems, and its Consumer Protection Law of 1990 allows consumers to access the personal data companies store about them.[168] Canada's Federal Court of Appeal declared that people "have a legitimate interest in knowing what personal information the state possesses about them" and should be "able to verify the accuracy of personal information and if possible that it was legally obtained."[169] The EU Data Protection Directive provides rights of access and correction. The OECD Privacy Guidelines and the APEC Privacy Framework also contain access and correction provisions.[170] These are just a few among many examples.

Providing notice to people about the uses of their personal information and giving them rights to access and correct it can be costly and time consuming. Why do so many laws provide people with access and correction rights? What problems are caused when people are not informed about the information entities have about them?

I refer to the failure to provide individuals with notice and input about their records as "exclusion." Exclusion reduces accountability on the part of government agencies and businesses that maintain records about individuals. Exclusion is related to insecurity because the lack of accountability often goes hand in hand with inadequate security in record systems of personal data. Exclusion differs from insecurity in that exclusion is not primarily a harm caused by the lack of protection against data leakage or contamination. Rather, it is a harm created by being shut out from participating in the use of one's personal data, by not being informed about how that data is used, and by not being able to do anything to affect how it is used.

One might contend that exclusion is not harmful in and of itself but is merely a factor that leads to downstream harms like information dissemination. Exclusion, however, can cause harm even if it does not lead to the dissemination of data. As with secondary use and insecurity, exclusion creates a sense of vulnerability and uncertainty. When people are unable to participate in the maintenance and use of their information, they can be rendered powerless. Some might argue that there are many aspects of life in which we are powerless, and that there is nothing special about powerlessness with respect to personal information. But in a world where people's information is increasingly used to make important decisions about them, powerlessness in this arena can be significantly troublesome. Exclusion divests people of control over their lives in a substantial way.

For the most part, tort law has not recognized exclusion as a harm. In certain kinds of special relationships, however, tort law has developed strong duties and responsibilities. The law of fiduciary duties creates special duties of accountability within certain relationships. A fiduciary relationship exists when one party stands in a special position of power over another person.[171] New York Chief Justice Benjamin Cardozo described the relationship best:

> Many forms of conduct permissible in a workaday world for those acting at arm's length, are forbidden to those bound by fiduciary ties. A trustee is held to something stricter than the morals of the market place. Not honesty alone, but the punctilio of an honor the most sensitive, is then the standard of behavior.[172]

In these relationships, such as between doctors and patients, fiduciary duties require informed consent. As one court has noted, when "soliciting the patient's consent, a physician has a fiduciary duty to disclose all information material to the patient's decision."[173] In some instances, obtaining informed consent might require disclosing to a person how her data might be used in the future.

The primary legal protection against exclusion is statutory. Numerous U.S. privacy statutes guard against exclusion by mandating transparency and granting individuals the right to access their information. For example, the Privacy Act provides people the right to access their records. So do the Cable Communications Policy Act, the Fair Credit Reporting Act, and the Children's Online Privacy Protection Act.[174] Several privacy statutes offer people a way to correct inaccurate information in their records.[175] Although these statutes stop short of requiring informed consent, they do give people some ability to discover the information gathered about them.

Some statutes also allow people to opt out of certain uses of information. The Gramm-Leach-Bliley Act, for example, allows people to refuse to allow financial institutions to share their data with third parties.[176] The opt-out right, which assumes consent unless an individual affirmatively indicates a preference for not sharing the information, does not ensure that consent is informed beyond providing customers with notice that information may be shared. Accordingly, it would most likely fail to constitute informed consent within a fiduciary relationship.

The law thus partially protects against exclusion. It provides people with some rights over their information when in the possession of others, but it stops short of allowing individuals to exercise a significant degree of control over their data.

Information Dissemination

Thus far, I have discussed problems that arise out of the collection of information, as well as problems that arise from the storage and use of data. "Information dissemination" is one of the broadest groupings of privacy problems. These problems consist of revealing personal data or the threat of spreading information. This group includes (1) breach of confidentiality, (2) disclosure, (3) exposure, (4) increased accessibility, (5) blackmail, (6) appropriation, and (7) distortion.

Breach of Confidentiality

The frankest and freest and privatest product of the human mind and heart is a love letter; the writer gets his limitless freedom of statement and expression from his sense that no stranger is going to see what he is writing. Sometimes there is a breach-of-promise case by and by; and when he sees his letter in print it makes him cruelly uncomfortable and he perceives that he never would have unbosomed himself to that large and honest degree if he had known that he was writing for the public.

—*Mark Twain*[177]

Three may keep a secret, if two are dead.

—*Benjamin Franklin*[178]

Mrs. McCormick was involved in a contentious divorce and custody battle with her husband. McCormick's doctor told her husband that McCormick was suffering from "major depression and alcoholism." McCormick sued her doctor. According to the court, a "majority of the jurisdictions faced with the issue have recognized a cause of action against a physician for the unauthorized disclosure of confidential information unless the disclosure is compelled by law or is in the patient's interest or the public interest." Unlike the tort of public disclosure, the tort of breach of confidentiality does not require that the disclosure be "highly offensive." The court reasoned that while the public-disclosure tort "focuses on the *content*, rather than the *source* of the information," the breach-of-confidentiality tort centers on the source of the data. Thus the "unauthorized revelation of confidential medical information should be protected without regard to the degree of its offensiveness."[179] In the United States, the tort of breach of confidentiality applies not only to physicians, but also to bankers and other professionals who maintain relationships of trust.[180] Additionally, some courts have extended liability to third parties who induce a betrayal of confidence.[181]

England, which rejects Warren and Brandeis's privacy torts, recognizes a breach-of-confidence tort. Unlike the American version, which applies only in a few narrow contexts, the English tort applies much more generally and extends even to spouses and lovers.[182] One English court declared "The fact is that when people kiss and later one of them tells, that second person is almost certainly breaking a confidential arrangement."[183] In *A v. B*, for example, a soccer player sought to stop a magazine from publishing stories by two of his lovers about their extramarital affairs with him. The Court of Appeal refused to grant the injunction because free-speech interests won out in the balance, but the court did recognize a breach of confidence. It held that a "duty of confidence will arise whenever the party subject to the duty is in a situation where he either knows or ought to know that the other person can reasonably expect his privacy to be protected." According to the court, even those engaged in extramarital trysts have duties of confidentiality, but these duties are lesser than those of a marital relationship.[184] Other common-law jurisdictions recognize a breach-of-confidence tort akin to that of England, including Canada, Australia, New Zealand, and Scotland.[185]

Why does the law recognize a separate cause of action for breach of confidentiality? Why not rectify such harms with the tort of public disclosure? The answer, I posit, is that disclosure and breach of confidentiality cause different kinds of injuries. Both involve revealing a person's secrets, but breaches of confidentiality also violate trust in a specific relationship. The harm from a breach of confidentiality, then, is not simply that information has been disclosed, but that the victim has been betrayed. When it recognized a cause of action for breach of confidentiality in 1920, an American court in *Simonsen v. Swenson* noted that "the physician is bound, . . . upon his own professional honor and the ethics of his high profession, to keep secret [a patient's information]. . . . A wrongful breach of such confidence, and a betrayal of such trust, would give rise to a civil action for the damages naturally flowing from such wrong."[186]

Protection against breach of confidentiality helps promote certain relationships that depend upon trust. The disclosure tort also protects relationships of trust, but disclosure must result in the release of embarrassing secrets or discrediting data before courts will consider it harmful. Breach of confidentiality requires only a betrayal of trust, regardless of the nature of the data revealed.

There are certainly instances where we might find a breach of confidentiality desirable. In *Simonsen*, for example, the court concluded that a doctor should not be held liable for disclosing the fact that a patient had syphilis, which at the time was believed to be highly contagious. The court held that protecting public health outweighed any privacy interest the plaintiff might have.[187] Likewise, in *Tarasoff v. Regents of the University of California*, a psychotherapy patient murdered a young woman with whom he was obsessed. The California Supreme Court concluded that the patient's psychotherapist had a duty to the woman because he had knowledge that his patient posed a danger to her:

[T]he therapist's obligations to his patient require that he not disclose a confidence unless such disclosure is necessary to avert danger to others, and even then that he do so discreetly, and in a fashion that would preserve the privacy of his patient to the fullest extent compatible with the prevention of the threatened danger.[188]

The law, however, is inconsistent in its recognition of breach of confidentiality as a harm. U.S. Fourth Amendment law fails to recognize breach of confidentiality as a harm. In *United States v. Miller,* federal law-enforcement officials issued subpoenas to two banks to produce a customer's financial records. The banks complied with the subpoenas, but the customer was not notified of the disclosure of the records until later in the course of prosecution. The defendant contended that the subpoenas violated his Fourth Amendment rights. The Supreme Court concluded, however, that the customer lacked a reasonable expectation of privacy in the financial records maintained by his bank: "[T]he Fourth Amendment does not prohibit the obtaining of information revealed to a third party and conveyed by him to Government authorities." Moreover, the Supreme Court contended, "All of the documents obtained, including financial statements and deposit slips, contain only information voluntarily conveyed to the banks and exposed to their employees in the ordinary course of business."[189]

A few years later, the Supreme Court employed similar reasoning in *Smith v. Maryland,* where it held that people lack a reasonable expectation of privacy in the phone numbers they dial because people "know that they must convey numerical information to the phone company" and, therefore, cannot "harbor any general expectation that the numbers they dial will remain secret."[190]

Miller and *Smith* are the leading cases in what has become known as the "third-party doctrine." This doctrine provides that if information is possessed or known by third parties, then, for purposes of the Fourth Amendment, an individual lacks a reasonable expectation of privacy in the information. In the information age, much of what we do is recorded by third parties. The third-party doctrine therefore places an extensive amount of personal information outside the protection of the Fourth Amendment.[191]

The third-party doctrine is based on the secrecy paradigm: when others know the information, it is no longer completely secret. But the fact that the information is known to third parties would not be relevant to the Court's analysis if the harm were understood to be a breach of confidentiality. When people establish a relationship with banks, Internet service providers, phone companies, and other businesses, they are not disclosing their information to the world. They are giving it to a party with implicit (and often explicit) promises that the information will be confidential.[192]

More than ten American states have rejected the reasoning of the third-party doctrine in interpreting their own constitutional protections against search and seizure.[193] Dissent from the third-party doctrine is not limited to American courts. In 2004, the Supreme Court of India, after looking to U.S. Fourth Amendment law for guidance in a case similar to *Miller*, declared that bank customer records "must continue to remain confidential vis-à-vis the person, even if they are no longer at the customer's house and have been voluntarily sent to a Bank." Therefore, the court concluded, "[W]e cannot accept the line of *Miller* in which the [U.S. Supreme] Court proceeded on the basis that the right to privacy is referable to the right of 'property' theory."[194]

In the United States, tort law, unlike Fourth Amendment law, recognizes breach of confidentiality as a distinct harm. The breach-of-confidentiality tort applies to the patient-physician relationship and to other relationships as well. As mentioned previously, some courts have held that the tort applies to banks. In *Peterson v. Idaho First National Bank*, the court observed, "All agree that a bank should protect its business records from the prying eyes of the public, moved by curiosity or malice. No one questions its right to protect its fiduciary relationship with its customers, which, in sound banking practice, as a matter of common knowledge, is done everywhere." Not divulging customers' financial information to others "is an implied term of the contract between a banker and his customer." Moreover, the court reasoned, "Inviolate secrecy is one of the inherent and fundamental precepts of the relationship of the bank and its customers or depositors."[195] Many other courts have agreed.[196]

Disclosure

[I]t ain't going to be possible to keep out anywhere the light of the press. Now what I'm going to do is to set up the biggest lamp yet made over and make it shine all over the place. We'll see who's private then.

—*George Flack, a journalist in Henry James,*
The Reverberator *(1888)*[197]

The law in the United States has developed a number of protections against disclosures of true information about people. The tort of public disclosure of private facts, inspired by Warren and Brandeis's article, creates a cause of action for one who publicly discloses a private matter that is "highly offensive to a reasonable person" and "is not of legitimate concern to the public."[198] In *Whalen v. Roe*, the Supreme Court recognized that the "right to privacy" based on substantive due process also encompassed the "individual interest in avoiding disclosure of personal matters."[199] Although the Supreme Court has not further elaborated on this branch of the right to privacy, it is recognized in many circuits and thus enables plaintiffs to sue government officials for disclosing personal information.[200] Further, a number of statutes restrict disclosure of information from government records, school records, cable-company records, video records, motor-vehicle records, and health records.[201] Various states have restricted the disclosure of particular forms of information, such as medical data and alcohol and drug abuse.[202]

In other countries, constitutions and laws limit the disclosure of private information. Argentina's Civil Code restricts "publishing photos, divulging correspondence, mortifying another's customs or sentiments or disturbing his privacy by whatever means."[203] Several Canadian provinces provide a tort action for invasion of privacy, akin to Warren and Brandeis's public-disclosure tort.[204] In France, courts have created tort remedies for the disclosure of personal secrets.[205] Mexico's Federal Civil Code allows people to sue for "moral damage" if one prints photographs of an individual that inflict "an injury in his sentiments, affections, or intimate life."[206] New Zealand has also recognized a tort akin to the public-disclosure tort that provides a remedy for the disclosure of "private facts that would be considered highly offensive to an objective reasonable person."[207] The South Korean Supreme Court held that disclosing the face and voice of a victim of botched plastic surgery would give rise to liability.[208]

Japan has also recognized the public-disclosure tort. In a famous case in 1964, a politician sued acclaimed author Yukio Mishima for chronicling his extramarital affairs in the novel *After the Banquet*, which was a fusion of fact and fiction. The court derived the right to privacy from Article 13 of the Japanese constitution, which provides that "[a]ll of the people shall be respected as individuals." According to the court, there was a "legal right and assurance that one's private life will not be wantonly opened to the public."[209] Mishima had to pay 800,000 yen, about $2,200 at the time, then the largest verdict in Japan after World War II.[210]

Why does the law protect people against disclosure of true information about them? Some critics of these protections contend that they infringe upon free speech. Eugene Volokh argues that "the right to information privacy—my right to control your communication of personally identifiable information about me—is a right to have the government stop you from speaking about me."[211] Others have charged that protection against disclosure inhibits our ability to judge others and determine whether they are worthy of our trust. According to Richard Posner, disclosure protections provide people the "power to conceal information about themselves that others might use to their disadvantage."[212]

"Disclosure" occurs when certain true information about a person is revealed to others. Disclosure differs from breach of confidentiality because the harm in disclosure involves the damage to reputation caused by the dissemination; the harm in breach of confidentiality is the violation of trust in the relationship. Disclosure can harm even if the information is revealed by a stranger. In "The Right to Privacy," Warren and Brandeis took issue with the argument that express or implied contractual duties of confidentiality could adequately protect privacy. In particular, they noted that strangers were increasingly able to gather personal information:

> The narrower doctrine [of breach of contract] may have satisfied the demands of society at a time when the abuse to be guarded against could rarely have arisen without violating a contract or a special confidence; but now that modern devices afford abundant opportunities for the perpetration of such wrongs without any participation by the injured party, the protection granted by the law must be placed upon a broader foundation.

Warren and Brandeis pointed to new technologies of photography. Previously, cameras had been large and expensive, and people had to pose for their picture to be taken. This gave rise to a relationship with implicit contractual terms. But the invention of the "snap camera," a smaller camera that could take candid photographs, "rendered it possible to take pictures surreptitiously." This led Warren and Brandeis to conclude that "the doctrines of contract and of trust are inadequate to support the required protection."[213]

Although protecting against disclosure can limit free speech, disclosure protections can promote the same interests free speech furthers. Protection from disclosure, like free speech, advances individual autonomy. The risk of disclosure can prevent people from engaging in activities that further their own self-development.[214] As with free speech, disclosure protections further democratic self-governance. A substantial amount of political discourse does not occur on public soapboxes, but rather in private conversations. Privacy encourages uninhibited speech by enabling individuals to direct frank communication to those people they trust and who will not cause them harm because of what they say. Communication essential for democratic participation does not occur only at public rallies or on nationwide television broadcasts, but often takes place between two people or in small groups. Without protections against disclosure, people might be more reluctant to criticize aspects of their public lives, such as their employers. The threat of disclosure probably will not end all conversations, but it will alter what is said. Disclosure can also inhibit people from associating with others, impinging upon freedom of association, and can destroy anonymity, which is sometimes critical for the promotion of free expression. Julie Cohen points out that protection against disclosure also facilitates the reading and consumption of ideas.[215] Therefore, protections against disclosure promote democratic aims, including the same aims that are furthered by free speech.

Disclosure can also threaten people's security. People want to protect information that can be used by others to harm them physically, emotionally, financially, or reputationally. For example, in *Remsburg v. Docusearch, Inc.*, a deranged man was obsessed with Amy Lynn Boyer. He purchased Boyer's Social Security number and employment address from a database company called Docusearch, then went to Boyer's workplace and murdered her. The court concluded that "threats posed by stalking and identity theft lead us to conclude that the risk of criminal misconduct is sufficiently foreseeable so that an investigator has a duty to exercise reasonable care in disclosing a third person's personal information to a client."[216]

Critics of protection against disclosure often tout the benefits of the free flow of information. For example, law professor Diane Zimmerman argues that "gossip is a basic form of information exchange that teaches about other lifestyles and attitudes, and through which community values are changed or reinforced."[217] For Zimmerman, gossip can educate us about human behavior, and more disclosures about people's private lives might change hypocritical social norms that societies proclaim in public but flout in private. Disclosing private information about people might change attitudes. This argument is frequently raised in support of the outing of gays.[218] Outing gays, the argument goes, will help alter society's perception of gays by demonstrating that mainstream people or role models are gay.

It is true that if every person's private life were exposed, society might change its attitudes and beliefs. But in reality, the revelation of people's personal secrets often does damage to the individuals without having much effect on changing norms. Such disclosures can just as readily entrench existing norms as change them. The outing of gays often occurs haphazardly, and the number of people outed will rarely be enough to force a change in social opinion.[219] Moreover, there are other ways to alter norms and attitudes than disclosing people's secrets. For example, Alfred Kinsey's best-selling studies of human sexuality in 1948 and 1953 revealed a great discord between the public and private dimensions of sex. Professors John D'Emilio and Estelle Freedman note, "Kinsey's statistics pointed to a vast hidden world of sexual experience sharply at odds with publicly espoused norms."[220] Because his data were systematic and not linked to specific individuals, Kinsey's study managed to be effective without invading people's privacy in the process.

In many instances, disclosure of information about a person will not enhance our ability to judge her; in fact, it may distort our assessments.[221] Disclosure protections also guard against irrational judgments based on stereotypes or misinformation. Likewise, society may want to inhibit certain rational judgments, such as employment decisions based on genetic information. Even if employers are correct that a prospective employee with a genetic risk for developing a certain condition is, on balance, riskier to hire than a prospective employee without this predisposition, a rational discriminatory employment decision of this kind has its costs. Such decisions may penalize people for things they cannot control and deter people from learning their genetic makeup.[222]

Disclosure can also be harmful because it makes a person a "prisoner of his recorded past."[223] People grow and change, and disclosures of information from their past can inhibit their ability to reform their behavior, to have a second chance, or to alter their life's direction. Moreover, when information is released publicly, it can be used in a host of unforeseeable ways, creating problems related to those caused by secondary use.

The law often protects against disclosure when the information is kept secret but not when others know about it. As one court observed, appearing in public "necessarily involves doffing the cloak of privacy which the law protects."[224] In *Penwell v. Taft Broadcasting Co.*, the court held that a husband and wife wrongfully arrested in public had no privacy interest against the broadcast of video footage of the arrest because it was filmed in public and was "left open to the public eye."[225] Moreover, if a fact about a person is known to others, many courts conclude that it is no longer private. This was the case in *Sipple v. Chronicle Publishing Co.*, where newspapers "outed" Oliver Sipple, who heroically saved President Gerald Ford from an assassination attempt. The court concluded that his sexuality was not private because it was well known in the gay community.[226] In *Duran v. Detroit News, Inc.*, a former Colombian judge was attempting to lie low because of death threats and a bounty placed on her head by a drug lord. When a newspaper disclosed her address, a court found no privacy interest because she had revealed it to a few people.[227] A few courts, however, have come to different conclusions regarding whether there is a privacy interest in information communicated to others. For example, in *Times Mirror Co. v. Superior Court*, a newspaper article disclosed the identity of a murder witness. Although the witness had confided in a few friends and family members, she had not "rendered otherwise private information public by cooperating in the criminal investigation and seeking solace from friends and relatives."[228]

Lior Strahilevitz aptly observes that disclosure involves spreading information beyond existing networks of information flow.[229] The harm of disclosure is not so much the elimination of secrecy as it is the spreading of information beyond expected boundaries. People often disclose information to a limited circle of friends, and they expect the information to stay within this group. Some courts, however, focus on secrecy and do not examine people's expectations of information flow.

Exposure

> Let not thy privy members be
> layd upon to be view'd
> it is most shameful and abhord,
> detestable and rude.
>
> Retaine not urine nor the winde
> which doth thy body vex
> so it be done with secresie
> let that not thee perplex.
>
> —*Richard Weste*, The Booke of Demeanor and the Allowance and
> Disallowance of Certaine Misdemeanors in Companie *(c. 1619)*[230]

In an 1881 case, *DeMay v. Roberts*, a young unmarried man accompanied a doctor into the room where the doctor was assisting a woman in labor. The court held that the young man had no business being in the room: "It would be shocking to our sense of right, justice and propriety to doubt even but that for such an act the law would afford an ample remedy."[231] Why is it "shocking" for a stranger to watch a woman give birth to a baby?

In 2004, in *National Archives & Records Administration v. Favish*, the U.S. Supreme Court rejected a request under the Freedom of Information Act (FOIA) for autopsy photos of Vincent Foster, Jr., a deputy counsel to President Clinton who had committed suicide by shooting himself. The Court concluded that the photos fell under the exemption for records that "could reasonably be expected to constitute an unwarranted invasion of personal privacy." The Supreme Court contended, "Family members have a personal stake in honoring and mourning their dead and objecting to unwarranted public exploitation that, by intruding upon their own grief, tends to degrade the rites and respect they seek to accord to the deceased person who was once their own."[232]

A related sentiment emerged when the media sought to obtain the autopsy photos of Dale Earnhardt, a famous race-car driver who died while racing in 2001. In response, the Florida legislature passed a law restricting the disclosure of autopsy photographs without good cause. A Florida court upheld the law against a free-speech challenge, stating that the "publication of a person's autopsy photographs constitutes a unique, serious, and extraordinarily intrusive invasion of the personal privacy of that person's surviving family members."[233] One of the earliest cases involving death photos is an 1858 case from France, *l'affaire Rachel.* A well-known actress's sister hired a photographer to take pictures of the actress on her deathbed. The photographer improperly showed them to an artist who made sketches of the pictures and began selling them. A French court declared, "No one may, without the explicit consent of the family, reproduce and bring to the public eye the image of an individual on her deathbed whatever the celebrity of the person involved."[234]

Why is it indecent to publish autopsy photographs? What harm does it cause the families? Imagine that a newspaper prints candid photographs of a person naked or of a person defecating. The person would likely be appalled. But why? We all have genitals. We all defecate. There are no big surprises here.

These are all illustrations of a problem I call "exposure." Exposure involves exposing to others certain physical and emotional attributes about a person. These are attributes that people view as deeply primordial, and their exposure often creates embarrassment and humiliation. Grief, suffering, trauma, injury, nudity, sex, urination, and defecation all involve primal aspects of our lives—ones that are physical, instinctual, and necessary.[235] We have been socialized into concealing these activities.[236]

Although exposure is similar to disclosure—both involve the dissemination of true information—they diverge in an important respect. Exposure involves information about our bodies and health, whereas disclosure involves a much broader range of data that implicate a person's reputation. People have particularly strong reactions of humiliation when they suffer from exposure, even if the information revealed has no effect on how others judge their reputation.

Exposure creates injury because we have developed social practices to conceal aspects of life that we find animal-like or disgusting. Further, in certain activities, we are vulnerable and weak, such as when we are nude or going to the bathroom. Norms about nudity and bodily functions have changed throughout history. Martha Nussbaum points out that ancient Romans used toilets, whereas "courtiers in Elizabethan England urinated and defecated in corners of palaces, until the stench made it necessary to change residences."[237] In various cultures and at different times in history, levels of reticence and modesty concerning the body have differed greatly. Today's norms and practices, however, call for the concealment of many aspects of the body. We protect against the exposure of these bodily aspects because this protection safeguards human dignity as defined by modern society. Dignity is a part of being civilized; it involves the ability to transcend one's animal nature.[238]

The need for privacy, and therefore the prevention of exposure, is created by the fact that we have social relationships and concomitant norms of dignity and decorum. "The private arises as a necessary space for the production of civilized behavior," law professor William Ian Miller contends. "Private space enables a civilized public space."[239] Another theory, cultural historian Rochelle Gurstein posits, is that certain activities "leave the body vulnerable"—they "leave us defenseless precisely because we are not our usual selves at these moments."[240]

When these practices are disrupted by exposure, people can experience a severe and sometimes debilitating humiliation and loss of self-esteem. Exposure thus impedes a person's ability to participate in society. Even though most people would not view a victim of exposure as a lesser person or as being less civilized, victims feel that way. This is in contrast to disclosure, where information often affects a person's reputation.

Disclosure is a power that controls through the imposition of social sanctions and condemnation. Exposure works in a different way, by stripping people of their dignity.[241] Exposure interacts with powerful and potent social norms. When people willingly transgress these norms, society has a strong interest in shaming them, and it is socially beneficial for these norms to be internalized and to result in feelings of shame. However, exposure involves people unwillingly placed in transgression of these norms. We do not view the victims as blameworthy, and there is little social value in their suffering. Nevertheless, because of the internalization of these norms, exposure victims experience strong feelings of shame.

American tort law does not recognize a separate cause of action for exposure; the tort of public disclosure covers both disclosure and exposure.[242] Generally, exposure cases have fared better than disclosure cases.[243] For example, in *Daily Times Democrat v. Graham*, air jets blew up a woman's dress while she was at a county fair, exposing her underwear. At that very moment, a photographer for the local newspaper took her photograph, and the picture was printed on the front page of the paper. The woman sued under the public-disclosure tort. The newspaper contended that the picture was taken in public, and that, accordingly, there was no privacy interest. This reasoning was based on the secrecy paradigm—that once something is disclosed to the public, it is no longer secret. However, the court concluded that the woman still had a right to be protected from "an indecent and vulgar" violation of privacy under the tort of public disclosure.[244]

Failing to distinguish between disclosure and exposure has adversely affected the recognition of exposure harms in some instances. In *McNamara v. Freedom Newspapers, Inc.*, for example, a newspaper published a picture of a high-school athlete whose genitalia were accidentally exposed while playing soccer. The student sued under the tort of public disclosure of private facts. According to the student, "[T]he Newspaper violated the bounds of public decency." The court conceptualized the injury as one of disclosure and concluded that the picture was not private because "[the student] was voluntarily participating in a spectator sport at a public place."[245] The harm in this case, however, is more appropriately classified as one of exposure. Had the court conceptualized the disruption as one of exposure, the fact that it occurred in a public place would have been much less relevant to the analysis.

Increased Accessibility

Obscurity often brings safety.

—Aesop, "*The Tree and the Reed*" (sixth century B.C.)[246]

Federal courts, along with many state courts and agencies, are developing systems to place their records online.[247] These records are readily available at local courthouses or government offices. Nevertheless, placing them online has given rise to an extensive debate over privacy. Some argue that the information is already publicly available, and that therefore it should be available on the Internet in the same manner as it is in physical form at the localities. But many administrative bodies charged with examining the issue have hesitated because of the increased accessibility the Internet will bring. The U.S. Judicial Conference Committee concluded, for example, that "any benefits of public remote electronic access to criminal files were outweighed by the safety and law enforcement risks such access would create."[248]

If the information is already available to the public, what is the harm in increasing its accessibility? Increased accessibility does not involve a direct disclosure. Secret information is not revealed. Confidentiality is not breached. Rather, information that is already available to the public is made easier to access. With increased accessibility, a difference in quantity becomes a difference in quality—it heightens the risk of the harms of disclosure.

Increased accessibility to personal information has many benefits. It enhances openness by allowing people to locate information that they are seeking more easily. Ready accessibility of records, for example, can assist in investigating the background of a person whom one is planning to hire. Robert Gellman notes, "Some basic functions and institutions depend on the public availability of records to operate. The U.S. system of land ownership relies on the public availability of records, although that has not always been the case. The public availability of bankruptcy records is also integral to the process."[249]

Increased accessibility, however, creates problems, such as the greater possibility of disclosure. Information can readily be exploited for purposes other than those for which it was originally made publicly accessible. For example, companies are gathering data from public records for commercial and marketing purposes or for profiling and other analysis.[250] Peter Winn notes that increased access to court records will cause harms to participants in the judicial system: "They will lose . . . their interest in privacy—their identities will be subject to potential misuse by thieves, and their children may be exposed to sexual predators."[251]

Under the secrecy paradigm, courts often view privacy as a binary status—information is either completely private or completely public. Accordingly, once information is released into the public domain, it is no longer private. In U.S. law, the secrecy paradigm is pervasive. For example, according to the Restatement of Torts, the public-disclosure tort does not apply "when the defendant merely gives further publicity to information about the plaintiff that is already public."[252] For the harm of increased accessibility, however, prior publicity is not dispositive. One should focus on the extent to which the information is made more accessible. Most courts, however, struggle with recognizing this harm because of their commitment to the secrecy paradigm.[253] In *Walls v. City of Petersburg*, for example, public employees were compelled to answer a questionnaire asking about the criminal histories of their family members, their complete marital history, their children, and their financial status. The court dismissed their claim that their constitutional right to information privacy was violated, reasoning that there was no privacy interest in the information because it was already available in public records.[254]

In *United States Department of Justice v. Reporters Committee for Freedom of the Press*, the Supreme Court recognized the problem of increased accessibility. Earlier in this chapter, I noted how this case recognized the problem of aggregation when the Court concluded that the disclosure of FBI "rap sheets" violated a privacy interest under FOIA. In addition to concluding that there was a difference between scattered pieces of information and a fully assembled dossier, the Court recognized that "there is a vast difference between the public records that might be found after a diligent search of courthouse files, county archives, and local police stations throughout the country and a computerized summary located in a single clearinghouse of information."[255] Here, the Court has recognized the harm of increased accessibility.

Blackmail

> The robber on the highway who was bold and wicked enough to hold a pistol at the head of his fellow man, and demand his money or his life, was an innocent offender, compared with the cowardly assassin of honour and reputation, who sheltered by darkness and secrecy, would seek in cold blood to gratify his sordid views by wounding the peace and blasting the happiness of his terrified victim.
>
> *—A judge sentencing a blackmailer in Britain in 1838*[256]

In nineteenth-century England, sodomy was a serious offense. Although no longer a capital offense, as it had been in the seventeenth century, sodomy still carried harsh penalties of ten years to life in prison. Blackmailers would threaten wealthy elites with disclosure of their homosexual activities unless the blackmailers were paid handsomely. The law began to recognize that these forms of extortion should be criminalized. One nineteenth-century English judge contended that blackmail was "one of the worst offenses known to the law."[257] When a blackmail case came to court, courts would awkwardly ignore whether there was any truth to the blackmailer's charges.[258] Certainly not all victims of blackmail were innocent, but courts offered protection even to those accused of transgressing society's strong sexual taboos and criminal laws. Why were these people protected? If society so vehemently condemned sodomy at the time, why punish the blackmailers rather than those who may have been guilty of sodomy?

Blackmail has long posed a conundrum for legal scholars.[259] Blackmail involves coercing an individual by threatening to expose her personal secrets if she does not accede to the demands of the blackmailer, which often involve paying hush money.[260] Blackmail is criminalized in most industrialized societies.[261] Why should society restrict contracts not to divulge secrets? Blackmail does not seem to be about preventing disclosure, for, as Joseph Isenbergh argues, prohibiting a blackmailer compensation for silence will likely make disclosure more probable.[262] If this is the case, then what interest does the crime of blackmail protect?

Scholars have offered a panoply of hypotheses. Richard Posner argues that blackmail is illegal because it neither maximizes wealth nor provides any net social benefit.[263] In contrast, Walter Block and Gary Anderson contend that blackmail, as distinct from extortion, involves a transaction just like any other, in which both parties bargain for the result they desire.[264] Jennifer Brown finds that blackmail undermines the criminal justice system by enabling private contracts that withhold information from the justice system.[265] Richard Epstein proposes that blackmail is socially detrimental because it "breeds fraud and deceit."[266] According to Wendy Gordon, blackmail is illegal because it involves the blackmailer treating the victim as a means (to earn money) rather than an end.[267] Finally, Richard McAdams argues that blackmail inhibits the development of social norms by stifling the enforcement, discussion, and critique of norms.[268]

I posit that blackmail is criminalized because of the power relationship it creates. Blackmail allows a person to be dominated and controlled by another. With blackmail, the harm is not in the actual disclosure of the information, but in the control exercised by the one who makes the threat over the data subject. In some cases, blackmail can also involve information more akin to exposure than disclosure. Breach of confidentiality is also related to blackmail because a confidant can threaten to disclose a secret in return for money. Blackmail differs from disclosure, exposure, and breach of confidentiality in that it involves a threat of disclosure rather than an actual disclosure.

A rough analogy may be made to the crimes of battery and assault. Battery involves actual physical harm, whereas assault is putting a person in fear of physical harm.[269] But there are important differences between blackmail and assault. Unlike assault, where the violence threatened is illegal, with blackmail, the threatened disclosure can be perfectly legal. Indeed, the disclosure might be socially beneficial in that it might reveal that the blackmail victim committed a crime or heinous act. The threat of disclosure, however, is so profoundly disempowering that society still wants to protect against it. Toward the end of Henrik Ibsen's play *Hedda Gabler*, Judge Brack, who knows a damaging secret about Hedda Gabler, says to her, "My dearest Hedda, believe me, I shall not abuse the position." Hedda replies, "In your power, all the same. At the mercy of your will and demands. And so a slave! A slave!"[270] The more people know about us, the more they can exercise control over us. This is why telling one's deepest secrets to another makes one vulnerable. Prohibiting blackmail prevents people from taking advantage of us with our personal information.

The purpose of restricting blackmail is not to limit disclosure but to prevent the threat of disclosure from being used as a tool for exerting power and dominion over others. Our society prohibits slavery, labor below the minimum wage, dangerous workplace conditions, and quid pro quo sexual harassment even if the victim seemingly consents. The rationale for these prohibitions stems in part from the fact that these acts are so coercive that the consent is not voluntary, and so they give a person excessive power over another. Blackmail involves a similar kind of coercive power. Indeed, criminal codes classify blackmail as a form of extortion, which involves the use of fear or threats to force someone to submit to another's will.[271]

Laws that make blackmail a crime thus prohibit the use of disclosure, exposure, or breach of confidentiality as a means for exercising power over another person. Threatening to disseminate information can achieve levels of domination that may not be socially beneficial. This is why the threat is usually treated as a wrongful act itself.

Appropriation

> If a man's name be his own property, as no less an authority than the United States Supreme Court says it is, it is difficult to understand why the peculiar cast of one's features is not also one's property, and why its pecuniary value, if it has one, does not belong to its owner, rather than to the person seeking to make an unauthorized use of it.
>
> —Edison v. Edison Polyform Manufacturing Co. *(1907)*,
> *granting Thomas Edison's demand that a company refrain*
> *from using his name to promote its products*[272]

In 1902, in *Roberson v. Rochester Folding Box Co.*, a flour company included a lithograph of Abigail Roberson, a minor, on 25,000 advertisement flyers with the caption "Flour of the Family," without her consent. Roberson claimed that she "ha[d] been greatly humiliated by the scoffs and jeers of persons who ha[d] recognized her face and picture on this advertisement, and her good name ha[d] been attacked, causing her great distress and suffering, both in body and mind." Roberson became so ill that she had to see a physician. The portrait, however, was neither racy nor libelous. "The likeness is said to be a very good one," the court noted, and Roberson was "caused to suffer mental distress where others would have appreciated the compliment to their beauty implied in the selection of the picture for such purposes." The court refused to recognize a remedy based on Warren and Brandeis's article, concluding that such an action was the proper domain of the legislature.[273]

Roberson caused quite a stir. An editorial in the *New York Times* lambasted the decision and noted that it "excited as much amazement among lawyers and jurists as among the promiscuous lay public."[274] Another editorial in the same paper declared, "If there be . . . no law now to cover these savage and horrible practices . . . then the decent people will say that it is high time that there were such a law."[275]

Shortly after the decision, a comment in the *Yale Law Journal* criticized the *Roberson* decision for not recognizing a remedy for the "undoubted injury to the plaintiff."[276] The strong criticism of the decision even led one of the judges of the majority to defend the opinion in the *Columbia Law Review*.[277] A year later, New York passed a law creating a cause of action to redress the type of injury Roberson suffered.[278] The law remains in force today.[279]

The tort of appropriation was the first privacy tort to be recognized after Warren and Brandeis's article. The tort of appropriation occurs when "[o]ne . . . appropriates to his own use or benefit the name or likeness of another." To be liable for appropriation, "the defendant must have appropriated to his own use or benefit the reputation, prestige, social or commercial standing, public interest or other values of the plaintiff's name or likeness."[280]

Why did *Roberson* create such a response? What spurred such an extensive public discussion and prompt legislative action? What is problematic about using a person's name or photograph in an advertisement? After all, one's name and image are often not secret. The picture of Roberson was flattering and did not ruin her reputation. What was the injury?

"Appropriation" is the use of one's identity or personality for the purposes and goals of another. Appropriation, like the privacy disruptions of disclosure and distortion, involves the way an individual desires to present herself to society.

Beyond the United States, the law of many other countries protects against appropriation of one's name or likeness. French law provides people with a "right of monopoly over exploitation of one's image, name, and notoriety."[281] France's protection of the unauthorized use of people's photographs traces back to *l'affaire Rachel* in 1858 (discussed earlier in the section on exposure).[282] Germany has a remedy for the "[m]isuse of another's name, likeness, ideas or personal history that causes economic or emotional damage to 'personality development.' "[283] The European Court of Human Rights has recognized a person's right to control her image even when taken in public. In *Von Hannover v. Germany*, Princess Caroline of Monaco sued three German magazines to halt the publication of photos of her in various public places. The court concluded that "the concept of the private life extends to aspects relating to personal identity, such as a person's name, or a person's picture."[284] In Canada, the Supreme Court held that a magazine violated the Quebec Charter when it published a photograph of a young woman who was sitting outside in public without her consent: "Since the right to one's image is included in the right to respect for one's private life, it is axiomatic that every person possesses a protected right to his or her image."[285]

In the United States, the tort of appropriation has currently lost its way because courts and commentators have not been able to adequately explain the injury that is redressed by the tort. Two competing accounts of the injury predominate in cases and commentary.[286] Many commentators describe the harm caused by the use of one's likeness for commercial purposes as an affront to dignity. For example, Edward Bloustein argued that the harm caused to an individual by appropriation is the "demeaning and humiliating . . . commercialization of an aspect of personality."[287]

Another rationale for the tort is as a protection of property rights. Prosser, who was profoundly influential in the creation of the four modern privacy torts, viewed the interest protected by the appropriation tort as "not so much a mental as a proprietary one."[288] According to Jonathan Kahn, the "early association of appropriation claims with such intangible, non-commensurable attributes of the self as dignity and the integrity of one's persona seems to have been lost, or at least misplaced, as property-based conceptions of the legal status of identity have come to the fore."[289] Courts have transformed the tort's targeted harm from one of appropriation to one of intellectual property. Most contemporary cases recognize that the appropriation tort protects a "valuable right of property."[290] Loss of property seems to be more readily recognized by courts today than the more amorphous feelings of embarrassment or loss of dignity.[291]

To the extent that the tort remains a way to protect against the loss of dignity, why should we inhibit social use of identities simply to prevent people from feeling demeaned when their identities are commercialized? After all, we allow people to sell their identities to endorse products. Further, we allow vigorous criticism and satire, which can be quite humiliating and injurious to people's dignity.

I contend that there is another important dimension of the harm of appropriation—an interference with freedom and self-development. Early appropriation cases allude to this aspect of the harm. In 1905, in

Pavesich v. New England Life Insurance Co., a life-insurance advertisement used a photograph of Paolo Pavesich next to a photograph of "an ill-dressed and sickly looking person." Under Pavesich's picture, the advertisement stated, in part, "In my healthy and productive period of life I bought insurance in the New England Mutual Life Insurance Co." The ad seemed flattering for Pavesich, for he was the paragon of all the success and good fortune that would come to those who purchased insurance. Pavesich, however, was not flattered, and he sued. In contrast to the *Roberson* court, the *Pavesich* court recognized a cause of action, reasoning that "the body of a person cannot be put on exhibition . . . without his consent. The right of one to exhibit himself to the public at all proper times, in all proper places, and in a proper manner is embraced within the right of personal liberty." The use of one's likeness for advertising purposes can bring a person to "a realization that his liberty has been taken away from him . . . that he is for the time being under the control of another, that he is no longer free, and that he is in reality a slave."[292] The court spoke in terms of loss of liberty, not in terms of loss of monetary value. The injury was that Pavesich had been used against his will. Similarly, according to Justice John Clinton Gray's dissent in *Roberson*, "[W]e may not say that the plaintiff's complaint is fanciful, or that her alleged injury is purely a sentimental one." He concluded that "the conspicuous display of her likeness in various public places has . . . humiliated her by the notoriety and by the public comments it has provoked."[293] Justice Gray alluded to what I believe to be the crux of the harm: unwanted notoriety. The appropriation of Roberson's image forced her to become a public figure. In addition to bringing her unwillingly into the public sphere, the appropriation defined her public role and public persona.

The interest safeguarded by protections against appropriation is control of the way one presents oneself to society. The products and causes people publicly endorse shape their public image. When people are associated with products, they become known in terms of these products. Many public figures take great care with their endorsements because these endorsements shape their public image. For example, in 1903, Thomas Edison sought to enjoin the Edison Polyform Manufacturing Company from using his picture on bottles of a pain reliever that Edison himself had invented earlier in his career.[294] Similarly, Jacqueline Onassis sued a clothing company for the use of a lookalike in an advertisement because "she has never permitted her name or picture to be used in connection with the promotion of commercial products," and her "name has been used sparingly only in connection with certain public services, civic, art and educational projects which she has supported."[295] Thus appropriation can be harmful even if it is not humiliating, degrading, or disrespectful. Being unwillingly used to endorse a product resembles, in certain respects, being compelled to speak and to represent certain viewpoints. As the Federal Supreme Court of Germany declared in an opinion forbidding the use of a person's photograph on an advertisement without his consent, "[T]he person depicted is deprived of the freedom to deal with this item from his individual sphere on the basis of his own resolution."[296]

Protection against appropriation establishes what society considers appropriate for others to do in shaping a person's identity. The harm, then, is an impingement on the victim's freedom in the authorship of her self-narrative, not merely her loss of profits. Prosser, however, used the term "appropriation," which is a word that pertains to property. Perhaps a better word to describe the harm is "exploitation." I continue to use the word "appropriation," however, because it has become commonly known in relation to this kind of harmful activity.

Distortion

> Because it is my name! Because I cannot have another in my life! Because I lie and sign myself to lies! Because I am not worth the dust on the feet of them that hang! How may I live without my name? I have given you my soul; leave me my name!
>
> —*John Proctor in Arthur Miller,* The Crucible *(1953)*[297]

Defamation law has existed for centuries. Consisting of the torts of libel and slander, defamation law protects against falsehoods that injure a person's reputation. Defamation law has its origins in the ancient Roman law of *injuria*.[298] During the early Middle Ages, defamation was considered so contemptible that it was punished by slicing off the tongue.[299] Today, in the United States, in order to be liable for defamation, one must make "a false and defamatory statement concerning another."[300] A "defamatory" statement "tends so to harm the reputation of another as to lower him in the estimation of the community or to deter third persons from associating or dealing with him."[301] False light, a more recent tort inspired by Warren and Brandeis's article, protects against giving "publicity to a matter concerning another that places the other before the public in a false light" that is "highly offensive to a reasonable person."[302] It safeguards "the interest of the individual in not being made to appear before the public in an objectionable false light or false position, or in other words, otherwise than as he is."[303]

Countries around the world protect against falsehoods that injure a person's reputation. Hungary's constitution, for example, declares that "everyone has the right to the good standing of his reputation." Poland guarantees that every person "shall have the right to legal protection . . . of his honor and good reputation." Portugal's constitution protects people's right to "good name and reputation." Russia safeguards "one's honor and good name." Sri Lanka's constitution provides that a person "shall not be subjected to unlawful attacks on his or her reputation."[304] The United Nations Universal Declaration of Human Rights of 1948 declares that a person shall not be subjected to "attacks upon his honor and reputation."[305] These are just a few examples. Beyond constitutional protections, countless nations have laws protecting against defamation. For example, defamation law in India applies when the falsehood lowers a person's "moral or intellectual character."[306] In Japan, the law protects against defamation that damages "the social reputation that a person enjoys due to his or her personal merits such as personality, character, fame, and credibility."[307] According to a Japanese proverb, "A person lives for one generation; a good name lasts forever."[308] Defamation law exists in all Western European nations.[309]

Beyond false light, defamation, and other reputational torts, a number of privacy statutes ensure against false information in record systems. In the United States, the Privacy Act, for example, enables a person to access and correct her records maintained by government agencies. Likewise, the Fair Credit Reporting Act provides recourse for a person who wants to correct her credit records, and the Family Educational Rights and Privacy Act enables students to review and ensure the accuracy of their school records.[310] Additionally, longstanding privacy principles, such as the Fair Information Practices and the OECD Privacy Guidelines, contain provisions for ensuring the accuracy of records. The European Union Data Protection Directive contains a similar provision.[311]

Why are these harms of inaccuracy understood as privacy injuries? Why does the law protect against these harms? Why should people have a right to be judged accurately?

I refer to these harms as "distortion." Distortion is the manipulation of the way a person is perceived and judged by others. It involves the victim being inaccurately characterized. I include distortion in the taxonomy of privacy because of its significant similarity to other privacy disruptions. Distortion, like disclosure, involves the spreading of information that affects the way society views a person. Both distortion and disclosure can result in embarrassment, humiliation, stigma, and reputational harm. They both involve the ability to control information about oneself and to have some limited dominion over the way one is viewed by society. Distortion differs from disclosure, however, because with distortion, the information revealed is false and misleading.

Throughout most of Western history, one's reputation and character have been viewed as indispensable to self-identity and the ability to engage in public life. For centuries, the loss of social regard has had deleterious effects on one's wealth, prosperity, and employment.[312] Social regard, acceptance, and honor are extremely valuable, and they have power over us because they are integral to how we relate to others. Robert Post observes that defamation law also exists for "the protection of an individual's interest in dignity, which is to say his interest in being included within the forms of social respect; and the enforcement of society's interest in its rules of civility, which is to say its interest in defining and maintaining the contours of its own social constitution."[313]

Reputation is not merely an individual creation. Although it is true that people work very hard to build their reputations, one's reputation is the product of other people's judgments. Reputation is a currency through which we interact with each other. Protection against distortion structures our interactions because it protects this currency. Distortion not only affects the aggrieved individual but also the society that judges that individual. It interferes with our relationships to that individual, and it inhibits our ability to assess the character of those we deal with. We are thus deceived in our relationships with others; these relationships are tainted by false information that prevents us from making sound and fair judgments. Distortion's direct impact is felt by the aggrieved individual, but it also affects society. We want to avoid arbitrary and undeserved disruption of social relations.

The enigmatic and devious Iago's comments in William Shakespeare's *Othello* capture the importance of reputation:

> Good name in man and woman, dear my lord,
> Is the immediate jewel of their souls;
> Who steals my purse steals trash: 'tis something, nothing;
> 'Twas mine, 'tis his, and has been slave to thousands.
> But he that filches from me my good name
> Robs me of that which not enriches him
> And makes me poor indeed.[314]

Using the power of reputation, Iago orchestrates a series of distortions to make Othello believe that his wife, Desdemona, is having an affair with his lieutenant, Cassio. These distortions induce a murderous rage in Othello, during which he suffocates his wife. *Othello* illustrates the profound destructiveness of distortion, which tears apart relationships, dissolves trust, and instigates violence.

Invasion

The final grouping of privacy harms I label "invasion." Invasions differ from the problems of information collection, processing, and dissemination because they do not always involve information. I discuss two types of invasion: (1) intrusion and (2) decisional interference.

Intrusion

> The soul selects her own society
> Then shuts the door;
> On her divine majority
> Obtrude no more
>
> —*Emily Dickinson (1890)*[315]

For hundreds of years, the law has strongly guarded the privacy of the home.[316] According to William Blackstone, "[T]he law . . . has so particular and tender a regard to the immunity of a man's house, that it stiles it his castle."[317] The law protects the home from trespass by others, as well as from nuisances.[318] Thomas Cooley observed in his famous treatise on constitutional law in 1868, "[I]t is better oftentimes that crime should go unpunished than that the citizen should be liable to have his premises invaded, his trunks broken open, his private books, papers, and letters exposed to prying curiosity, and to the misconstructions of ignorant and suspicious persons."[319] The Fourth Amendment protects the home, as well as one's body and baggage, from unreasonable searches by government officials.[320] One of the torts inspired by Warren and Brandeis's article is intrusion upon seclusion, which creates a cause of action when one intrudes "upon the solitude or seclusion of another or his private affairs or concerns" if the intrusion is "highly offensive to a reasonable person."[321]

Protection against intrusion exists around the world. The constitutions of countless countries protect against unreasonable search and seizure by the government.[322] For example, Mexico's constitution provides, "No one shall be disturbed in his person, family, domicile, documents or possessions except by virtue of a written order by the competent authority stating the legal grounds and the justification for the action taken."[323] The Canadian Charter of Rights and Freedoms protects against "unreasonable search and seizure."[324] Countries also protect against intrusions by individuals upon other individuals. Argentina's Civil Code protects against "intrusive telephone calls, and neighbor's intrusions into one's private life."[325] The New Zealand Harassment Act of 1997 prohibits "[w]atching, loitering near, or preventing or hindering access to or from, that person's place of residence, business, employment, or any other place that the person frequents for any purpose."[326] Why has the home been so zealously protected? Why is it important to protect a private realm from intrusions?

"Intrusion" involves invasions or incursions into one's life. It disturbs the victim's daily activities, alters her routines, destroys her solitude, and often makes her feel uncomfortable and uneasy. Protection against intrusion involves protecting the individual from unwanted social invasions, affording people what Warren and Brandeis called "the right to be let alone."[327]

Intrusion is related to disclosure because disclosure is often made possible by intrusive information-gathering activities. Intrusion into one's private sphere can be caused not only by physical incursion and proximity but also by gazes (surveillance) or questioning (interrogation). Intrusion has a certain resemblance to surveillance in that being stared at for extended periods of time can be quite invasive, penetrating, disturbing, frightening, and disruptive. Intrusion is also related to interrogation because people can experience interrogation as a kind of intrusion into their affairs.

The harm caused by intrusion, however, differs from that caused by other types of disruption because intrusion interrupts one's activities through the unwanted presence or activities of another person. The case *Galella v. Onassis* provides a good illustration of how intrusion is related to forms of information gathering but distinct from them. Galella, a paparazzo, routinely harassed Jacqueline Onassis and her children with the late President John F. Kennedy, John and Caroline. To capture pictures, Galella jumped into John's path as he was riding his bike, interrupted Caroline's tennis, and, in the words of the trial judge, "insinuated himself into the very fabric of Mrs. Onassis' life."[328] Galella's activities involved monitoring, akin to surveillance, but they were also physically intrusive.

Intrusion need not involve spatial incursions: spam, junk mail, junk faxes, and telemarketing are disruptive in a similar way because they sap people's time and attention and interrupt their activities. Although many forms of intrusion are motivated by a desire to gather information or result in revealing information, intrusion can cause harm even if no information is involved. In particular, intrusion often interferes with solitude—the state of being alone or able to retreat from the presence of others. Indeed, Warren and Brandeis wrote from a tradition of solitude inspired by Ralph Waldo Emerson, Henry David Thoreau, and Emily Dickinson.[329]

For centuries, however, solitude has been criticized as self-indulgent.[330] Aristotle observed, "Surely it is strange, too, to make the supremely happy man a solitary; for no one would choose the whole world on condition of being alone, since man is a political creature and one whose nature is to live with others."[331] Under this view, solitude is a form of retreat from solidarity, a condition of being isolated and self-interested in which a person can escape her social responsibilities.[332] Too much of such freedom from intrusion can lead to a scattered community where people distance themselves into isolated enclaves. Why do we want to allow people to have a realm in which they can avoid the presence of others in society?

"[I]ndividuals need a place of sanctuary where they can be free from societal control," the Supreme Court of India aptly stated. "The importance of such sanctuary is that individuals can drop the mask, desist for a while from projecting to the world the image they want to be accepted as themselves, an image that may reflect the values of their peers rather than the realities of their natures."[333] The protection of a realm of solitude does not merely benefit the individual; it is built into society's structure for a social purpose. Hannah Arendt notes that although the Greeks viewed the public sphere as having paramount importance, the private sphere was essential to shaping the dimensions and quality of life in the public sphere:

> A life spent entirely in public, in the presence of others, becomes, as we would say, shallow. While it retains its visibility, it loses the quality of rising into sight from some darker ground which must remain hidden if it is not to lose its depth in a very real, non-subjective sense.[334]

In other words, solitude does not detract from a rich public life but in fact enhances it. Solitude enables people to rest from the pressures of living in public and performing public roles.[335] Too much envelopment in society can be destructive to social relationships. Without refuge from others, relationships can become more bitter and tense.[336] Moreover, a space apart from others has enabled people to develop artistic, political, and religious ideas that have had lasting influence and value when later introduced into the public sphere.[337]

Generally, U.S. courts recognize intrusion-upon-seclusion tort actions only when a person is at home or in a secluded place.[338] This approach is akin to courts recognizing a harm in surveillance only when it is conducted in private, not in public. However, beyond solitude, people often expect space apart from others even when they are with other people. According to sociologist Irwin Altman, we need "personal space," a kind of zone or aura around us to separate ourselves from others. Spatial distance provides for "comfort, ease, and relaxation." Animals maintain "remarkably constant" distances from other animals of the same species. In one series of studies, people placed themselves very close to others, which sparked strong reactions of hostility and unease. The intruded-upon subjects quickly reestablished appropriate spatial boundaries.[339] Robert Post observes that the tort of intrusion upon seclusion upholds rules of civility and social respect. We each have certain "territories of the self," and norms of civility require that we respect others' territories. We can, however, "invite intimacy by waiving our claims to a territory and allowing others to draw close."[340]

Some courts are beginning to recognize realms of exclusion where people can shut others out, even in public.[341] Realms of *exclusion* are not realms of *seclusion;* they are structures for personal space that allow us to interact with others without the interference of the rest of society. Communication and association with others often require freedom from intrusion. For example, when we talk to a friend in a restaurant or another public place, we still need space from other people in order to converse freely. In *Sanders v. American Broadcasting Companies,* an undercover reporter accepted work as a "telepsychic" and surreptitiously videotaped conversations she had at work with her coworkers, including Sanders. Even though Sanders worked in a cubicle where he could readily be seen and overheard by other employees, the court concluded that he had a viable privacy interest: "[T]he concept of 'seclusion' is relative. The mere fact that a person can be seen by someone does not automatically mean that he or she can legally be forced to be subject to being seen by everyone."[342]

Decisional Interference

I avoid looking down at my body, not so much because it's shameful or immodest but because I don't want to see it. I don't want to look at something that determines me so completely.

—*Offred in Margaret Atwood,* The Handmaid's Tale *(1986)*[343]

In 1965, in *Griswold v. Connecticut,* the U.S. Supreme Court held that the Constitution prohibited the government from banning the use of contraceptives by married couples. Although the word "privacy" is not explicitly mentioned anywhere in the Constitution, the Court reasoned that the Constitution provides for a "right to privacy" in the "penumbras" of many of the amendments in the Bill of Rights. The Court noted that "[v]arious guarantees [by the Bill of Rights] create zones of privacy."[344]

In *Eisenstadt v. Baird*, the Court extended the reasoning in *Griswold* to the use of contraceptives by unmarried persons as well. The Court explained that privacy "is the right of the individual, married or single, to be free from unwarranted governmental intrusion into matters so fundamentally affecting a person as the decision whether to bear or beget a child."[345] Subsequently, the Court held in *Roe v. Wade* that the right to privacy "encompass[es] a woman's decision whether or not to terminate her pregnancy."[346]

Griswold, Eisenstadt, and *Roe* all protect against what I call "decisional interference"—that is, governmental interference with people's decisions regarding certain matters in their lives. These cases extend to decisions relating to sex and sexuality, as well as parents' child-rearing decisions.[347]

Many commentators have argued that the language of privacy is inappropriate for decisional-interference cases because they primarily concern a harm to autonomy and liberty, not to privacy. Thus Laurence Tribe argues that the central issue in *Roe v. Wade* is "not privacy, but autonomy."[348] Similarly, Louis Henkin contends that the Supreme Court's substantive due process right-to-privacy cases are about protecting a "zone of autonomy, of presumptive immunity to governmental regulation," not about protecting privacy.[349] What relationship does decisional interference have to the other forms of privacy in the taxonomy?

The decisional-interference cases are deeply connected to information privacy. Legal scholar Neil Richards notes that the "canonical 'decisional' privacy case law has long had a substantial informational component." *Griswold* "relied extensively upon several lines of cases now commonly considered as falling on the information privacy side of the informational/decisional binary of information privacy scholars."[350] In particular, the Supreme Court explained in *Whalen v. Roe* that the constitutionally protected "zone of privacy" extends not only to the "interest in independence in making certain kinds of important decisions" but also to the "individual interest in avoiding disclosure of personal matters."[351] This gave rise to the constitutional right to information privacy, which, although not developed further by the Supreme Court, has been recognized by most federal circuit courts.[352] *Whalen* involved a challenge to a requirement that physicians report to the state the names and addresses of patients who received prescriptions for certain classes of drugs. The *Whalen* Court linked decisional interference with disclosure by suggesting that "[t]he mere existence in readily available form of the information about patients' use of [the] drugs creates a genuine concern that the information will become publicly known and that it will adversely affect their reputations. This concern makes some patients reluctant to use [the drugs]."[353]

By creating a risk of disclosure, the statute inhibited patients' decisions regarding their health care. The Court ultimately rejected the plaintiff's challenge because the state provided adequate protection against the improper disclosure of the patient information.[354] Thus *Whalen* illustrates how decisional interference is related to disclosure. *Whalen* also shows how decisional interference bears similarities to increased accessibility because the existence of information in a government database can increase the potential accessibility of that information. Decisional interference also resembles insecurity, secondary use, and exclusion in that all three of these information-processing harms can have a chilling effect on a person's decisions regarding her health and body.

Decisional interference and exposure generally involve the same aspects of the self, such as one's body and sexual activities. Decisional interference, therefore, does not apply to all decisions but only to a subset of decisions; this aspect of decisional interference resembles exposure in its focus on those aspects of life that are socially considered the most private.

Decisional interference bears a similarity to the harm of intrusion because both involve invasions into realms where we believe that people should be free from the incursions of others. In *On Liberty*, John Stuart Mill declared that "there is a sphere of action in which society, as distinguished from the individual, has, if any, only an indirect interest; comprehending all that portion of a person's life and conduct which affects only himself, or if it also affects others, only with their free, voluntary, and undeceived consent and participation."[355] Although his book *Liberty, Equality, Fraternity* critiqued Mill's *On Liberty*, James Fitzjames Stephen in 1873 wrote, "[T]here is a sphere, none the less real because it is impossible to define its limits, within which law and public opinion are intruders likely to do more harm than good. To try to regulate the internal affairs of a family, the relations of love or friendship, or many other things of the same sort, by law or by the co-ercion of public opinion, is like trying to pull an eyelash out of a man's eye with a pair of tongs. They may put out the eye, but they will never get hold of the eyelash."[356]

Whereas intrusion involves the unwanted general incursion of an-other's presence or activities, decisional interference involves unwanted incursion by the government into an individual's decisions about her personal life. The resemblance is demonstrated by examining the first in the Court's line of right-to-privacy cases, its 1891 decision in *Union Pa-cific Railway Co. v. Botsford*. There, the Court held that a female plaintiff in a civil action could not be forced to submit to a surgical examination: "To compel any one, and especially a woman, to lay bare the body, or to submit it to the touch of a stranger, without lawful authority, is an indig-nity, an assault, and a trespass." The Court emphasized the importance of what Judge Cooley had termed the right "to be let alone" that Warren and Brandeis had used in their article one year earlier. Although the in-trusion at issue in *Botsford* clearly implicated the harms of intrusion and exposure, it also resembled decisional interference. The Court captured this parallel in stating that the right "to be let alone" was "carefully guarded by the common law" and consisted of "the right of every indi-vidual to the possession and control of his own person, free from all re-straint or interference of others, unless by clear and unquestionable au-thority of law."[357] Neil Richards points out that *Griswold* "suggests that a fear of government intrusion into private zones (both physical and so-cial) in pursuit of information was a large part of the rationale behind the conclusion that the Constitution protects a right of privacy."[358]

Another case that illustrates the connection between decisional in-terference and intrusion is *Stanley v. Georgia*, which involved a chal-lenge to an obscenity statute that punished the private possession of obscene material. *Stanley* was cited as support for the constitutional right to privacy in *Roe v. Wade* and *Eisenstadt v. Baird*. Although the ma-terial in *Stanley* was obscene and could properly be banned under the First Amendment, the Court concluded that "the Constitution pro-tects the right to receive information and ideas . . . regardless of their social worth." The Court noted that this "right takes on an added di-mension" in a "prosecution for mere possession of printed or filmed matter in the privacy of a person's own home." It is a fundamental right "to be free, except in very limited circumstances, from unwanted governmental intrusions into one's privacy."[359] The Court quoted Justice Brandeis's dissent in *Olmstead v. United States*, a Fourth Amendment wiretapping case, in which Brandeis argued that the "makers of our Constitution . . . conferred, as against the government, the right to be let alone—the most comprehensive of rights and the right most valued by civilized men."[360]

It is particularly interesting that the Court invoked "the right to be let alone," which was Warren and Brandeis's principle justifying the privacy torts. The criminalization of the private possession of obscene material, the Court's reasoning suggests, necessitates governmental intrusion into one's home. The Supreme Court noted that people have "the right to be free from state inquiry into the contents of [their] library." Linking decisional interference with intrusion, it stressed that "a State has no business telling a man, sitting alone in his own house, what books he may read or what films he may watch."[361] Further capturing the relationship between the two categories, Robert Post contends that the intrusion tort protects "territories of the self," which are critical to remaining "an independent and autonomous person."[362]

In *Lawrence v. Texas*, the Court further demonstrated the frequent overlap between decisional interference and intrusion in striking down a law that prohibited consensual homosexual sodomy. The Court reasoned that "adults may choose to enter upon this relationship in the confines of their homes and their own private lives and still retain their dignity as free persons." The statute was unconstitutional because of "its [unjustified] intrusion into the personal and private life of the individual." Moreover, the Court stated:

> Liberty protects the person from unwarranted government intrusions into a dwelling or other private places. In our tradition the State is not omnipresent in the home. And there are other spheres of our lives and existence, outside the home, where the State should not be a dominant presence. Freedom extends beyond spatial bounds.[363]

The Court thus linked decisional interference to intrusion.

Decisional interference also bears an indirect resemblance to blackmail in that laws restricting consensual private sexual behavior often give rise to blackmail. The *Lawrence* Court noted that in 1955, when crafting the Model Penal Code, the American Law Institute recommended against criminalizing "consensual sexual relations conducted in private" in part because "the statutes regulated private conduct not harmful to others," and because "the laws were arbitrarily enforced and thus invited the danger of blackmail."[364] Indeed, as Angus McLaren recounts, blackmail historically occurred in the shadow of laws that punished consensual sexual activities in private.[365]

~ 6

Privacy: A New Understanding

For quite a long time, the concept of privacy has been a source of chagrin. Despite the profound importance and increasing prevalence of privacy issues, efforts to conceptualize privacy have been plagued by a curse of difficulties. Attempts to locate a common denominator for the manifold things that constitute privacy have proven unsatisfying. Conceptions that attempt to locate the core or essence of privacy have been too broad or too narrow. Despite many good insights, the philosophical discourse about privacy has left a sense of emptiness and dissatisfaction.

Yet we need to conceptualize privacy because it affects the way we craft legal solutions to particular problems. Even if we eschew attempts to conceptualize privacy, we are relying in part on implicit understandings of privacy whenever we discuss it. Judges, legislators, policymakers, and commentators all have some notion of privacy in mind when they address privacy issues. The way we conceptualize privacy is of paramount importance for the information age because we are beset with a number of complex privacy problems that cause great disruption to numerous important activities of high social value.

Therefore, I have proposed a new way to conceptualize privacy. Under my conception, we should understand privacy as a set of protections against a plurality of distinct but related problems. These problems are not related by a common denominator or core element. Instead, each problem has elements in common with others, yet not necessarily the same element—they share family resemblances with each other. We label the whole cluster "privacy," but this term is useful primarily as a shorthand way of describing the cluster. Beyond that, it is more fruitful to discuss and analyze each type of problem specifically.

I am not arguing that we must always avoid referring to privacy in the abstract; sometimes it is more efficient to do so. Rather, such abstract references to privacy often fail to be useful when we need to conceptualize privacy to solve legal and policy problems. By shifting the focus to a plurality of related problems, we can better understand what is at stake in particular situations. We can better recognize each situation for what it is rather than conflating it with other situations.

I proposed a framework of four general types of privacy problems with sixteen different subgroups. First, *information collection* consists of problems that arise in the gathering of information about individuals. I identified two distinct forms of information collection: surveillance and interrogation. A second group of problems, *information processing*, involves difficulties that arise in the storage, usage, and analysis of personal data. I listed five types of information processing: aggregation, identification, insecurity, secondary use, and exclusion. Third, *information dissemination* involves the transfer and publicizing of personal data. I described seven forms of information dissemination: breach of confidentiality, disclosure, exposure, increased accessibility, blackmail, appropriation, and distortion. Finally, *invasion* involves interference with one's personal life. I identified two forms: intrusion and decisional interference.

I do not base this framework on a top-down normative vision about what I believe privacy ought to be. Rather, it is a bottom-up descriptive account of the kinds of privacy problems that are addressed in various discussions about privacy, laws, cases, constitutions, guidelines, and other sources. The problems identified in the taxonomy are not eternal and unchanging. Reasonable people may certainly disagree about the inclusion of certain problems and the exclusion of others. Even with such disagreement, the primary function of my approach to conceptualizing privacy has been to shift the kind of theoretical discussions we have about privacy. Instead of looking for a unified conception of privacy, we can free ourselves to focus on the various problems. Shifting the focus in this way will provide greater clarity and guidance in addressing privacy issues.

My taxonomy of privacy endeavors to serve as a more contextual approach to conceptualizing privacy. Of course, in advocating a contextual conception of privacy, the issue remains: At what level of generality should the contexts be defined? Although my taxonomy consists of a much more finely grained set of categories beyond the general category of "privacy," I define each type of problem with a fair degree of generality. As I have argued, if we seek to conceptualize privacy in too contextual a manner, it is difficult to develop a framework that will apply beyond just a few circumstances. The purpose of a framework is to guide analysis. Merely calling for more context in conceptualizing privacy throws the issue back into the hands of those who are struggling over a particular problem without telling them how to make sense of it. Thus it is useful to define problems with some breadth so long as the generalizations are not overly reductive or distorting.

The taxonomy focuses on problems. I explored a number of other ways to focus the taxonomy—based on the nature of the information or matters, individual preferences, and reasonable expectations of privacy. There is tremendous variability in the particular kinds of information or matters people consider private. No matter how sensitive something may be, it might not be private because it is widely known to others. Privacy is in part a condition of the information or matter, such as whether it is concealed or held in confidence. On the other hand, privacy is not exclusively a condition because not all information or matters that are concealed are private. The taxonomy focuses on problems because they are often the starting point for discussion and for the formulation of legal and policy responses.

Since privacy is a pluralistic concept, its value should be understood pluralistically as well. Privacy does not have a uniform value. Its value varies across different contexts depending upon which form of privacy is involved and what range of activities are imperiled by a particular problem. Additionally, I have contended that the value of privacy should be understood in terms of its contribution to society. Many accounts of privacy's value have sought to understand it in terms of individual rights that conflict with the interests of society. Commentators have argued that privacy should be protected as an individual right that trumps competing interests even when these interests have greater social utility than privacy. In contrast, I have argued that when privacy protects the individual, it does so because it is in society's interest. Individual liberties should be justified in terms of their social contribution. Privacy is not just freedom from social control but is in fact a socially constructed form of protection. The value of privacy does not emerge from each form of privacy itself but from the range of activities it protects.

Privacy, in short, involves a cluster of protections against a group of different but related problems. These problems impede valuable activities that society wants to protect, and therefore society devises ways to address these problems. By creating these protections, society opens up a particular realm of freedom we call "privacy."

The Nature of Privacy Problems

To properly weigh privacy against conflicting interests, it is imperative that we have a complete understanding of the particular privacy problems involved in any given context. We must identify the privacy problems, examine the activities compromised by each, and recognize the nature of harms to these activities. A problem is a situation that creates harms to individuals and society. A privacy problem can create many different types of harm. Throughout the taxonomy, I discussed the harms created by privacy problems. Sometimes the law comprehends these harms well, but other times, the law fixates on one kind of harm to the exclusion of others or lacks the tools to address certain harms. The theory of privacy I have developed aims to improve our ability to recognize and comprehend the harms created by privacy problems.

Individual and Societal Harms

In the taxonomy, I identified sixteen different categories of problems. Each is problematic for a number of reasons. One of the difficulties the law experiences in grappling with privacy issues is understanding the nature of privacy problems. In particular, the law struggles with comprehending how and why privacy problems cause injury. Throughout the taxonomy, I have discussed a range of ways that the individual and society are harmed by privacy problems.

Physical Injuries. Certain kinds of harm, such as physical injuries, are very easy to articulate and understand. The law has long been able to comprehend physical pain and impairment, and therefore, the law has been able to provide adequate remedies to redress such injuries. In most cases, however, privacy problems do not cause physical injuries.

Financial Losses and Property Harms. In some cases, privacy problems result in financial losses or property harms. Insecurity, for example, can lead to fraud or identity theft. Some intrusions can involve trespass onto property or interference with the enjoyment of one's property. The law is generally quite adept at rectifying financial losses and protecting property rights.

Reputational Harms. In a number of instances, privacy problems result in reputational injuries. President John Adams once asserted that the "man . . . without attachment to reputation, or honor, is undone."[1] Reputational harms impair a person's ability to maintain "personal esteem in the eyes of others" and can taint a person's image in the community. They can result in "social rebuffs" or lost business or employment.[2] The law has long recognized reputational injuries because it has protected against defamation since ancient Roman times. Moreover, the law has understood reputational harms as distinct from physical and property injuries.[3]

Emotional and Psychological Harms. In many instances, privacy problems do not create physical, financial, or reputational harm. Rather, they result in feelings of emotional distress, humiliation, and outrage. Some might contend that certain forms of emotional harm created by privacy problems are mere anxieties and that they are too tenuous and subjective to be afforded protection. But one British privacy expert aptly observed, "Privacy itself is in one sense irrational: it is about people's feelings. But feelings are *there*, they are facts. And if people's anxieties aren't relieved, they tend to find outlets which are likely to be painful."[4]

American law has slowly grown to comprehend psychological harms. For a long time, tort law recognized only tangible harms. When Samuel Warren and Louis Brandeis wrote their 1890 article on privacy, they acknowledged that the psychological nature of privacy harms would present a challenge for the law. "[I]n very early times," they argued, "the law gave a remedy only for physical interference with life and property." They noted, however, that the law developed to recognize nonphysical injuries: "From the action of battery grew that of assault. Much later there came a qualified protection of the individual against offensive noises and odors, against dust and smoke, and excessive vibration. The law of nuisance was developed." In addition to physical property, they observed, the law also recognized intellectual property. Warren and Brandeis were attempting to justify why the law should also recognize the nonphysical harms of privacy, which consisted of an "injury to the feelings."[5]

Concerned that privacy harms might strike some as too ethereal, Warren and Brandeis aimed to demonstrate that they were genuine harms that deserved a remedy. Privacy harms, they wrote, can subject people to "mental pain and distress far greater than could be inflicted by mere bodily injury."[6] Today, the privacy torts they recommended are recognized in most jurisdictions. The development of the privacy torts is mirrored by the increasing recognition of psychological harms in American law. Until the twentieth century, courts were reluctant to recognize psychological harms in part because of "fear of imaginary injuries and fictitious suits" and "the difficulty of monetarily valuing emotional harm."[7] But in the twentieth century, American law significantly expanded its recognition of psychological harms.[8] A tort to redress intentional infliction of emotional distress arose, and the tort currently provides a remedy when one "by extreme and outrageous conduct intentionally or recklessly causes severe emotional distress."[9] A tort protecting against negligent infliction of emotional distress also grew and developed throughout the past century.

Relationship Harms. Several of the problems in the taxonomy involve damage to relationships. Breach of confidentiality, for example, thwarts expectations of trust within relationships. Information gathering can also interfere with relationships by making people less likely to communicate or associate with each other. Legal scholar Nancy Levit observes, "The development of protection for relational interests evidences a communitarian view of the role of tort law. . . . The vision being promoted is one of the responsible social interaction: a commitment to the value of the permanency of relationships and to appropriate treatment within those relationships."[10]

American law recognizes relationship harms, although it does so inconsistently. In legal proceedings, evidentiary privileges restrict the disclosure of communications between attorney and client, priest and penitent, husband and wife, and psychotherapist and patient.[11] Often this information is highly relevant and probative. The rationale for protecting these relationships is the importance of fostering candid communication and preserving the relationships themselves. This justification is rooted in society's interests; it is not based solely on preventing individuals from suffering emotional distress.

Relationship harms are also implicated by information collection and dissemination about the groups one associates with. In several cases, the U.S. Supreme Court has held that the First Amendment restricts the interrogation of individuals about their membership in various groups.[12] The Supreme Court has declared that there is a "vital relationship between freedom to associate and privacy in one's associations." For members of dissident or unpopular groups, disclosing their identities would subject them "to economic reprisal, loss of employment, threat of physical coercion, and other manifestations of public hostility."[13] Protection against these relationship harms stems from the social value of preserving associations. As Alexis de Tocqueville declared:

> The most natural privilege of a man next to the right of acting for himself, is that of combining his exertions with those of his fellow creatures and of acting in common with them. The right of association therefore appears to be as almost inalienable in its nature as the right of personal liberty. No legislator can attack it without impairing the foundations of society.[14]

Vulnerability Harms. Several of the problems discussed in the taxonomy result in making people more vulnerable and less secure. Vulnerability harms involve the creation of the risk that a person might be harmed in the future. For example, the problem of insecurity results in increasing people's risk that a future harm will occur, such as being victimized by identity theft or fraud. Such risk-enhancing activities increase the chance that the individual will suffer physical, financial, reputational, or psychological harms.

In many ways, vulnerability harms are akin to environmental harms.[15] Vulnerability harms are often created not by singular egregious acts but by a gradual series of relatively minor acts that add up over time. In this way, some privacy problems resemble certain forms of pollution. There is often no single wrongdoer; instead, this digital pollution occurs through the combined activities of a multitude of institutions, each with differing motives and aims.

Many contemporary privacy problems are systemic in nature. Information-processing problems frequently are the result of what I call "architectures of vulnerability."[16] Architectures of vulnerability consist of the designs or structures for the processing of personal information that make people vulnerable to a host of dangers. Information economies often have structural flaws that create problems such as insecurity. When inadequate security practices lead to personal data leaks, they expose people to potential future harm. Architectures of vulnerability result in people being worse off—they are akin to a disease that weakens the immune system.

Chilling Effects. Some privacy problems create another kind of harm: they inhibit people from engaging in certain activities. This kind of harm is often referred to as a "chilling effect."[17] Legal scholar Frederick Schauer defines it as follows: "A chilling effect occurs when individuals seeking to engage in activity protected by the first amendment are deterred from doing so by governmental regulation not specifically directed at that protected activity."[18] Government monitoring of dissident groups can make people less likely to attend political rallies or criticize popular views. On a number of occasions, American courts have recognized chilling effects as injuries. The chilling-effect doctrine understands that First Amendment rights, such as free speech and free association, can be inhibited indirectly, not just through direct legal restrictions.[19]

The value of protecting against such chilling effects is not measured simply in terms of the value to those particular individuals. Chilling effects harm society because, among other things, they reduce the range of viewpoints being expressed and limit the degree of freedom with which to engage in political activity.

Power Imbalances. Many privacy problems result in power imbalances that adversely affect social structure but do not result in direct harm to specific individuals. The problem of exclusion, for example, often does not cause psychological harm, but it puts people in a position of powerlessness. Power imbalances can occur when a particular activity upsets the balance of social or institutional power in undesirable ways. Sociologist Robert Merton notes, " 'Privacy' is not merely a personal predilection; it is an important functional requirement for the effective operation of social structure."[20] Although particular individuals may not be directly injured, power imbalances can affect people's lives because they shape the social and political atmosphere in which people live. In some cases, they have direct effects on individuals because they can result in chilling effects or vulnerability harms. Often, the aggrandizement of power by institutions does not arise out of malicious aims, but it nevertheless creates dangers such as drift in purposes and abuse. Joel Reidenberg aptly notes, "[D]ata privacy is a societal value and a requisite element of democracy. Society as a whole has an important stake in the contours of the protection of personal information."[21]

In a related manner, the Fourth Amendment's requirement of judicial oversight of government searches does not protect only the specific individuals being searched; it is a protection of society as a whole against excessive government power. The Fourth Amendment is enforced through the exclusionary rule, by which a criminal defendant can exclude evidence obtained improperly from trial. If we view the Fourth Amendment as protecting the privacy rights of the defendant, it is hard to justify why we should protect her privacy at the cost of the safety of the rest of the community. Instead, if we view the Fourth Amendment as protecting privacy as a social value, we are enforcing privacy rights because of the larger value to the community in ensuring that the police follow appropriate procedures when conducting searches. Priscilla Regan observes, "A public value of privacy derives not only from its protection of the individual as an individual but also from its usefulness as a restraint on the government or on the use of power."[22] The Fourth Amendment rectifies a set of power imbalances; it aims to provide a structural balance of power between the government and citizens.

Recognizing and Redressing Harms

Even when it appears that the law recognizes a problem, the law can also falter in understanding its nature and effects. In other words, there is a distinction between recognizing a problem and understanding a problem. The law sometimes acknowledges the privacy problems involved in a given context but fails to effectively redress the harms caused by the problems. For example, in the U.S. Privacy Act of 1974, Congress sought to regulate the collection, processing, and dissemination of personal information by government agencies.[23] On the surface, the act embodies a pluralistic conception of privacy that recognizes many of the problems in the taxonomy, such as information collection, processing, and dissemination. The act falls short, however, because its enforcement provisions do not adequately address the harms created by these problems. In many instances, enforcement of the Privacy Act occurs through lawsuits by individuals for damages. Collecting damages, however, is very difficult.[24] For example, in *Doe v. Chao*, the Department of Labor improperly disclosed coal-mine workers' Social Security numbers. Several sued under the federal Privacy Act, which prohibits the disclosure of personal information. One of the plaintiffs, Buck Doe, explained his injury:

> He was "greatly concerned and worried" about the disclosure of his SSN; that he felt his privacy had been violated in "words he cannot describe"; that he felt the consequences of the disclosure of his SSN could be "devastating" for himself and his wife, and that the disclosure of his SSN had "torn [him] all to pieces."

But Doe could not prove these damages based on his "own conclusory allegations that he felt 'embarrassed,' 'degraded,' or 'devastated,' and suffered a loss of self-esteem." According to the court, Doe "did not produce any evidence of tangible consequences stemming from his alleged angst over the disclosure of his SSN. He claimed no medical or psychological treatment, no purchase of medications (prescription or over-the-counter), no impact on his behavior, and no physical consequences."[25] Although the Privacy Act provides for liquidated damages (a minimum amount of damages without regard to a person's actual damages), the U.S. Supreme Court concluded that Doe could only collect liquidated damages once he had proven actual damages.[26]

Although one of the Privacy Act's central purposes is to protect against exclusion, insecurity, and other information-processing problems, it fails because its enforcement structure focuses too much on the individual and not enough on the harms of vulnerability and power imbalances. These harms often cannot be adequately rectified by requiring proof of physical or financial harm. Often, no immediate fraud or identity theft has resulted from a particular data leak. A concrete injury may never emerge, or it could occur years later. The law frequently struggles to recognize a harm until an actual misuse of the information occurs. To be effective, any individual enforcement mechanisms must be structured to address the larger architectural harms. To the extent that enforcement occurs by way of individual lawsuits, it must involve true liquidated damages without requiring proof of any specific individual harm.

Courts sometimes struggle with recognizing a harm in the processing and dissemination of data by businesses. For example, in *U.S. West, Inc. v. Federal Communications Commission*, a communications carrier challenged privacy regulations for telephone customer information as a violation of free speech. The regulations required that the companies first obtain the consent of their customers before using their personal information for new purposes beyond those for which the data were collected. In order for the regulations to survive constitutional muster, they had to serve a substantial interest. The court concluded that privacy did not rise to the level of a substantial interest:

> [T]he government must show that the dissemination of the information desired to be kept private would inflict specific and significant harm on individuals, such as undue embarrassment or ridicule, intimidation or harassment, or misappropriation of sensitive personal information for the purposes of assuming another's identity.

The court further stated that a "general level of discomfort from knowing that people can readily access information about us does not necessarily rise to the level of a substantial state interest . . . for it is not based on an identified harm."[27]

The *U.S. West* court focused too heavily on harm to particular individuals and did not see the larger social harms. The court was fixated on finding a physical, financial, reputational, or psychological harm. It did not see the power imbalance caused by the aggregation and secondary uses of personal information by the telephone company. Aggregation, secondary use, and many other information-processing problems affect the way that power is allocated between individuals and large corporations. These problems affect the structure of our society as a whole. The problems are different from the disclosure of a secret, the exposure of a nude body, or the pervasive surveillance of an individual. They are problems that go to the heart of what type of society we are constructing as we move headlong into the information age.

Information can be used to make important decisions about people's lives; it is often subjected to a bureaucratic process that lacks discipline and control; and the individual has scant knowledge of how the information is processed and used.

The law frequently struggles with recognizing harms that do not result in embarrassment, humiliation, or physical or psychological injury.[28] For example, after the September 11 attacks, several airlines gave their passenger records to federal agencies in direct violation of their privacy policies. A group of passengers sued Northwest Airlines for disclosing their personal information. One of their claims was that Northwest Airlines breached its contract with the passengers. In *Dyer v. Northwest Airlines Corp.*, the court rejected the contract claim in part because the passengers "failed to allege any contractual damages arising out of the alleged breach."[29] A similar difficulty in recognizing harm is illustrated by *Smith v. Chase Manhattan Bank*. A group of people sued Chase Manhattan Bank for selling their personal information to third parties. The sale of the information violated Chase's privacy policy, which stated that the information would remain confidential. The court held that even presuming these allegations were true, the plaintiffs could not prove any actual injury: "[T]he 'harm' at the heart of this purported class action, is that class members were merely offered products and services which they were free to decline. This does not qualify as actual harm. The complaint does not allege any single instance where a named plaintiff or any class member suffered any actual harm due to the receipt of an unwanted telephone solicitation or a piece of junk mail."[30]

These cases illustrate a difficulty in the legal system in addressing privacy problems. The actions of Northwest Airlines and Chase Manhattan Bank constituted breaches of confidentiality. The harm involved in a breach of confidentiality consists of more than emotional distress. The harm is one that affects social structure because it involves the extent to which promises of confidentiality can be trusted. If companies can promise confidentiality but suffer no consequences in violating their word, then promises of confidentiality become unreliable, and trust between companies and their customers gradually erodes. The effects often extend beyond the specific companies that break their promises; unpunished breaches of confidentiality can erode trust in promises of confidentiality more generally. Countless transactions depend upon the viability of promises of confidentiality, and ensuring that these promises remain dependable has a social value.

Secondary use is also implicated in *Dyer* because the data collected for one purpose was then given to the government for an entirely different purpose. The secondary-use problem did not cause financial injuries or even psychological ones. Instead, the harm was one of power imbalance. Data was disseminated in a way that ignored airline passengers' interests in the data despite promises made in the privacy policy. Even if the passengers were unaware of the policy, there is a social value in ensuring that companies adhere to established limits on the way they use personal information. Otherwise, any stated limits become meaningless, and companies have discretion to use data with few bounds. This state of affairs can leave nearly all consumers in a powerless position. The harms are not primarily injuries to particular individuals—they involve structural harms.

Privacy and Cultural Difference

The privacy problems in the taxonomy have been recognized, at least partially, in nearly every industrialized information-age society. Cultural differences manifest themselves most in terms of ascribing different values to privacy and countervailing interests. My project focuses primarily on understanding and distinguishing privacy problems because this approach transcends cultural variation more than other ways of understanding privacy. Once we move to ascribing values, however, cultural differences begin to play a greater role.

In analyzing a privacy problem, we must first identify the problem, assess its value and the value of any conflicting interests, and then seek a reconciliation or determine which prevails in a balancing. The balance might come out differently across various societies because of differences in the values ascribed to privacy and its conflicting interests. Despite contrasting balances, it is important to note that there is a significant degree of consensus about the kinds of problems involved. This is the first step toward addressing privacy issues, but difficulties in conceptualizing these problems often prematurely halt the balancing process even before privacy and conflicting interests are placed on the scale.

It is often not fruitful to speak in broad generalities about whether a particular country or society respects "privacy." Speaking in terms of the more specific problems in the taxonomy will be much more helpful. In any given society, certain aspects of life (for example, sex or nudity) may be protected against exposure, but some cultures do not protect them all. The harm of exposure exists in many cultures, though not to the same degree. In many primitive communal societies, people live openly and tolerate much greater degrees of visibility than people in modern industrialized societies. Nevertheless, these societies may still recognize privacy violations. For example, the Mehinacu tribe, which lives deep in the tropical rain forests of Brazil, appears to have little privacy. Mehinacu families share houses that are arrayed around a central common area. Gossip is rampant, and nearly everything is in an open area. Nevertheless, the Mehinacu have enclaves of seclusion, paths away from others where people can engage in clandestine affairs. The tribe has norms against gawking, reporting certain of each other's transgressions, interrogating people about intimate matters, and entering into another family's space.[31]

Therefore, although the problems in the taxonomy are not universal, they are widely recognized. Different societies protect against them differently, a reflection of different values ascribed both to privacy and to the interests that conflict with it. It is certainly true that societies do not experience some of the privacy problems with the same degree of intensity. For example, Professor Dan Rosen notes that people have less seclusion in Japan than in many other industrialized societies because of very crowded conditions. Japan's exceptionally crammed subways, for example, lead to extensive physical contact that is alien to people in many other societies. This does not mean, however, that the Japanese prefer less personal space or that they fail to recognize the harm of intrusion. Even despite the extensive bodily contact, the Japanese find certain conduct intrusive, such as groping or glaring.[32] Living conditions and life experiences within different societies alter people's tolerance of a lack of interpersonal distance. Of course, these living conditions could also be the product of a different set of values and desires with respect to privacy. But generally, across a wide array of societies, people recognize the problems in the taxonomy as problematic to some degree. We see evidence of this recognition in the laws, politics, literature, and other cultural products that embody a society's values.

Nevertheless, some commentators focus more on the differences than the similarities and conclude that cultural attitudes toward privacy are so divergent that little can be done to bridge the gaps. There is no shared worldwide understanding of privacy, they argue, just a number of localized notions. For example, Professor James Whitman argues that American and European privacy law emerge from two very distinct underlying conceptions of privacy: "[T]here are, on the two sides of the Atlantic, two different cultures of privacy, which are home to different intuitive sensibilities, and which have produced two significantly different laws of privacy." According to Whitman, "American privacy law is a body caught in the gravitational orbit of liberty values, while European law is caught in the orbit of dignity." Europeans have a deeper concern for honor and dignity, whereas Americans have prized liberty in the form of freedom from government control. "Continental jurists," Whitman observes, "have always tried to understand 'privacy' as a species of personal honor." Whitman concludes that Warren and Brandeis tried to import "a continental-style of privacy into American law," and that this was an "unsuccessful continental transplant." Because of the difference between American and European conceptions, Whitman concludes that "there is little reason to suppose that Americans will be persuaded to think of their world of values in a European way any time soon; American law simply does not endorse the general norm of personal dignity found in Europe."[33]

Many commentators have embraced Whitman's thesis because his characterizations of American and European society resonate at a general level. America and Europe certainly have created different legal regimes to regulate privacy. Through the European Union Data Protection Directive, Europe regulates privacy with a comprehensive set of rules. The approach in the United States is "sectoral," a patchwork of laws that protect privacy in certain areas, but with significant gaps and omissions. Joel Reidenberg notes, "[T]he United States has resisted all calls for omnibus or comprehensive legal rules for fair information practice in the private sector. Legal rules have developed on an ad hoc, targeted basis, while industry has elaborated voluntary norms and practices for particular problems."[34]

It is erroneous, however, to view differences between the protection of privacy in different countries in too essentialist a manner—as rooted in fundamentally incompatible conceptions of privacy. Divergences between the ways different societies protect privacy do not necessarily stem from conceptual differences about privacy. Comparative-law

scholar Francesca Bignami explains that differences in American and
European privacy protections are often the product of diverging enforcement strategies. In the 1970s, she notes, American and European
privacy laws had a great degree of similarity, but different ways of enforcing the law led to significant differences. Europe enforces its laws
through privacy agencies; the United States does not.[35] Many privacy
problems in the United States are enforced primarily by aggrieved
individuals bringing suit. Enforcement by individuals can be very
effective, but for certain problems, individual enforcement mechanisms alone are inadequate. Problems involving vulnerability harms
and power imbalances, for example, are difficult to remedy at the individual level.

Although certainly there are differences between the American and
European approaches to privacy, one should not lose sight of the remarkable similarities. The taxonomy illustrates that there is widespread recognition of each privacy problem across geographic borders.
In any particular country, there is rarely a unified conception of privacy
embodied in its norms and law. American attitudes and law about privacy, for example, are incredibly diverse. American privacy law does
not orbit around one central concept but embodies a jumble of conflicting ideas and values.

Viewed in totality, the degree to which so many countries recognize
the same set of privacy problems is more significant than the divergences. By and large, American and European law recognize nearly all
the problems in the taxonomy. Americans may not have the same notion of dignity and honor as Europeans, but Americans still view privacy problems that infringe upon dignity as harmful. Indeed, reputational and psychological harms are well recognized in U.S. law.

In addition, countries often inform their cultural understanding of
privacy by drawing on other countries' views. Although countries protect privacy differently, there is a significant cross-pollination of ideas
regarding privacy problems. The basic framework for the European
Union Data Protection Directive emerges from an American privacy
report written for the Department of Health, Education, and Welfare
(HEW) in 1973 as part of the effort that led to the passage of the federal Privacy Act of 1974.[36] The HEW report recommended a code of
Fair Information Practices, which have influenced many laws in the
United States. The HEW report also helped shape the OECD Privacy

Guidelines of 1980, which form the basis of privacy laws in countries around the world. Colin Bennett notes that there has been a convergence in the privacy law of modern industrialized nations: "[W]hile the nomenclature and codification may vary from country to country, the substance and purpose of these [privacy] principles are basically the same."[37]

Although the problems in the taxonomy are not universal, there is a remarkable degree of consensus about them. With increasing globalization, this consensus is likely to grow because countries share personal information for security and business purposes.

The Benefits of a Pluralistic Conception of Privacy

In this book, I have attempted to provide a framework for understanding privacy problems. Currently, too many courts and policymakers struggle with identifying the presence of a privacy problem. Protecting privacy requires careful balancing because neither privacy nor its countervailing interests are absolute values. Unfortunately, because of conceptual confusion, courts and legislatures often fail to recognize privacy problems, and thus no balancing ever takes place. This does not mean that privacy should always win in the balance, but it should not be dismissed just because it is ignored or misconstrued.

When privacy is translated into the legal system, it is a form of protection against certain harmful or problematic activities. The activities that affect privacy are not necessarily socially undesirable or worthy of sanction or prohibition. This fact makes addressing privacy issues complex. In many instances, there is no indisputable villain whose activities lack social value. Instead, many privacy problems emerge as a result of efficacious activities, much as pollution is an outgrowth of industrial production. With the taxonomy, I have attempted to demonstrate that these activities are not without cost; they have certain nontrivial effects on people's lives and well-being.

Courts and policymakers often have great difficulty in arriving at a coherent assessment of the various privacy problems they must address. One common pitfall is viewing "privacy" as involving a particular kind of problem to the exclusion of all others. As illustrated throughout this book, courts generally find no privacy interest if information is in the public domain, if people are monitored in public, if information is gathered in a public place, if no intimate or embarrassing details are revealed, or if no new data is collected about a person. If courts and legislatures focused instead on privacy *problems*, many of these distinctions and determinative factors would matter much less in the analysis. Thus, in analyzing surveillance issues, courts currently focus on whether the surveillance occurs in public or in private, even though problems and harms can emerge in all settings. Aggregation creates problems even when all the data are already available in the public domain. The same is true of increased accessibility. For disclosure, the secrecy of the information becomes a central dispositive factor, but this approach often misses the crux of the disclosure harm, which is not the revelation of total secrets, but the spreading of information beyond expected boundaries. In intrusion analyses, courts often fail to recognize harm when people are intruded upon in public places, but the nature of the harm is not limited solely to private places.

At other times, the privacy problem at issue is misconstrued. For example, identification is often understood as a harm created by revealing one's name, but the essence of the problem is being linked to a stream of data, not only a name. Insecurity is often not adequately addressed by the law because a materialized harm has not yet occurred. But insecurity remains a problem even where there has been no actual disclosure or leakage of embarrassing details. Appropriation is understood primarily as a harm to property interests, and its dignitary dimensions are thus frequently ignored by courts. Further complicating matters is the fact that privacy problems are inconsistently recognized across different areas of the law. For example, tort law readily recognizes and redresses breach of confidentiality, but Fourth Amendment law ignores it.

Courts and legislatures respond well to more traditional privacy problems, such as intrusions that are physical in nature, disclosures of deep secrets, or distortion. This is due, in part, to the fact that these problems track traditional conceptions of privacy. In the secrecy paradigm, a privacy violation is understood as the uncovering of a person's hidden world. Physical intrusions are problems that even people in ancient times could experience and understand. But some of the privacy problems we face today are different in nature and do not track traditional conceptions of privacy. They involve efforts to gain knowledge about individuals without physically intruding on them or even gathering data directly from them (aggregation), or problems that emerge from the way that data is handled and maintained (insecurity), the way it is used (secondary use), and the inability of people to participate in its processing (exclusion). Modern privacy problems emerge not just from disclosing deep secrets, but from making obscure information more accessible (increased accessibility) or from consistent observation or eavesdropping (surveillance).

The taxonomy lays down a framework to understand the range of privacy problems, the similarities, differences, and relationships among them, and what makes them problematic. The taxonomy also seeks to emphasize how privacy problems arise. Often, technology is involved in various privacy problems because it facilitates the gathering, processing, and dissemination of information. Privacy problems, however, are caused not by technology alone, but primarily through *activities* of people, businesses, and governments. These activities disrupt other activities that we value and thus create a problem. The way to address privacy problems is to reconcile conflicts between activities. To demonstrate the importance of understanding the different types of privacy problems, as well as the social value of privacy, I will provide a few examples.

Drug Testing

In *Board of Education v. Earls*, a school district in Tecumseh, Oklahoma, required all middle- and high-school students to undergo drug testing before participating in any extracurricular activity. Some of the students challenged the policy under the Fourth Amendment. The U.S. Supreme Court recognized that drug testing involves a search under the Fourth Amendment. Because of "special needs beyond the normal need for law enforcement," the Court concluded that the Fourth Amendment's warrant and probable-cause requirements were impractical for school searches.[38] Therefore, the Court proceeded to determine whether the drug-testing policy was "reasonable" under the Fourth Amendment, a determination that required balancing the privacy interest against the school's interest in testing.

In analyzing the privacy interest, the Court viewed it in terms of exposure and disclosure. For example, the Court focused on the fact that the drug testing occurred through obtaining urine samples. The Court noted that "[u]rination is an excretory function traditionally shielded by great privacy." Thus the Court focused on the way that urination was monitored: "[T]he degree of intrusion on one's privacy caused by collecting a urine sample depends upon the manner in which production of the urine sample is monitored." The Court concluded that the disruption was "negligible" because school officials waited outside closed restroom stalls and merely listened to detect normal sounds of urination. In addition to focusing on exposure, the Court also examined the potential for disclosure. The Court concluded that this disruption was also minor because the policy required that the test results be kept in confidential files and "released to school personnel only on a 'need to know' basis."[39]

The Court analyzed these problems from the standpoint of the individual, focusing on the specific harms to the students. In contrast, in analyzing the competing interest, the Court described it in broader social terms, defining it as addressing the "drug abuse problem among our Nation's youth." The Court stated, "[T]he nationwide drug epidemic makes the war against drugs a pressing concern in every school."[40] When the privacy interests of a few individuals are balanced against redressing "the nationwide drug epidemic," the scales readily tip toward the government's interest.

The Court improperly characterized the privacy interests as individual ones and missed other problems caused by drug testing. Drug testing certainly involves exposure and disclosure, but it also involves distortion. One court has observed, "[U]rine testing—unaided by blood or breath testing—is a blunt instrument. A single positive urine test is silent as to when and how much of the drug was taken, the pattern of the . . . drug use, or whether the [person] was intoxicated when the test was given."[41] Drug testing can also lead to erroneous results, which, even if later corrected, can still cause fear and anxiety in the interim. Furthermore, drug testing is a form of interrogation by physical means, forcing people to undergo an analysis of their urine to detect drugs. Drug-testing programs, such as the one in *Earls*, alter the nature of the communities in which they are implemented. They create a regime of suspicion and distrust, and they force students to justify themselves to take advantage of beneficial educational opportunities. Drug testing thus shapes the environment in which students learn. It does not merely probe for drug use or cause embarrassment but also teaches and instructs. Justice Sandra Day O'Connor observed, dissenting in *Vernonia School District v. Acton*, where the Court upheld a drug-testing program for student athletes:

> [I]ntrusive, blanket searches of schoolchildren, most of whom are innocent, for evidence of serious wrongdoing are not part of any traditional school function of which I am aware. Indeed, many schools, like many parents, prefer to trust their children unless given reason to do otherwise. As James Acton's father said on the witness stand, "[suspicionless testing] sends a message to children that are trying to be responsible citizens . . . that they have to prove that they're innocent . . . , and I think that kind of sets a bad tone for citizenship."[42]

The Court's balancing in *Earls* thus overlooked the most important privacy harms caused by the drug-testing policy—those that implicated social structure.

Moreover, the Court neglected to address the problem of insecurity. The students contended that the school was careless about keeping the test results secure. Files were not carefully secured and were left where they could be accessed by unauthorized people, such as other students.[43] The Court dismissed this contention because there were no allegations of any improper disclosures.[44] It failed to recognize that disclosure differs from insecurity because the harm caused by disclosure is the actual leakage of information; insecurity is the injury of being placed in a weakened state, of being made more vulnerable to a range of future harms.

Government Data Mining

Increasingly, the U.S. government is engaging in data mining. Data mining involves excavating repositories of personal data to glean nuggets of new information. In many instances, combining different pieces of information can yield new insights into an individual's personality and behavior. Data mining often consists of analyzing personal information for patterns of suspicious behavior. In 2002, for example, the media revealed that the Department of Defense was developing a data-mining project called Total Information Awareness under the leadership of Admiral John Poindexter. The program involved collecting extensive information about people, such as financial, educational, health, and other data. The information would then be analyzed for behavior patterns to identify terrorists. According to Poindexter, "The only way to detect . . . terrorists is to look for patterns of activity that are based on observations from past terrorist attacks as well as estimates about how terrorists will adapt to our measures to avoid detection."[45] When the program came to light, a public outcry erupted that led to the demise of the program when the U.S. Senate voted to deny it funding. Nevertheless, many components of Total Information Awareness continue in various government agencies in a less systematic and more clandestine fashion.[46]

Beyond Total Information Awareness, the government engages in a number of data-mining programs—about 200 according to a 2004 government report.[47] One example is the Multi-State Anti-Terrorism Information Exchange (MATRIX), a database of personal information used by various states.[48] Another is the National Security Administration (NSA) data-mining program on telephone records. After September 11, the NSA obtained customer records from several major phone companies and analyzed them to identify potential terrorists.[49] The telephone-call database was reported to be the "largest database ever assembled in the world."[50] The government has also been devising a series of data-mining programs for airline passenger screening.[51]

Some scholars argue that data mining does not pose a significant threat to privacy. Much of the information involves relatively innocuous daily transactions and is not particularly sensitive or revealing. Moreover, Richard Posner argues:

> The collection, mainly through electronic means, of vast amounts of personal data is said to invade privacy. But machine collection and processing of data cannot, as such, invade privacy. Because of their volume, the data are first sifted by computers, which search for names, addresses, phone numbers, etc., that may have intelligence value. This initial shifting, far from invading privacy (a computer is not a sentient being), keeps most private data from being read by any intelligence officer.[52]

Posner's argument is one commonly made about the privacy of personal information in large databases. The data is stored and analyzed by computers. No human might actually see the information. The primary concern with data mining, according to Posner, is that the information might be used to blackmail people or leaked in order to "ridicule or embarrass."[53]

Posner focuses only on problems of information dissemination (disclosure and blackmail), but data mining also implicates several problems of information collection and information processing. Data mining often begins with the collection of personal information, usually from various third parties that possess people's data. Under current Supreme Court Fourth Amendment jurisprudence, when the government gathers data from third parties, there is no Fourth Amendment protection because people lack a "reasonable expectation of privacy" in information exposed to others. As I argued extensively in my book *The Digital Person*, the lack of Fourth Amendment protection of third-party records results in the government's ability to access an extensive amount of personal information with minimal limitation or oversight.[54] Many scholars have referred to the collection of information as a form of surveillance. "Dataveillance," a term coined by Roger Clarke, refers to the "systemic use of personal data systems in the investigation or monitoring of the actions or communications of one or more persons."[55] Christopher Slobogin has referred to the gathering of personal information in business records as "transactional surveillance."[56] Surveillance can create chilling effects on important activities, especially ones essential for democracy, such as free speech and free association.[57]

Surveillance, however, like disclosure, is just one of the problems created by data mining. Far too often, discussions of government data mining define the problem solely in terms of surveillance or disclosure. I have argued that this way of understanding the problem has been embodied by the metaphor of George Orwell's novel *Nineteen Eighty-four*.[58] In Orwell's novel, a totalitarian government known as Big Brother engages in repressive surveillance of its citizens.[59] The problem, as understood by Orwell's metaphor, is one of surveillance, which chills people's behavior. Privacy is violated when people can no longer conceal information they want to hide. But data mining is problematic even if no information we want to hide is uncovered. Another set of problems is implicated by the processing of personal information, and they are better understood with the metaphor of Franz Kafka's novel *The Trial*. In Kafka's novel, an unwieldy bureaucratic court system "arrests" the protagonist but refuses to inform him of the charges. It maintains a dossier about him that he is unable to see. His case is processed in clandestine proceedings.[60] Kafka's *The Trial* captures a different set of problems than Orwell's *Nineteen Eighty-four*. In *The Trial*, the problem is not inhibited behavior but a suffocating powerlessness and vulnerability created by the court system's use of personal data and its exclusion of the protagonist from having any knowledge or participation in the process. The harms consist of those created by bureaucracies—indifference, errors, abuses, frustration, and lack of transparency and accountability. For example, data mining creates the problem of exclusion because people are often prevented from having access and knowledge about how their information is being used, as well as barred from being able to correct errors in that data. Many data-mining programs are conducted in secret and lack transparency. People often are denied the ability to correct errors or to challenge being singled out on the basis of a particular profile. There is little control over how long the data is kept and what it can be used for. The problem of secondary use is implicated because there are few limitations on how data might be used in the future. There is little public accountability or judicial oversight of data-mining programs. The Fourth Amendment, for example, primarily regulates the collection of information and says little about what the government can do with data after it is already in the government's possession.[61] Data mining thus creates many information-processing problems that lead to structural harms, such as vulnerability harms and power imbalances. Data mining allows executive officials and agencies relatively insulated from public accountability to exercise significant power over citizens.

Analyzing data mining with the aid of the taxonomy reveals the manifold problems that data mining creates. The taxonomy helps prevent us from focusing on only a few of the problems to the exclusion of others. In short, the taxonomy provides us with a way to evaluate activities such as data mining with greater comprehensiveness and clarity.

Disclosure of Surveillance Camera Footage

As demonstrated in the previous discussion, many cases involve a combination of several different kinds of privacy problems. Analyzing the privacy issues in these cases involves understanding the distinctions between these different problems. In *Peck v. United Kingdom*, a case before the European Court of Human Rights (ECHR), a person attempted suicide by slitting his wrists with a knife on a public street. A closed-circuit television (CCTV) surveillance camera was recording him, and the person monitoring the camera notified the police. After recovering from his injuries, he was dismayed to see a photograph of himself carrying a knife, taken from the CCTV footage, appear in a newspaper in an article titled "Gotcha." The article "referred to the [person] as having been intercepted with a knife and a potentially dangerous situation being defused as a result of the CCTV system." A television station broadcast footage from the CCTV recording of the incident, but his face was not adequately obscured, and he could be identified by people who knew him. The BBC show *Crime Beat* also broadcast the footage. Although the BBC had an agreement with the government to obscure faces in the CCTV footage, it failed to adequately obscure his face, and it completely failed to mask his identity in the trailers for its show. The person sued the government, but the High Court in England dismissed his case. He subsequently sought redress with the ECHR.[62]

According to the English government, there was no violation of privacy because the plaintiff's "actions were already in the public domain," and revealing the footage "simply distributed a public event to a wider public." The ECHR disagreed. It noted that even if the surveillance of a person in public does not invade privacy, "the recording of the data and the systemic or permanent nature of the record" may create a privacy problem. The court observed that although he was in public, he "was not there for the purposes of participating in any public event and he was not a public figure." The extent to which he could be observed by a passerby was much less than the extent to which he could be observed from the footage made public. The court noted that the government could have asked for the person's consent to release the video to the media or could have obscured his face in the images itself to ensure that it was properly done. The court therefore awarded him damages for his distress from the violation.[63]

The court's opinion recognizes that not all privacy problems are the same, although the court did not directly state this. The person's actions may not have been private in the sense that they were secret or concealed. Instead, the privacy problems involved a combination of identification, secondary use, disclosure, accessibility, and perhaps even distortion. The problem of identification occurred because the broad dissemination of images of his actions allowed him to be identified by many people, whereas he might not have been readily identified by anybody at the scene where he attempted suicide. Secondary use is implicated because the CCTV camera footage was originally for use in preventing crime and promoting safety and was then provided to the media. Disclosure is obviously implicated because the footage displaying him in a desperate moment was broadcast to millions. Accessibility is involved since the video that would ordinarily be seen by just a handful of officials was disseminated publicly on television. Finally, distortion may be involved because some of the disclosures involved merely showing the person with the knife. People may have thought that he was attempting to attack others. Obviously, disclosing that he was attempting suicide would also be a privacy violation, but the difficulty in deciding how to characterize the events emerges only because of the improper release of the video.

Recognition of the plurality of privacy problems makes it easier to analyze the situation in this case. The European Court of Human Rights issued a nuanced opinion that thoughtfully examined the situation and understood many of the problems involved.

The Future of Privacy

Privacy has long been a conceptual jungle that has entangled law and policy and prevented them from effectively addressing privacy problems. This book has attempted to provide a way out of the thicket. With a framework for identifying and understanding privacy problems, courts and policymakers can better balance privacy considerations against countervailing interests. The theory of privacy I have developed is not meant to be the final word. It cannot be, because privacy is evolving. In the future, new technologies and ways of living will create new privacy problems and transform old ones. But we need a framework, a way of conceptualizing privacy that does not get bogged down and befuddled by its manifold complexities. This book is the beginning of what I hope will be a more comprehensive and clear understanding of privacy.

Notes

1. Privacy: A Concept in Disarray

1. Olmstead v. United States, 277 U.S. 438, 478 (1928) (Brandeis, J., dissenting).

2. Ruth Gavison, "Privacy and the Limits of Law," 89 *Yale Law Journal* 421, 455 (1980); James Rachels, "Why Privacy Is Important," in *Philosophical Dimensions of Privacy: An Anthology* 290, 292 (Ferdinand David Schoeman ed., 1984); Beate Rössler, *The Value of Privacy* 1 (2005); Arthur R. Miller, *The Assault on Privacy* 212 (1971).

3. Lake v. Wal-Mart Stores, Inc., 582 N.W.2d 231, 235 (Minn. 1998); Pub. Utilities Comm'n v. Pollak, 343 U.S. 451, 467 (1952) (Douglas, J., dissenting).

4. See, e.g., Gavison, "Privacy and the Limits of Law," 422 (lamenting the lack of a useful, distinct, and coherent concept of privacy); Alan F. Westin, *Privacy and Freedom* 7 (1967) ("Few values so fundamental to society as privacy have been left so undefined in social theory").

5. Miller, *Assault on Privacy*, 25.

6. Jonathan Franzen, *How to Be Alone* 42 (2003).

7. Julie C. Inness, *Privacy, Intimacy, and Isolation* 3 (1992).

8. Hyman Gross, "The Concept of Privacy," 43 *New York University Law Review* 34, 35 (1967).

9. Colin J. Bennett, *Regulating Privacy: Data Protection and Public Policy in Europe and the United States* 25 (1992).

10. Robert C. Post, "Three Concepts of Privacy," 89 *Georgetown Law Journal* 2087, 2087 (2001).

11. The "reasonable-expectation-of-privacy" test currently employed by the Court to determine the applicability of the Fourth Amendment to a particular situation was first articulated in Justice John Marshall Harlan's concurring opinion in Katz v. United States, 389 U.S. 347 (1967). A person must demonstrate an "actual

(subjective) expectation of privacy" and "the expectation [must] be one that society is prepared to recognize as 'reasonable.' " Id. at 360–61 (Harlan, J., concurring).

12. Griswold v. Connecticut, 381 U.S. 479 (1965); Eisenstadt v. Baird, 405 U.S. 438 (1972); Roe v. Wade, 410 U.S. 113 (1973); Whalen v. Roe, 429 U.S. 589 (1977); Lawrence v. Texas, 539 U.S. 558 (2003).

13. See Alaska Const. art. I, §22 ("The right of the people to privacy is recognized and shall not be infringed"); Ariz. Const. art. II, §8 ("No person shall be disturbed in his private affairs, or his home invaded, without authority of law"); Cal. Const. art. I, §1 ("All people are by their nature free and independent and have inalienable rights. Among these are enjoying and defending life and liberty, acquiring, possessing, and protecting property, and pursuing and obtaining safety, happiness, and privacy"); Fla. Const. art. I, §23 ("Every natural person has the right to be let alone and free from governmental intrusion into his private life except as otherwise provided herein"); see also Haw. Const. art. I, §6; Ill. Const. art. I, §6; La. Const. art. I, §5; Mont. Const. art. II, §10; S.C. Const. art. I, §10; Wash. Const. art. I, §7. For a further discussion of state constitutional protections of privacy, see Timothy O. Lenz, " 'Rights Talk' About Privacy in State Courts," 60 *Albany Law Review* 1613 (1997); Mark Silverstein, Note, "Privacy Rights in State Constitutions: Models for Illinois?" 1989 *University of Illinois Law Review* 215 (1989).

14. Brazilian Constitution art. 5; South African Constitution §14 (1996); Constitution of The Republic of Korea, art. 17, quoted in Electronic Privacy Information Center & Privacy International, *Privacy and Human Rights* 288, 904, 917 (2005).

15. Although Canada's Charter of Rights and Freedoms does not explicitly protect a right to privacy, the Supreme Court of Canada has interpreted it to imply such a right. *Privacy and Human Rights*, 323. The Constitutional Court in France declared in 1995 that the French constitution has an implied right of privacy. *Privacy and Human Rights*, 463–64. Germany's Basic Law protects the privacy of communications, and the Federal Constitutional Court in 1983 recognized the protection of a person's "right to informational self-determination" under Basic Law (*Grundgesetz*), art. 10 (1949). See Federal Constitutional Court, decision of Dec. 15, 1983, 1 BvR 209, quoted in *Privacy and Human Rights*, 480. Although the word "privacy" does not appear in Japan's constitution, the Supreme Court has recognized a right to privacy since 1963. *Privacy and Human Rights*, 620. Likewise, even though privacy is not mentioned in India's constitution, the Supreme Court of India has declared, "The right to privacy has since been widely accepted as implied in our Constitution." Distt. Registrar & Collector, Hyderabad & Anr v. Canara Bank Etc, [2004] INSC 668, available at http://www.commonlii.org/in/cases/INSC/2004/668.html.

16. Organization for Economic Cooperation and Development (OECD), Guidelines on the Protection of Privacy and Transborder Flows of Personal Data (1980).

17. Directive of the European Parliament and the Council of Europe on the Protection of Individuals with Regard to the Processing of Personal Data and on the Free Movement of Such Data (1995).

18. Asia-Pacific Economic Cooperation (APEC), Privacy Framework, Nov. 2004.

19. William Prosser, "Privacy," 48 *California Law Review* 383 (1960).

20. Privacy Act, Pub. L. No. 93-579, 5 U.S.C. §552a; Family Educational Rights and Privacy Act of 1974, Pub. L. No. 93-380, 20 U.S.C. §§1221 note, 1232; Right to Financial Privacy Act of 1978, Pub. L. No. 95-630, 12 U.S.C. §§3401–3422; Privacy Protection Act of 1980, Pub. L. No. 96-440, 42 U.S.C. §2000aa; Electronic Communications Privacy Act of 1986, Pub. L. No. 99-508 and Pub. L. No. 103-414, 18 U.S.C §§2510–2522, 2701–2709; Video Privacy Protection Act of 1988, Pub. L. No. 100-618, 18 U.S.C. §§2710–2711; Driver's Privacy Protection Act of 1994, Pub. L. No. 103-322, 18 U.S.C. §§2721–2725.

21. United Nations Universal Declaration of Human Rights, GA Res 217A(III), UN Doc A/Res/810 (1948).

22. European Convention of Human Rights art. 8 (1950).

23. Deborah Nelson, *Pursuing Privacy in Cold War America* xii–xiii (2002) ("Since the end of the 1950s, the cry 'the death of privacy' has rung out from a wide variety of sources: journalism, television, film, literature, law enforcement, philosophy, medical discourse, and more"). A barrage of books warned of the growing threat to privacy, including Morris Ernst and Alan Schwartz's *Privacy: The Right to Be Let Alone* (1962), Edward Long's *The Intruders* (1967), Jerry Martin Rosenberg's *The Death of Privacy* (1969), Arthur Miller's *The Assault on Privacy* (1971), John Curtis Raines's *Attack on Privacy* (1974), and Robert Ellis Smith's *Privacy: How to Protect What's Left of It* (1979). A number of books in Britain and Germany in the 1970s likewise examined the issue. Bennett, *Regulating Privacy*, 46–57 (citing and discussing the books).

24. Vance Packard, *The Naked Society* 12 (1964).

25. Myron Brenton, *The Privacy Invaders* 21, 225 (1964).

26. Westin, *Privacy and Freedom*, 3.

27. Bruno Bettelheim, "The Right to Privacy Is a Myth," *Saturday Evening Post*, July 27, 1968, at 8.

28. Thomas Nagel, "The Shredding of Public Privacy," *Times Literary Supplement*, Aug. 14, 1998, at 15.

29. See, e.g., Roger Rosenblatt, "Who Killed Privacy?" *New York Times Magazine*, Jan. 31, 1994; Robert O'Harrow, Jr., "Privacy Eroding, Bit by Byte," *Washington Post*, Oct. 15, 2004, at E1; Craig Mullins, "Data Privacy Policies," *DBAzine.com Online*, Mar. 4, 2006, http://www.dbazine.com/blogs/blog-cm/craigmullins/blogentry.2006-03-04.7587002706 ("Our privacy is evaporating"); Jonathan Turley, " 'Big Brother' Bush and Connecting the Data Dots," *Los Angeles Times*, June 24, 2006 ("Privacy is dying in America"); Stephen J. Kobrin, "With Technology Growing, Our Privacy Is Shrinking," *Philadelphia Inquirer*, Jan. 3, 2001 ("Privacy is threatened by the digital age"); Bob Sullivan, "Privacy Lost: Privacy Under Attack, but Does Anybody Care?" MSNBC, Oct. 17, 2006, http://www.msnbc.msn.com/id/15221095/ (noting that many say that privacy is "vanishing" and "slipping away"); Alan Stafford, "Privacy in Peril," *PC World*, Sept. 30, 2005; Joyce Slaton, "Homeland Insecurity: Is Your Privacy in Danger?" *SF Gate*, Dec. 12, 2002, available at http://www.sfgate.com/cgi-bin/article.cgi?file=/gate/archive/2002/12/12/csea.DTL; Jennifer Granick, "Computer Privacy in Distress," *Wired News*, Jan. 17, 2007, available at http://www.wired.com/news/columns/0,72510-0.html.

30. Simson Garfinkel, *Database Nation: The Death of Privacy in the 21st Century* (2001); Charles Sykes, *The End of Privacy* (1999); Reg Whitaker, *The End of Privacy*

(2000); Jeffrey Rosen, *The Unwanted Gaze: The Destruction of Privacy in America* (2000).

31. Nelson, *Pursuing Privacy*, xii.

32. Franzen, *How to Be Alone*, 40.

33. Eric Goldman, "The Privacy Hoax," *Forbes*, Oct. 14, 2002.

34. Calvin C. Gotlieb, "Privacy: A Concept Whose Time Has Come and Gone," in *Computers, Surveillance, and Privacy* 156, 156 (David Lyon & Elia Zuriek eds. 1996).

35. Richard A. Epstein, "The Legal Regulation of Genetic Discrimination: Old Responses to New Technology," 74 *Boston University Law Review* 1, 12 (1994).

36. Richard Posner, *The Economics of Justice* 271 (1981).

37. Fred H. Cate, *Privacy in the Information Age* 29 (1997).

38. Amitai Etzioni, "The Myth of Privacy Invasion," *Christian Science Monitor*, Sept. 10, 2001, at 9.

39. See Florida Star v. B.J.F., 491 U.S. 524, 527 (1989).

40. See Dietemann v. Time, Inc., 449 F.2d 245, 246 (9th Cir. 1971).

41. "Beyond X-ray Vision: Can Big Brother See Right Through Your Clothes?" *Discover*, July 2002, at 24; Guy Gugliotta, "Tech Companies See Market for Detection: Security Techniques Offer New Precision," *Washington Post*, Sept. 28, 2001, at A8.

42. See Kyllo v. United States, 533 U.S. 27, 29 (2001).

43. See Standards for Privacy of Individually Identifiable Health Information, 65 Fed. Reg. 82,461, 82,467 (Dec. 28, 2000) (codified at 45 C.F.R. pts. 160 & 164).

44. See *In re* GeoCities, 127 F.T.C. 94, 97–98 (1999).

45. Jorge Luis Borges, "Everything and Nothing," in *Labyrinths* 248, 249 (Donald A. Yates & James E. Irby eds., J.E.I. trans., 1964).

46. J. Thomas McCarthy, *The Rights of Publicity and Privacy* §5.59 (2d ed. 2005).

47. Lillian R. BeVier, "Information About Individuals in the Hands of Government: Some Reflections on Mechanisms for Privacy Protection," 4 *William and Mary Bill of Rights Journal* 455, 458 (1995) (footnote omitted).

48. Tom Gerety, "Redefining Privacy," 12 *Harvard Civil Rights–Civil Liberties Law Review* 233, 234 (1977); Kim Lane Scheppele, *Legal Secrets* 184–85 (1988).

49. Judith Jarvis Thomson, "The Right to Privacy," in *Philosophical Dimensions of Privacy: An Anthology* 272, 272 (Ferdinand David Schoeman ed., 1984).

50. Report of the Committee on Privacy (HMSO 1972) Cmnd 5012 (Sir Kenneth Younger, Chairman), at ¶¶658, 665.

51. See, e.g., Joel R. Reidenberg, "Privacy in the Information Economy: A Fortress or Frontier for Individual Rights?" 44 *Federal Communications Law Journal* 195, 208 (1992) ("The American legal system does not contain a comprehensive set of privacy rights or principles that collectively address the acquisition, storage, transmission, use and disclosure of personal information within the business community"); Paul M. Schwartz, "Privacy and Democracy in Cyberspace," 52 *Vanderbilt Law Review* 1609, 1611 (1999) ("At present, however, no successful standards, legal or otherwise, exist for limiting the collection and utilization of personal data in cyberspace").

52. National Commission on Terrorist Attacks upon the U.S., *The 9/11 Commission Report* 394 (2004).

53. Ludwig Wittgenstein, *Philosophical Investigations* §§66–67 (G.E.M. Anscombe trans., 1958).

54. See John Dewey, *Logic: The Theory of Inquiry* (1938), in 12 *The Later Works of John Dewey* 1, 106–10 (Jo Ann Boydston ed., 1988).

2. Theories of Privacy and Their Shortcomings

1. Some of the conceptions concentrate on means to achieve privacy; others focus on the ends or goals of privacy. Further, there is overlap between conceptions, and the conceptions discussed under different headings are by no means independent of each other. For example, control over personal information can be seen as a subset of limited access to the self, which in turn bears significant similarities to the right to be let alone. These headings are therefore not taxonomic; rather, they track how scholars have chosen to theorize about privacy. I use the headings to discuss the primary representatives of conceptual approaches in the discourse.

2. See, e.g., Julie C. Inness, *Privacy, Intimacy, and Isolation* 56 (1992) (noting that intimacy is the "common denominator" of privacy); Arthur Miller, *The Assault on Privacy* 25 (1971) (stating that control is the "basic attribute" of privacy); David M. O'Brien, *Privacy, Law, and Public Policy* 16 (1979) (conceptualizing privacy as "fundamentally denoting an existential condition of limited access"); Edward J. Bloustein, "Privacy as an Aspect of Human Dignity: An Answer to Dean Prosser," 39 *New York University Law Review* 962, 963 (1964) (proposing a "general theory of individual privacy which will reconcile the divergent strands of legal development"); Charles Fried, "Privacy," 77 *Yale Law Journal* 475, 475 (1968) (seeking to "isolate from restrictions and intrusions in general whatever is peculiar about invasions of privacy"); Ruth Gavison, "Privacy and the Limits of Law," 89 *Yale Law Journal* 421, 423 (1980) (developing a "distinct and coherent" conception of privacy); Tom Gerety, "Redefining Privacy," 12 *Harvard Civil Rights–Civil Liberties Law Review* 233, 263 (1977) ("Intimacy is the chief restricting concept in the definition of privacy"); Richard B. Parker, "A Definition of Privacy," 27 *Rutgers Law Review* 275, 277 (1974) (seeking to articulate "some characteristic common to all or some of [a list of invasions of 'different personal interests']").

3. Samuel D. Warren & Louis D. Brandeis, "The Right to Privacy," 4 *Harvard Law Review* 193 (1890).

4. See, e.g., Irwin P. Kramer, "The Birth of Privacy Law: A Century Since Warren and Brandeis," 39 *Catholic University Law Review* 703, 704 (1990); Ruth Gavison, "Too Early for a Requiem: Warren and Brandeis Were Right on Privacy vs. Free Speech," 43 *South Carolina Law Review* 437, 438 (1992) (Warren and Brandeis "single-handedly created a tort"); James H. Barron, "Warren and Brandeis, The Right to Privacy, 4 Harvard L. Rev. 193 (1890): Demystifying a Landmark Citation," 13 *Suffolk University Law Review* 875, 877 (1979) (there is "near unanimity among courts and commentators that the Warren-Brandeis conceptualization created the structural and jurisprudential foundation of the tort of invasion of privacy").

5. Harry Kalven, Jr., "Privacy in Tort Law—Were Warren and Brandeis Wrong?" 31 *Law and Contemporary Problems* 326, 327 (1966); Benjamin E. Bratman, "Brandeis and Warren's 'The Right to Privacy' and the Birth of the Right to Privacy," 69 *Tennessee Law Review* 623, 624 (2002).

6. Elbridge L. Adams, "The Right of Privacy, and Its Relation to the Law of Libel," 39 *American Law Review* 37, 37 (1905).

7. See, e.g., Richard C. Turkington, "Legacy of the Warren and Brandeis Article: The Emerging Unencumbered Constitutional Right to Informational Privacy," 10 *Northern Illinois University Law Review* 479, 481–82 (1990) (observing that the article "has acquired legendary status in the realm of legal scholarship" and "has had as much impact on the development of law as any single publication in legal periodicals").

8. Warren & Brandeis, "Right to Privacy," 195.

9. Robert E. Mensel, "'Kodakers Lying in Wait': Amateur Photography and the Right to Privacy in New York, 1885–1915," 43 *American Quarterly* 24, 28 (1991).

10. Warren & Brandeis, "Right to Privacy," 196.

11. Robert Ellis Smith, *Ben Franklin's Web Site: Privacy and Curiosity from Plymouth Rock to the Internet* 108–09 (2000); Gini Graham Scott, *Mind Your Own Business: The Battle for Personal Privacy* 37–38 (1995).

12. Warren & Brandeis, "Right to Privacy," 197, 193. Cooley's treatise was originally published in 1880, and a second edition was published in 1888. See Thomas M. Cooley, *Law of Torts* (2d ed. 1888).

13. Warren & Brandeis, "Right to Privacy," 205, 200, 197, 198, 207.

14. Daniel J. Solove, Marc Rotenberg, & Paul M. Schwartz, *Information Privacy Law* 31 (2d ed. 2006).

15. David W. Leebron, "The Right to Privacy's Place in the Intellectual History of Tort Law," 41 *Case Western Reserve Law Review* 769, 807–09 (1991).

16. Union Pac. Ry. Co. v. Botsford, 141 U.S. 250, 251 (1891).

17. Olmstead v. United States, 277 U.S. 438, 466 (1928).

18. Id. at 478 (Brandeis, J., dissenting).

19. Katz v. United States, 389 U.S. 347 (1967).

20. See, e.g., Eisenstadt v. Baird, 405 U.S. 438, 454 n.10 (1972); Stanley v. Georgia, 394 U.S. 557, 564 (1969); *Katz*, 389 U.S. at 350.

21. Time, Inc. v. Hill, 385 U.S. 374, 413 (1967) (Fortas, J., dissenting).

22. Doe v. Bolton, 410 U.S. 179, 213 (1973) (Douglas, J., concurring) (citations omitted) (quoting Kent v. Dulles, 357 U.S. 116, 126 (1958)).

23. Gavison, "Privacy and the Limits of Law," 438.

24. See, e.g., O'Brien, *Privacy, Law, and Public Policy*, 5; Gerety, "Redefining Privacy," 263.

25. Anita L. Allen, *Uneasy Access: Privacy for Women in a Free Society* 7 (1988).

26. Ferdinand Schoeman, "Privacy: Philosophical Dimensions of the Literature," in *Philosophical Dimensions of Privacy: An Anthology* 1, 14 (Ferdinand David Schoeman ed., 1984).

27. See Bloustein, "Privacy as an Aspect of Human Dignity," 970.

28. E. L. Godkin, "Libel and Its Legal Remedy," 12 *Journal of Social Science* 69, 80 (1880).

29. E. L. Godkin, "The Rights of the Citizen, IV—To His Own Reputation," *Scribner's Magazine*, July–Dec. 1890, at 65. For a discussion of this article's influence on Warren and Brandeis, see Richard C. Turkington & Anita L. Allen, *Privacy Law: Cases and Materials* 40–41 (1999).

30. Sissela Bok, *Secrets: On the Ethics of Concealment and Revelation* 10–11 (1983).

31. Hyman Gross, "The Concept of Privacy," 43 *New York University Law Review* 34, 35–36 (1967) (emphasis removed).

32. Ernest Van Den Haag, "On Privacy," in *Nomos XIII: Privacy* 149, 149 (J. Roland Pennock & J.W. Chapman eds., 1971).

33. Allen, *Uneasy Access*, 10. For additional proponents of limited-access conceptions, see Edward Shils, "Privacy: Its Constitution and Vicissitudes," 31 *Law and Contemporary Problems* 281, 281 (1966) (privacy "is constituted by the absence of interaction or communication or perception within contexts in which such interaction, communication, or perception is practicable"); Adam Carlyle Breckenridge, *The Right to Privacy* 1 (1970) ("Privacy, in my view, is the rightful claim of the individual to determine the extent to which he wishes to share of himself with others").

34. O'Brien, *Privacy, Law, and Public Policy*, 15, 16.

35. Gavison, "Privacy and the Limits of Law," 423, 426, 433.

36. Id. at 433.

37. Gavison openly recognizes that her theory excludes these things. See id. at 436.

38. Id.

39. Richard A. Posner, *The Economics of Justice* 272–73 (1981).

40. Richard A. Posner, *Economic Analysis of Law* 46 (5th ed. 1998).

41. Posner, *Economics of Justice*, 234.

42. Id. at 271. Posner's conception of privacy is infused with his own normative assessment of privacy as a form of deception. According to Posner, the "economist sees a parallel to the efforts of sellers to conceal defects in their products." Posner, *Economic Analysis of Law*, 46.

43. Sidney M. Jourard, "Some Psychological Aspects of Privacy," 31 *Law and Contemporary Problems* 307, 307 (1966).

44. Griswold v. Connecticut, 381 U.S. 479 (1965); Roe v. Wade, 410 U.S. 113 (1973).

45. 429 U.S. 589, 599-600 (1977).

46. William J. Stuntz, "Privacy's Problem and the Law of Criminal Procedure," 93 *Michigan Law Review* 1016, 1022 (1995).

47. Katz v. United States, 389 U.S. 347, 351 (1967).

48. 486 U.S. 35, 40 (1988).

49. 488 U.S. 445, 450-51 (1989); see also California v. Ciraolo, 476 U.S. 207 (1986) (holding that the Fourth Amendment did not apply to surveillance of property from airplane flying at 1,000 feet); Dow Chem. Co. v. United States, 476 U.S. 227 (1986) (holding that the Fourth Amendment did not apply to aerial surveillance of property with high-tech camera that could enlarge objects so that objects half an inch in diameter could be seen).

50. Edward J. Bloustein, *Individual and Group Privacy* 123–86 (1978).

51. See, e.g., Arnold Simmel, "Privacy Is Not an Isolated Freedom," in *Nomos XIII: Privacy* 71, 81 (J. Roland Pennock & J.W. Chapman eds., 1971).

52. See Shils, "Privacy," 305.

53. Kenneth L. Karst, " 'The Files': Legal Controls over the Accuracy and Accessibility of Stored Personal Data," 31 *Law and Contemporary Problems* 342, 344 (1966).

54. Amitai Etzioni, *The Limits of Privacy* 196 (1999).

55. Judith Wagner DeCew, *In Pursuit of Privacy: Law, Ethics, and the Rise of Technology* 48 (1997).

56. Inness, *Privacy, Intimacy, and Isolation*, 6.

57. Stanley I. Benn, "Privacy, Freedom, and Respect for Persons," in *Nomos XIII: Privacy* 2 (J. Roland Pennock & J. W. Chapman eds., 1971).

58. Alan Westin, *Privacy and Freedom* 7 (1967).

59. See, e.g., Breckenridge, *Right to Privacy*, 1 (noting that privacy is "the individual's right to control dissemination of information about himself"); Executive Office of the President, Office of Science and Technology, *Privacy and Behavioral Research* 2 (Washington, D.C., G.P.O. 1967) ("The right to privacy is the right of the individual to decide for himself how much he will share with others his thoughts, his feelings, and the facts of his personal life"); Randall P. Benzanson, "The Right to Privacy Revisited: Privacy, News, and Social Change, 1890–1990," 80 *California Law Review* 1133, 1135 (1992) ("I will advance a concept of privacy based on the individual's control of information"); Oscar M. Ruebhausen & Orville G. Brim, Jr., "Privacy and Behavioral Research," 65 *Columbia Law Review* 1184, 1189 (1965) ("The essence of privacy is no more, and certainly no less, than the freedom of the individual to pick and choose for himself the time and circumstances under which, and most importantly, the extent to which, his attitudes, beliefs, behavior and opinions are to be shared with or withheld from others"); Ian Goldberg, Austin Hill, & Adam Shostack, "Trust, Ethics, and Privacy," 81 *Boston University Law Review* 407, 418 (2001) ("We build our own definition of privacy on what we consider the most elegant definition, 'informational self-determination,' which refers to a person's ability to control the flow of his own personal information"). Anne Wells Branscomb focuses almost exclusively on the importance of control over information for privacy. See Anne Wells Branscomb, *Who Owns Information? From Privacy to Public Access* (1994).

60. Miller, *Assault on Privacy*, 25.

61. Fried, "Privacy," 482–83.

62. President Clinton's Information Infrastructure Task Force (IITF), *Principles for Providing and Using Personal Information* 5 (1995).

63. United States Dep't of Justice v. Reporters Comm. for Freedom of the Press, 489 U.S. 749, 763 (1989).

64. Schoeman, "Privacy," 3.

65. Parker, "Definition of Privacy," 280.

66. Richard S. Murphy, "Property Rights in Personal Information: An Economic Defense of Privacy," 84 *Georgetown Law Journal* 2381, 2383 (1996).

67. Westin, *Privacy and Freedom*, 324.

68. According to the Restatement of Torts, "One who appropriates to his own use or benefit the name or likeness of another is subject to liability to the other for invasion of his privacy." Restatement (Second) of Torts §652C (1977).

69. John Locke, *Second Treatise of Government* §27, at 19 (1980) (1690).

70. See James Boyle, *Shamans, Software, and Spleens: Law and the Construction of the Information Society* 54 (1996).

71. 17 U.S.C. §102(a) (1994).

72. Shils, "Privacy," 290.

73. Henry James, *The Portrait of a Lady* 253 (Geoffrey Moore ed., Penguin Books 1986) (1881).

74. Jerry Kang, "Information Privacy in Cyberspace Transactions," 50 *Stanford Law Review* 1193, 1202, 1246 (1998).

75. Miller, *Assault on Privacy*, 213.

76. 8 F.3d 1222 (7th Cir. 1993) (Posner, J.).

77. Id. at 1228.

78. Id. at 1233.

79. Gerety, "Redefining Privacy," 262–63.

80. Inness, *Privacy, Intimacy, and Isolation*, 58.

81. Fried, "Privacy," 483, 477.

82. DeCew, *In Pursuit of Privacy*, 53.

83. Daniel A. Farber, "Book Review: Privacy, Intimacy, and Isolation by Julie C. Inness," 10 *Constitutional Commentary* 510, 514–15 (1993).

84. O'Brien, *Privacy, Law, and Public Policy*, 13.

85. Id. at 14.

86. Id.

87. DeCew, *In Pursuit of Privacy*, 2.

88. Allen, *Uneasy Access*, 8.

89. Paul M. Schwartz, "Privacy and Democracy in Cyberspace," 52 *Vanderbilt Law Review* 1609, 1661 (1999).

90. See id. at 1661–64; see also Julie E. Cohen, "Examined Lives: Informational Privacy and the Subject as Object," 52 *Stanford Law Review* 1373 (2000); Paul M. Schwartz, "Internet Privacy and the State," 32 *Connecticut Law Review* 815 (2000).

91. For example, Anita Allen contends that privacy is not merely a matter of individual choice but must in certain instances be "coerced" by the government. Anita Allen-Castellitto, "Coercing Privacy," 40 *William and Mary Law Review* 723 (1999).

92. Paul Freund, Address at the American Law Institute, 52nd Annual Meeting 42–43 (1975); see also J. Braxton Craven, Jr., "Personhood: The Right to Be Let Alone," 1976 *Duke Law Journal* 699, 702 n.15 (1976) (citing Freund's formulation of personhood).

93. Bloustein, "Privacy as an Aspect of Human Dignity," 971. Bloustein's article was in response to William Prosser's 1960 article "Privacy," which examined over 300 privacy cases in the seventy years since Warren and Brandeis's 1890 article. Prosser concluded that "[t]he law of privacy comprises four distinct kinds of invasion of four different interests of the plaintiff, which are tied together by the common name, but otherwise have almost nothing in common." William Prosser, "Privacy," 48 *California Law Review* 383, 389 (1960).

94. Bloustein, "Privacy as an Aspect of Human Dignity," 973, 974.

95. Jeffrey H. Reiman, "Privacy, Intimacy, and Personhood," in *Philosophical Dimensions of Privacy*, 300, 314.

96. Benn, "Privacy, Freedom, and Respect for Persons," 26, 7.

97. Griswold v. Connecticut, 381 U.S. 479 (1965) (holding unconstitutional a statute criminalizing contraceptives for married couples because it invaded the "zone of privacy" created by the "penumbras" of the First, Third, Fourth, Fifth, and Ninth Amendments); Eisenstadt v. Baird, 405 U.S. 438 (1972) (extending *Griswold* to the use of contraceptives by unmarried individuals); Roe v. Wade 410 U.S. 113 (1973) (finding that the constitutional right to privacy encompasses the decision to procure an abortion).

98. Whalen v. Roe, 429 U.S. 589, 599–600 (1977).

99. See, e.g., Roe v. Wade, 410 U.S. 113, 152–53 (1973).

100. 505 U.S. 833, 851 (1992).

101. Michael Sandel, *Democracy's Discontent* 93 (1996).

102. Louis Henkin, "Privacy and Autonomy," 74 *Columbia Law Review* 1410, 1424 (1974).

103. DeCew, *In Pursuit of Privacy*, 44.

104. See, e.g., Joel Feinberg, "Autonomy, Sovereignty, and Privacy: Moral Ideas in the Constitution?" 58 *Notre Dame Law Review* 445 (1983); Henkin, "Privacy and Autonomy," 1424–25.

105. Jed Rubenfeld, "The Right of Privacy," 102 *Harvard Law Review* 737, 750 (1989).

106. Gavison, "Privacy and the Limits of Law," 438.

107. Rubenfeld, "Right of Privacy," 773, 754, 758, 770.

108. Id. at 782.

109. Id. at 784, 787, 794.

110. See Daniel J. Solove, *The Digital Person: Technology and Privacy in the Information Age* 44–47 (2004).

111. Rubenfeld, "Right of Privacy," 801–02.

112. Id. at 782.

113. Farber, "Book Review," 516.

114. Robert S. Gerstein, "Intimacy and Privacy," in *Philosophical Dimensions of Privacy*, 265, 265.

115. Inness, *Privacy, Intimacy, and Isolation*, 56, 76, 77, 78, 91.

116. Charles Fried, *An Anatomy of Values: Problems of Personal and Social Choice* 142 (1970).

117. James Rachels, "Why Privacy Is Important," in *Philosophical Dimensions of Privacy*, 290, 292.

118. Reiman, "Privacy, Intimacy, and Personhood," 304–06.

119. Gerety, "Redefining Privacy," 263, 268, 274.

120. DeCew, *In Pursuit of Privacy*, 56.

121. Farber, "Book Review," 515.

122. W. L. Weinstein, "The Private and the Free: A Conceptual Inquiry," in *Nomos XIII: Privacy*, 27, 33.

123. Priscilla M. Regan, *Legislating Privacy: Technology, Social Values, and Public Policy* 213 (1995).

124. Judith Jarvis Thomson, "The Right to Privacy," in *Philosophical Dimensions of Privacy*, 272, 280, 284.

125. H. J. McCloskey, "Privacy and the Right to Privacy," 55 *Philosophy* 37 (1980).

126. Kalven, "Privacy in Tort Law," 327.

127. Inness, *Privacy, Intimacy, and Isolation*, 36. For a summary of responses to Thomson and other reductionists, see Amy L. Peikoff, "The Right to Privacy: Contemporary Reductionists and Their Critics," 13 *Virginia Journal of Social Policy and the Law* 474 (2006).

128. Thomas Scanlon, "Thomson on Privacy," 4 *Philosophy and Public Affairs* 315, 322 (1975).

3. Reconstructing Privacy

1. Ludwig Wittgenstein, *Philosophical Investigations* §§91, 43 (G. E. M. Anscombe trans., 1958). After publishing his highly influential *Tractatus Logico-philosophicus* in

1921, Wittgenstein disappeared from the philosophical scene for over a decade. See Ludwig Wittgenstein, *Tractatus Logico-philosophicus* (D. F. Pears & B. F. McGuiness trans., 1961). When he returned, he had substantially altered his views, recognizing that he had made "grave mistakes" in *Tractatus*. See Wittgenstein, *Philosophical Investigations*, vi. Because Wittgenstein's thinking changed dramatically during his career, *Tractatus* is often referred to as "early" Wittgenstein, and *Philosophical Investigations*, along with other works such as *On Certainty*, is referred to as "late" Wittgenstein.

2. Wittgenstein, *Philosophical Investigations*, §§65, 66, 67. Wittgenstein uses the term "language-games" to describe the activities involving language. Id. at §7. Wittgenstein uses "games" as a metaphor to describe language as an active endeavor such as playing chess, tennis, or a card game. Wittgenstein thus sees language not as an abstract system of signs, but as a functioning aspect of our daily lives, as something we do, as a "form of life." Id. at §19. There are a "multiplicity" of language games, such as giving orders, describing appearances, reporting an event, speculating, singing, and telling a joke. See id. at §23. For more background on Wittgenstein's notion of family resemblances, see P. M. S. Hacker, *Insight and Illusion: Themes in the Philosophy of Wittgenstein* 131–34 (1986); Hanna Feinchel Pitkin, *Wittgenstein and Justice: On the Significance of Ludwig Wittgenstein for Social and Political Thought* 63–65 (1972).

3. Legal scholar Steven Winter develops a related view of conceptualization. He argues, "On the standard view, categories are descriptive, definitional, and rigidly bounded. The empirical evidence, in contrast, presents a picture of categorization as an imaginative and dynamic process that is flexible in application and elastic in scope." Steven L. Winter, *A Clearing in the Forest: Law, Life, and Mind* 69 (2001). Winter contends that categories are "radial"; they consist of a "central model" or paradigm example and related extensions radiating outward. Id. at 71. These extensions, "though related to the central case in some fashion, nevertheless cannot be generated by rule." Id.

4. Wittgenstein, *Philosophical Investigations*, §§68–69, 499. When describing the boundaries of categories, Wittgenstein uses the terms "blurred edges" and "indistinct picture." Id. at §71; see also Winter, *Clearing in the Forest*, 100–01 (contending that categories are not static entities but are tools created for particular purposes).

5. Judith Genova, *Wittgenstein: A Way of Seeing* 44 (1995).

6. Stanley Cavell, "Excursus on Wittgenstein's Vision of Language," in *The New Wittgenstein* 35 (Alice Crary & Rupert Read eds., 2000).

7. Genova, *Wittgenstein*, 35.

8. Richard Bruyer, "Privacy: A Review and Critique of the Literature," 43 *Alberta Law Review* 553, 576 (2006).

9. Raymond Wacks, *Law, Morality, and the Private Domain* 222 (2000).

10. Cass R. Sunstein, *Legal Reasoning and Political Conflict* 67 (1996).

11. For more background about the origins of pragmatism, see Richard Shusterman, *Practicing Philosophy: Pragmatism and the Philosophical Life* (1997); John J. Stuhr, *Genealogical Pragmatism: Philosophy, Experience, and Community* (1997); Michael Sullivan & Daniel J. Solove, "Can Pragmatism Be Radical? Richard Posner and Legal Pragmatism," 113 *Yale Law Journal* 687 (2003); Daniel J. Solove, "The Darkest Domain: Deference, Judicial Review, and the Bill of Rights," 84 *Iowa Law Review* 941, 970–71 (1999).

12. See Richard A. Posner, *Overcoming Law* (1995); Richard Rorty, *Consequences of Pragmatism: Essays, 1977–1980* (1982); Cornell West, *Keeping Faith: Philosophy and Race in America* (1993).

13. William James, *Pragmatism* 25 (Prometheus Books 1991) (1907). Pragmatists reject the view of philosophy "as a purely theoretical quest for eternal truths or knowledge of an ultimate and unchanging reality." *Pragmatism and Classical American Philosophy: Essential Readings and Interpretive Essays* 3 (John J. Stuhr ed., 2000); see also John Dewey, *Logic: The Theory of Inquiry* (1938), in 12 *The Later Works of John Dewey* 1, 72 (Jo Ann Boydston ed., 1988).

14. Although there are many interesting affinities in the thought of Wittgenstein and the pragmatists, there are many differences as well, and a complete account of the similarities and differences is beyond the scope of this book. For some interesting examinations of the relationship between pragmatic and Wittgensteinian thought, see Hilary Putnam, *Pragmatism* 27–56 (1995); Rorty, *Consequences of Pragmatism*, 19–36; Shusterman, *Practicing Philosophy*, 17–64.

15. Dewey, *Logic*, 72.

16. John Dewey, *Experience and Nature* (1925), in 1 *The Later Works of John Dewey* 1, 67 (Jo Ann Boydston ed., 1988).

17. Robert C. Post, "The Social Foundations of Privacy: Community and Self in the Common Law Tort," 77 *California Law Review* 957, 980, 981 (1989).

18. Serge Gutwirth, *Privacy and the Information Age* 34 (Raf Casert trans., 2002).

19. Gary T. Marx, "Murky Conceptual Waters: The Public and the Private," 3 *Ethics and Information Technology* 157 (2001).

20. Helen Nissenbaum, "Privacy as Contextual Integrity," 79 *Washington Law Review* 119, 137–38, 154–55 (2004).

21. Anita L. Allen, *Why Privacy Isn't Everything: Feminist Reflections on Personal Accountability* 2, 29–30 (2003).

22. See Dewey, *Logic*, 76, 111–12.

23. John Dewey, "In Reply to Some Criticisms" (1930), in 5 *The Later Works of John Dewey* 210, 216 (Jo Ann Boydston ed., 1984).

24. James, *Pragmatism*, 33.

25. See Dewey, *Logic*, 76.

26. See John Dewey, "What Pragmatism Means by Practical" (1908), in 4 *The Middle Works of John Dewey* 98, 100 (Jo Ann Boydston ed., 1977).

27. John Dewey, "The Quest for Certainty" (1929) *in* 4 *The Later Works of John Dewey* 16, 21 (Jo Ann Boydston ed., 1988).

28. Georges Duby, "Foreword" to *A History of Private Life*, vol. 1, *From Pagan Rome to Byzantium* viii (Paul Veyne ed. & Arthur Goldhammer trans., 1987).

29. United Nations Universal Declaration of Human Rights, GA Res 217A(III), UN Doc A/Res/810 (1948) ("No one shall be subjected to arbitrary interference with his privacy, family, home or correspondence, nor to attacks upon his honor and reputation").

30. Jürgen Habermas, *The Structural Transformation of the Public Sphere* 47–48 (1991).

31. Georges Duby, "Private Power, Public Power," in *A History of Private Life*, vol. 2, *Revelations of the Medieval World* 7 (Georges Duby ed. & Arthur Goldhammer trans., 1988).

32. David H. Flaherty, *Privacy in Colonial New England* 56 (1972).

33. Michelle Perrot, "The Family Triumphant," in *A History of Private Life*, vol. 4, *From the Fires of Revolution to the Great War* 121, 123 (Michelle Perrot ed. & Arthur Goldhammer trans., 1990).

34. Tamara K. Hareven, "The Home and the Family in Historical Perspective," 58 *Social Research* 253, 257 (1991).

35. Roger Chartier, "Community, State, and Family: Trajectories and Tensions: Introduction," in *A History of Private Life*, vol. 3 *Passions of the Renaissance* 400 (Roger Chartier ed. & Arthur Goldhammer trans., 1989); Beatrice Gottlieb, *The Family in the Western World from the Black Death to the Industrial Age* 52–53 (1993); Catherine Hall, "The Sweet Delights of Home," in *A History of Private Life*, vol. 4, 50; Michelle Perrot, "Roles and Characters," in *A History of Private Life*, vol. 4, 181–86.

36. Lawrence Stone, "The Public and the Private in Stately Homes of England, 1500–1990," 58 *Social Research* 227, 233 (1991); Perrot, "Roles and Characters," 181.

37. Hareven, "Home and the Family," 257.

38. Anita L. Allen, *Uneasy Access: Privacy for Women in a Free Society* 69 (1988); see generally Henrik Hartog, *Man and Wife in America: A History* (2000).

39. Reva B. Siegel, "'The Rule of Love': Wife Beating as Prerogative and Privacy," 105 *Yale Law Journal* 2117, 2122, 2118, 2152 (1996).

40. State v. Hussey, 44 N.C. 123, 126–27 (1852).

41. Siegel, "Rule of Love," 2158.

42. See, e.g., Catharine MacKinnon, *Toward a Feminist Theory of the State* 191 (1989). For an overview of the feminist critique of privacy, see Patricia Boling, *Privacy and the Politics of Intimate Life* (1996); Judith Wagner DeCew, *In Pursuit of Privacy: Law, Ethics, and the Rise of Technology* 81–94 (1997). For a critique of MacKinnon, see Allen, *Uneasy Access;* Ruth Gavison, "Feminism and the Public/Private Distinction," 45 *Stanford Law Review* 21 (1992).

43. Tom Gerety claims that any concept of privacy "must take the body as its first and most basic reference for control over personal identity." Tom Gerety, "Redefining Privacy," 12 *Harvard Civil Rights–Civil Liberties Law Review* 233, 266 & n.119 (1977).

44. Union Pac. Ry. Co. v. Botsford, 141 U.S. 250, 251 (1891).

45. Lake v. Wal-Mart Stores, Inc., 582 N.W.2d 231, 235 (Minn. 1998).

46. Radhika Rao, "Property, Privacy, and the Human Body," 80 *Boston University Law Review* 359 (2000). Rao critiques the tendency to reduce one's control over one's body to a simple property right. "[P]rivacy theory entitled the body to protection as the physical embodiment of a person, the subject of a privacy interest, whereas property theory reduces the body to a mere object of ownership." Id. at 445.

47. Peter Brown, "Late Antiquity," in *A History of Private Life*, vol. 1, 245–46.

48. Richard Sennett, *Flesh and Stone: The Body and the City in Western Civilization* 33 (1994). "Athenian democracy placed great emphasis on its citizens exposing their thoughts to others, just as men exposed their bodies. These mutual acts of disclosure were meant to draw the knot between citizens ever tighter." Id. Public nudity was limited to men. Women did not display their naked bodies in public. See id. at 34.

49. Simon Goldhill, *Love, Sex, and Tragedy: How the Ancient World Shapes Our Lives* 15, 19 (2004).

50. Witold Rybczynski, *Home: A Short History of an Idea* 28, 30 (1986). Of course, practices in these matters differed due to the influence of the customs of each specific society, as well as religious beliefs and the social status of individuals.

51. Goldhill, *Love, Sex, and Tragedy*, 112, 113; see also Peter Brown, *The Body and Society: Men, Women, and Sexual Renunciation in Early Christianity* 438 (1988) ("No longer were the body's taut musculature and its refined poise, signs of the athlete and the potential warrior, put on display, as marks of upper-class status").

52. Stone, "Public and the Private," 229 (1991).

53. Philippe Ariès, "Introduction" to *A History of Private Life*, vol. 3, 4; Roger Chartier, "Forms of Privatization: Introduction," in *A History of Private Life*, vol. 3, 163–64.

54. See Ariès, "Introduction," 5.

55. Sennett, *Flesh and Stone*, 343.

56. Stone, "Public and the Private," 228.

57. Id. at 244.

58. Barrington Moore, Jr., *Privacy: Studies in Social and Cultural History* 146 (1984). Historian Lewis Mumford observes, "In the castles of the thirteenth century, one notes the existence of a private bedroom for the noble owners; and one also finds, not far from it, perched over the moat, a private toilet: the first hint of the nineteenth-century luxury of a private toilet for every family." Lewis Mumford, *The City in History* 285 (1961).

59. John Stuart Mill, *On Liberty* 11 (David Spitz ed., 1975) ("Over himself, over his own body and mind, the individual is sovereign").

60. Jacques Gélis, "Forms of Privatization: The Child: From Anonymity to Individuality," in *A History of Private Life*, vol. 3, 310, 316.

61. Restatement (Second) of Torts §652D cmt. b.

62. Peck v. United Kingdom, [2003] ECHR 44 (2003), at ¶57.

63. B. Moore, *Privacy*, 256.

64. Mumford, *City in History*, 286.

65. Laura Gowing, *Domestic Dangers: Women, Words, and Sex in Early Modern London* 70 (1996); Anthony Giddens, *Modernity and Self-Identity: Self and Society in the Late Modern Age* 163 (1991).

66. Richard F. Hixson, *Privacy in a Public Society: Human Rights in Conflict* 11 (1987); Flaherty, *Privacy in Colonial New England*, 79. "The small size of colonial dwellings allowed children quite early in their lives to hear and see sexual activity among adults. Although curtains might isolate the parental bed, all family members commonly slept in the same room, especially during winters, where a single fireplace provided the heat." John D'Emilio & Estelle B. Freedman, *Intimate Matters: A History of Sexuality in America* 17 (2d ed. 1997).

67. Richard Godbeer, *Sexual Revolution in Early America* 93 (2002).

68. Thomas Nagel, *Concealment and Exposure and Other Essays* 16 (2002).

69. B. Moore, *Privacy*, 66.

70. Gowing, *Domestic Dangers*, 70–74, 192; Lawrence Stone, *The Family, Sex, and Marriage in England, 1500–1800*, 324 (Penguin Books ed. 1990).

71. D'Emilio & Freedman, *Intimate Matters*, 17; Flaherty, *Privacy in Colonial New England*, 92.

72. Flaherty, *Privacy in Colonial New England*, 93–94; Godbeer, *Sexual Revolution*, 867–88; D'Emilio & Freedman, *Intimate Matters*, 11 ("In Puritan theology, the entire community had responsibility for upholding morality").

73. Godbeer, *Sexual Revolution*, 100. "In New England, public confession and repentance both restored the individual to the congregation and at the same time confirmed the propriety of sexual rules." D'Emilio & Freedman, *Intimate Matters*, 27.

74. Godbeer, *Sexual Revolution*, 100.

75. Id. at 236, 300, 301.

76. "Sexual access to other persons is subject to some limitations in every known human society. There may possibly be a desire, which cannot always be gratified, to keep the human body inviolate, to prohibit or prevent intrusion in times of weakness or great emotional excitement, such as excretion or sexual intercourse." B. Moore, *Privacy*, 13.

77. Lawrence M. Friedman, *Crime and Punishment in American History* 34 (1993); D'Emilio & Freedman, *Intimate Matters*, 11.

78. Godbeer, *Sexual Revolution*, 102.

79. D'Emilio & Freedman, *Intimate Matters*, 49–50; Godbeer, *Sexual Revolution*, 228.

80. D'Emilio & Freedman, *Intimate Matters*, 83.

81. Id. at 138.

82. Id. at 138, 160, 133–35, 213.

83. Lawrence M. Friedman, "Name Robbers: Privacy, Blackmail, and Assorted Matters in Legal History," 30 *Hofstra Law Review* 1093, 1100 (2002).

84. D'Emilio & Freedman, *Intimate Matters*, 160.

85. Rochelle Gurstein, *The Repeal of Reticence* 91–145, 99 (1996).

86. Angus McLaren, *Sexual Blackmail: A Modern History* 274 (2002) ("At the beginning of the twentieth century the knowledge that a woman had had an abortion or an out-of-wedlock child or that a man was a homosexual or had had an adulterous affair could have disastrous consequences. By the 1990s a distinct shift had obviously occurred. The majority of the population had come to accept the notion that adults' private, consensual sexual acts should be left alone").

87. D'Emilio & Freedman, *Intimate Matters*, 242–43.

88. 381 U.S. 479, 485–86 (1965).

89. Lawrence M. Friedman, *Private Lives: Family, Individuals, and the Law* 173 (2004).

90. Lawrence v. Texas, 539 U.S. 558, 578 (2003).

91. Friedman, *Private Lives*, 94–95.

92. Goldhill, *Love, Sex, and Tragedy*, 99.

93. Argentine Constitution art. 18–19 (1994); Constitution of Finland §10; Constitution of Greece art. 9 (1975); Constitution of the Republic of Korea art. 16; quoted in Electronic Privacy Information Center & Privacy International, *Privacy and Human Rights* 212, 449, 507, 917–18 (2005).

94. Hixson, *Privacy in a Public Society*, 13. In the eighteenth century, William Blackstone declared that the law has "so particular and tender a regard to the immunity of a man's house that it stiles it his castle, and will never suffer it to be violated with impunity." 4 William Blackstone, *Commentaries on the Laws of England* 223 (1769).

95. Flaherty, *Privacy in Colonial New England*, 85.

96. B. Moore, *Privacy*, 115–16.

97. Semayne's Case, 77 Eng. Rep. 194, 195 (K.B. 1604). For more on the origins of the maxim, see Note, "The Right to Privacy in Nineteenth Century America," 94 *Harvard Law Review* 1892, 1894 n.18 (1981). The note, although anonymous, was written by legal historian David J. Seipp.

98. Quoted in Charles J. Sykes, *The End of Privacy* 83 (1999).

99. 116 U.S. 616, 630 (1886).

100. Payton v. New York, 445 U.S. 573, 589 (1980).

101. U.S. Const. amends. III and IV.

102. Silverman v. United States, 365 U.S. 505, 511 (1961).

103. Bell v. Maryland, 378 U.S. 226, 253 (1964) (Douglas, J., concurring).

104. Michelle Adams, "Knowing Your Place: Theorizing Sexual Harassment at Home," 40 *Arizona Law Review* 17, 23–24 (1998).

105. Hareven, "Home and the Family," 254–256.

106. William H. Gass, "Making Ourselves Comfortable," *New York Times*, Aug. 3, 1986, §7, at 1.

107. Rybczynski, *Home*, 25.

108. Flaherty, *Privacy in Colonial New England*, 45. In eighteenth-century New England, for example, families were twice as large on average as they are today, and a significant number of homes housed more than one family. See id. at 47.

109. Arlette Farge, "Community, State, and Family: Trajectories and Tensions: The Honor and Secrecy of Families," in *A History of Private Life*, vol. 3, 575–76.

110. See Flaherty, *Privacy in Colonial New England*, 43–44, 91.

111. See, e.g., Rybczynski, *Home*, 28.

112. Mumford, *City in History*, 286.

113. Flaherty, *Privacy in Colonial New England*, 76. Beds were crowded because of the scarcity of beds and the need for warmth. See id. at 78. At inns, strangers sometimes shared the same bed. See Gottlieb, *Family in the Western World*, 41.

114. Rybczynski, *Home*, 18; see also Flaherty, *Privacy in Colonial New England*, 34 (describing crowded one-room homes of sixteenth- and seventeenth-century England). Even in the sixteenth century, most homes lacked separate rooms. Rybczynski, *Home*, 18. When rooms were assigned purposes, the house became divided into distinct areas for women and men. See Hall, "Sweet Delights," 91. Houses in America followed the same pattern of development. Flaherty, *Privacy in Colonial New England*, 33–44.

115. Mumford, *City in History* 285.

116. Stone, "Public and the Private," 237.

117. Flaherty, *Privacy in Colonial New England*, 40; see also Rybczynski, *Home*, 41 ("There were no corridors in these houses—each room was connected directly to its neighbor—and architects prided themselves on aligning all the doors *enfilade*, so that there was an unobstructed view from one end of the house to the other").

118. Only the aristocracy could afford to purchase the space necessary to maintain privacy. "The wealthy naturally increased the amount of private space available to them, but for the rest of the population, the vast majority, the idea of privacy did not extend beyond the bedroom, and perhaps not beyond the bed curtains." Orest Ranum, "Forms of Privatization: The Refuges of Intimacy," in *A*

History of Private Life, vol. 3, 225. The rise of the bourgeoisie made solitude more widely available. See Joseph Bensman & Robert Lilienfeld, *Between Public and Private: The Lost Boundaries of the Self* 31 (1979).

119. Stone, "Public and the Private," 227, 232–34.

120. Mumford, *City in History*, 286, 243; Georges Duby, "Preface" to *A History of Private Life*, vol. 2, xii.

121. Gini Graham Scott, *Mind Your Own Business: The Battle for Personal Privacy* 32 (1995); Flaherty, *Privacy in Colonial New England*, 40.

122. Roger Chartier, "Figures of Modernity: The Practical Impact of Writing," in *A History of Private Life*, vol. 3, 134.

123. See Philippe Braunstein, "Toward Intimacy: The Fourteenth and Fifteenth Centuries," in *A History of Private Life*, vol. 2, 538.

124. See Ranum, "Forms of Privatization," 226–27.

125. Edward Shils, "Privacy: Its Constitution and Vicissitudes," 31 *Law and Contemporary Problems* 281, 289 (1966).

126. Ariès, "Introduction," 1–2.

127. Hareven, "Home and the Family," 259.

128. Mexican Constitution, art. 16 (amended 1996), quoted in Jorge A. Vagas, "Privacy Rights Under Mexican Law: Emergence and Legal Configuration of a Panoply of New Rights," 27 *Houston Journal of International Law* 73, 89 (2004); Constitution of the Republic of Chile art. 19 (1980); Germany, Basic Law *(Grundgesetz)* art. 10 (1949); Constitution of Belgium art. 29 (1831, latest revision 1993); Czech Republic, Charter of Fundamental Rights and Freedoms art. 7 (1993); quoted in *Privacy and Human Rights*, 352, 480, 270, 399.

129. Robert Ellis Smith, *Ben Franklin's Web Site: Privacy and Curiosity from Plymouth Rock to the Internet* 23–25 (2000).

130. Flaherty, *Privacy in Colonial New England*, 116–17.

131. Id. at 119, 122–23; Smith, *Ben Franklin's Web Site*, 50–51.

132. David J. Seipp, *The Right to Privacy in American History* 11 (1978).

133. Smith, *Ben Franklin's Web Site*, 50.

134. Cynthia A. Kierner, *Scandal at Bizarre: Rumor and Reputation in Jefferson's America* 64 (2004).

135. Flaherty, *Privacy in Colonial New England*, 120, 121.

136. Smith, *Ben Franklin's Web Site*, 50–51.

137. *Ex parte* Jackson, 96 U.S. 727, 733 (1877).

138. See Seipp, Note, "Right to Privacy," 1899.

139. Denis v. Leclerc, 1 Martin (O.S.) 297, 313 (La. 1811). See also Seipp, Note, "Right to Privacy," 1899 (collecting examples).

140. Seipp, Note, "Right to Privacy," 1900.

141. Joseph Story, 2 *Commentaries on Equity Jurisprudence: As Administered in England and America* 261, 262, 264 (3d ed., 1843). The desire for privacy of letters was not unique to America. In 1790 in France, "the National Assembly in Paris declared the secret of letters to be inviolable, and the French penal code incorporated this sweeping declaration." Many other countries enacted laws to safeguard the privacy of letters. Peter Gay, *Schnitzler's Century: The Making of Middle-Class Culture 1815–1914*, 258 (2002).

142. Seipp, *Right to Privacy*, 32 (quoting Western Union Rule 128).

143. Seipp, Note, "Right to Privacy," 1901.

144. Seipp, *Right to Privacy*, 31–35.

145. Id. at 31–42.

146. Smith, *Ben Franklin's Web Site*, 157.

147. Claude S. Fischer, *America Calling: A Social History of the Telephone to 1940*, 48, 71, 241 (1992). Some party lines had as many as ten to thirty parties. "As late as 1930, 63 percent of Bell's residential telephones were still on party lines. That proportion had decreased modestly over the previous four years, but was actually higher than it had been before World War I." Id. at 83.

148. Samuel Dash, Richard F. Schwartz, & Robert E. Knowlton, *The Eavesdroppers* 8, 25–26 (1959).

149. Orin S. Kerr, "The Fourth Amendment and New Technologies: Constitutional Myths and the Case for Caution," 102 *Michigan Law Review* 801, 841 (2004).

150. Olmstead v. United States, 277 U.S. 438, 466 (1928).

151. Samuel Dash, *The Intruders* 74 (2004).

152. Olmstead v. United States, 277 U.S. 438, 470 (1928) (Holmes, J., dissenting).

153. Dash, *Intruders*, 82; see Federal Communications Act of 1934, Pub. L. No. 90-351, §2520, 48 Stat. 1103 (codified as amended at 47 U.S.C. §605).

154. 389 U.S. 347, 353 (1967).

155. Pub. L. No. 90-351, ch. 119, 82 Stat. 212 (codified as amended at 18 U.S.C. §§2510–2522).

156. See generally *Privacy and Human Rights*.

157. B. Moore, *Privacy*, 59.

158. Id. at 67, 70.

159. Alan Westin, *Privacy and Freedom* 12 (1967).

160. Adam D. Moore, "Privacy: Its Meaning and Value," 40 *American Philosophical Quarterly* 215, 221–22, 223 (2003).

161. Restatement (Second) of Torts §652D cmt. h.

162. Mistry v. Interim National Medical & Dental Council, 1998 (4) SA 1127, available at http://www.worldlii.org/cgi-worldlii/disp.pl/za/cases/ZACC/1998/10 .html.

163. Regina v. Kang-Brown, [2005] ABQB 608 (Can LII).

164. Illinois v. Caballes, 543 U.S. 405, 408–09 (2005).

165. Smith v. Maryland, 442 U.S. 735, 741 (1979).

166. Orin S. Kerr, "Internet Surveillance Law After the USA Patriot Act: The Big Brother That Isn't," 97 *Northwestern University Law Review* 607, 611 (2003).

167. Orin S. Kerr, "A User's Guide to the Stored Communications Act—and a Legislator's Guide to Amending It," 72 *George Washington Law Review* 1208, 1229 n.142 (2004).

168. See Daniel J. Solove, "Reconstructing Electronic Surveillance Law," 72 *George Washington Law Review* 1264, 1288 (2004).

169. 136 F.3d 1055, 1069 (6th Cir. 1998).

170. Planned Parenthood v. American Coalition of Life Activists, 290 F.3d 1058, 1065 (9th Cir. 2002) (en banc).

171. Driver's Privacy Protection Act, 18 U.S.C. §§2721–2725; Daniel J. Solove, *The Digital Person: Technology and Privacy in the Information Age* 147 (2004).

172. Iris M. Young, *Justice and the Politics of Difference* 119–20 (1990).

173. Beate Rössler, *The Value of Privacy* 8 (2005). But see Ferdinand David Schoeman, "Privacy: Philosophical Dimensions of the Literature," in *Philosophical*

Dimensions of Privacy: An Anthology 1, 3 (Ferdinand David Schoeman ed., 1984) ("One difficulty with regarding privacy as a claim or entitlement to determine what information about oneself is to be available to others is that it begs the question about the moral status of privacy. It presumes privacy is something to be protected at the discretion of the individual to whom the information relates").

174. Luciano Floridi, "The Ontological Interpretation of Informational Privacy," 7 *Ethics and Information Technology* 185 (2005).

175. Katz v. United States, 389 U.S. 347, 361 (1967) (Harlan, J., concurring).

176. See, e.g., Hoskins v. Howard, 971 P.2d 1135, 1141 (Idaho 1998); Vernars v. Young, 539 F.2d 966, 969 (3d Cir. 1976); Pearson v. Dodd, 410 F.2d 701, 704 (D.C. Cir. 1969).

177. Video Voyeurism Prevention Act, 18 U.S.C. §1801 (applies to capturing an image of an "individual's naked or undergarment clad genitals, pubic area, buttocks, or female breast . . . under circumstances in which that individual has a reasonable expectation of privacy regarding such body part or parts"); Anti-Paparazzi Act, Cal. Civ. Code §1708.8(b) (applies to the capture of visual images or sound of "the plaintiff engaging in a personal or familial activity under circumstances in which the plaintiff had a reasonable expectation of privacy").

178. Hosking & Hosking v. Runting, [2005] 1 N.Z.L.R. 1, 117, 249–50 (C.A. 2004).

179. Hunter v. Southam, [1984] 2 S.C.R. 145.

180. H. Tomás Gómez-Arostegui, "Defining Private Life Under the European Convention of Human Rights by Referring to Reasonable Expectations," 35 *California Western International Law Journal* 153, 162 (2005).

181. Lior Jacob Strahilevitz, "A Social Networks Theory of Privacy," 72 *University of Chicago Law Review* 919, 937 (2005).

182. Minnesota v. Carter, 119 S. Ct. 469, 477 (1998) (Scalia, J., concurring).

183. Christopher Slobogin & Joseph E. Schumacher, "Reasonable Expectations of Privacy and Autonomy in Fourth Amendment Cases: An Empirical Look at 'Understandings Recognized and Permitted by Society,'" 42 *Duke Law Journal* 727, 732 (1993).

184. Alessandro Acquisti & Jens Grossklags, "Privacy and Rationality," in *Privacy and Technologies of Identity: A Cross-Disciplinary Conversation* 15, 16 (Katherine Strandburg & Daniela Stan Raicu eds. 2006).

185. Strahilevitz, "Social Networks Theory," 935–36.

186. Acquisti & Grossklags, "Privacy and Rationality," 17, 25.

187. Solove, *Digital Person*, 81–92; Paul M. Schwartz, "Privacy and Democracy in Cyberspace," 52 *Vanderbilt Law Review* 1609, 1661–64 (1999).

188. See Anthony Amsterdam, "Perspectives on the Fourth Amendment," 58 *Minnesota Law Review* 349 (1974) (suggesting that government could diminish a person's subjective expectation of privacy by announcing on television each night that we all can easily be subject to electronic surveillance).

189. See Smith v. Maryland, 442 U.S. 735, 740 n.5 (1979) ("[W]here an individual's subjective expectations had been 'conditioned' by influences alien to well-recognized Fourth Amendment freedoms, those subjective expectations obviously could play no meaningful role in ascertaining what the scope of Fourth Amendment protection was").

190. George Orwell, *Nineteen Eighty-four* 3 (Plume ed. 2003) (originally published in 1949).

191. See Dewey, *Experience and Nature*, 9. Thinking is thus a "tool" for solving problems. Michael Eldridge, *Transforming Experience: John Dewey's Cultural Instrumentalism* 4 (1998).

192. See, e.g., Dewey, *Experience and Nature*, 151; see also John Dewey, *How We Think* (1910).

193. Dewey, *Experience and Nature*, 65–66.

194. Dewey, *Logic*, 106–10.

195. Dewey, *Experience and Nature*, 154.

196. Alan Dershowitz, *Rights from Wrongs: A Secular Theory of the Origins of Rights* 6–9 (2004).

197. See Solove, *Digital Person*, 13–55 (discussing Kafka's *The Trial*, Orwell's *Nineteen Eighty-four*, and Huxley's *Brave New World*).

198. Henry David Thoreau, *Walden*, in *Walden and Other Writings* 113 (Barnes & Noble Books 1993) (1854).

199. B. Moore, *Privacy*, 73.

200. Id. at 14.

4. The Value of Privacy

1. U.S. Dep't of Health, Educ. & Welfare, *Records, Computers, and the Rights of Citizens* 33 (1973); Ruth Gavison, "Privacy and the Limits of Law," 89 *Yale Law Journal* 421, 437 (1980) (privacy enables people to "grow, maintain their mental health and autonomy, create and maintain human relations, and lead meaningful lives").

2. Michael A. Weinstein, "The Uses of Privacy in the Good Life," in *Nomos XIII: Privacy* 88, 97 (J. Roland Pennock & J. W. Chapman eds., 1971).

3. Alan Westin, *Privacy and Freedom* 35 (1967).

4. Paul Freund, "Privacy: One Concept or Many," in *Nomos XIII: Privacy*, 182, 195.

5. Westin, *Privacy and Freedom*, 39.

6. Joseph Bensman & Robert Lilienfeld, *Between Public and Private: The Lost Boundaries of the Self* 76 (1979).

7. Arnold Simmel, "Privacy Is Not an Isolated Freedom," in *Nomos XIII: Privacy*, 71, 73–74.

8. See, e.g., James Rachels, "Why Privacy Is Important," in *Philosophical Dimensions of Privacy: An Anthology* 290, 292 (Ferdinand David Schoeman ed., 1984) (privacy is essential to "our ability to create and maintain different sorts of social relationships with different people").

9. Robert S. Gerstein, "Intimacy and Privacy," in *Philosophical Dimensions of Privacy*, 265, 265.

10. Jeffrey Rosen, *The Unwanted Gaze: The Destruction of Privacy in America* 8 (2000).

11. Gavison, "Privacy and the Limits of Law," 455.

12. C. Keith Boone, "Privacy and Community," 9 *Social Theory and Practice* 1, 8 (1983).

13. Paul M. Schwartz, "Privacy and Democracy in Cyberspace," 52 *Vanderbilt Law Review* 1609, 1613 (1999).

14. Anita L. Allen, *Uneasy Access: Privacy for Women in a Free Society* 51 (1988).

15. Westin, *Privacy and Freedom*, 37.

16. See id. at 33–34.

17. Hannah Arendt, *The Human Condition* 38, 58 (1958).

18. Yao-Huai Lü, "Privacy and Data Privacy Issues in Contemporary China," 7 *Ethics and Information Technology* 7, 12 (2005).

19. Thomas More, *Utopia* 73 (Clarence H. Miller trans., 2001) (originally published in 1516). For more examples of utopian literature's distaste for privacy, see Jean Marie Goulemot, "Literary Practices: Publicizing the Private," in *A History of Private Life*, vol. 3, *Passions of the Renaissance* 376–78 (Roger Chartier ed. & Arthur Goldhammer trans., 1989).

20. Joseph Pulitzer, quoted in Brent Fisse & John Braithwaite, *The Impact of Publicity on Corporate Offenders* 1 (1983).

21. Bruno Bettelheim, "The Right to Privacy Is a Myth," *Saturday Evening Post*, July 27, 1968, at 8.

22. James B. Rule, *Private Lives and Public Surveillance: Social Control in the Computer Age* 21–22 (1974).

23. Kent Walker, "The Costs of Privacy," 25 *Harvard Journal of Law and Public Policy* 87, 91 (2002) ("The final consequence of increased privacy regulation of personal information is the loss of trust").

24. Francis Fukuyama, *Trust: The Social Virtues and the Creation of Prosperity* 26 (1995).

25. Steven L. Nock, *The Costs of Privacy: Surveillance and Reputation in America* 124 (1993).

26. Richard Posner, *Economic Analysis of Law* 46 (5th ed. 1998); Richard A. Epstein, "The Legal Regulation of Genetic Discrimination: Old Responses to New Technology," 74 *Boston University Law Review* 1, 12 (1994).

27. For an overview of the feminist critique of privacy, see Patricia Boling, *Privacy and the Politics of Intimate Life* (1996); Judith Wagner DeCew, *In Pursuit of Privacy: Law, Ethics, and the Rise of Technology* 81–94 (1997); Frances Olsen, "Feminist Critiques of the Public/Private Distinction," 10 *Constitutional Commentary* 327 (1993).

28. Reva B. Siegel, " 'The Rule of Love': Wife Beating as Prerogative and Privacy," 105 *Yale Law Journal* 2117, 2122 (1996).

29. Catharine MacKinnon, *Toward a Feminist Theory of the State* 194, 191 (1989).

30. Carole Pateman, "Feminist Critiques of the Public/Private Dichotomy," in *The Disorder of Women: Democracy, Feminism, and Political Theory* 121 (1989).

31. Westin, *Privacy and Freedom*, 348.

32. Harry Kalven, Jr., "Privacy in Tort Law—Were Warren and Brandeis Wrong?" 31 *Law and Contemporary Problems* 326, 329 (1966).

33. Rochelle Gurstein, *The Repeal of Reticence* 61–90 (1996).

34. Eve Fairbanks, "The Porn Identity," *New Republic*, Feb. 6, 2006.

35. Fred H. Cate, *Privacy in the Information Age* 28–29 (1997).

36. Virginia Postrel, "No Telling," *Reason Magazine*, June 1998, available at http://www.reason.com/news/show/30656.html.

37. Eugene Volokh, "Freedom of Speech and Information Privacy: The Troubling Implications of a Right to Stop People from Speaking About You," 52 *Stanford Law Review* 1049, 1050–51, 1115 (2000).

38. Solveig Singleton, "Privacy Versus the First Amendment: A Skeptical Approach," 11 *Fordham Intellectual Property, Media and Entertainment Law Journal* 97, 152 (2000).

39. Diane L. Zimmerman, "Requiem for a Heavyweight: A Farewell to Warren and Brandeis's Privacy Tort," 68 *Cornell Law Review* 291, 341 (1983); see also Kalven, "Privacy in Tort Law."

40. William J. Stuntz, "Against Privacy and Transparency," *New Republic*, Apr. 7, 2006.

41. Richard A. Posner, *Not a Suicide Pact: The Constitution in a Time of National Emergency* 141 (2006).

42. Ronald Dworkin, *Life's Dominion: An Argument About Abortion, Euthanasia, and Individual Freedom* 69–70 (1993).

43. Anita L. Allen, "Privacy," in *The Oxford Handbook of Practical Ethics* 485, 492 (Hugh LaFollette ed., 2003).

44. Beate Rössler, *The Value of Privacy* 69 (2005).

45. Anita Allen describes these theories as follows: "Kantian deontologists judge privacy on the basis of whether it represents satisfaction of duties, principles, or rules called for by due regard for the traits of personhood in virtue of which individuals have a special dignity and ought to be accorded with respect." Allen, *Uneasy Access*, 39.

46. Stanley I. Benn, *Privacy*, "Freedom, and Respect for Persons," in *Nomos XIII: Privacy* 2, 26 (J. Roland Pennock & J. W. Chapman eds., 1971).

47. Julie C. Inness, *Privacy, Intimacy, and Isolation* 95 (1992).

48. Rössler, *Value of Privacy*, 1, 117.

49. Charles Fried, "Privacy," 77 *Yale Law Journal* 475, 477, 478 (1968).

50. Bonome v. Kaysen, 32 Media L. Rep. 1520 (Mass. Super. 2004).

51. Thomas Powers, "Can We Be Secure and Free?" 151 *Public Interest* 3, 5 (Spring 2003).

52. Luciano Floridi, "The Ontological Interpretation of Informational Privacy," 7 *Ethics and Information Technology* 185 (2005).

53. See T. Alexander Aleinikoff, "Constitutional Law in the Age of Balancing," 96 *Yale Law Journal* 943 (1987).

54. James P. Nehf, "Incomparability and the Passive Virtues of Ad Hoc Privacy Policy," 76 *University of Colorado Law Review* 1, 35, 41 (2005).

55. Margaret Jane Radin, *Contested Commodities* 8–12 (1996).

56. Aleinikoff, "Constitutional Law," 982.

57. Frank N. Coffin, "Judicial Balancing: The Protean Scales of Justice," 63 *New York University Law Review* 16, 25 (1988).

58. Thomas I. Emerson, *The System of Freedom of Expression* 545, 549 (1970).

59. Richard F. Hixson, *Privacy in a Public Society: Human Rights in Conflict* 212 (1987).

60. See Daniel J. Solove, *The Digital Person: Technology and Privacy in the Information Age* 93–97 (2004).

61. Samuel D. Warren & Louis D. Brandeis, "The Right to Privacy," 4 *Harvard Law Review* 193, 207 (1890).

62. Restatement (Second) of Torts §652(I) cmt. a.

63. Smith v. City of Artesia, 772 P.2d 373, 376 (N.M.Ct. App. 1989).

64. Priscilla M. Regan, *Legislating Privacy: Technology, Social Values, and Public Policy* 200 (1995).

65. Hixson, *Privacy in a Public Society*, xiv.

66. Amitai Etzioni, *The Limits of Privacy* 196 (1999).

67. Hixson, *Privacy in a Public Society*, 93.

68. Etzioni, *Limits of Privacy*, 187–88, 194, 38, 198.

69. Id. at 198.

70. John Dewey, *Ethics* (1908), in 5 *The Middle Works of John Dewey* 268 (Jo Ann Boydston ed., 1978).

71. John Dewey, *Liberalism and Civil Liberties* (1936), in 11 *The Later Works of John Dewey* 374–75 (Jo Ann Boydston ed., 1991).

72. Id. at 373.

73. Spiros Simitis, "Reviewing Privacy in an Information Society," 135 *University of Pennsylvania Law Review* 707, 709 (1987). In analyzing the problems of federal legislative policymaking on privacy, Priscilla Regan demonstrates the need for understanding privacy in terms of its social benefits. See Regan, *Legislating Privacy*, xiv ("[A]nalysis of congressional policy making reveals that little attention was given to the possibility of a broader social importance of privacy").

74. Robert C. Post, "The Social Foundations of Privacy: Community and Self in the Common Law Tort," 77 *California Law Review* 957, 959 (1989).

75. See Julie Cohen, "Examined Lives: Informational Privacy and the Subject as Object," 52 *Stanford Law Review* 1373, 1427–28 (2000) ("Informational privacy, in short, is a constitutive element of a civil society in the broadest sense of the term"); Schwartz, "Privacy and Democracy in Cyberspace," 1613 ("[I]nformation privacy is best conceived of as a constitutive element of civil society"); see also Gavison, "Privacy and the Limits of Law," 455 ("Privacy is also essential to democratic government because it fosters and encourages the moral autonomy of the citizen, a central requirement of a democracy").

76. As Warren and Brandeis observed, "[T]he protection of society must come mainly through a recognition of the rights of the individual." Warren & Brandeis, "Right to Privacy," 219–20.

77. John Dewey, *Experience and Nature* (1925), in 1 *The Later Works of John Dewey* 1, 164 (Jo Ann Boydston ed., 1988).

78. Robert C. Ellickson, "The Evolution of Social Norms: A Perspective from the Legal Academy," in *Social Norms* 35, 35 (Michael Hechter & Karl-Dieter Opp eds., 2001).

79. Cass R. Sunstein, "Social Norms and Social Roles," 96 *Columbia Law Review* 903, 914 (1996).

80. Richard H. McAdams, "The Origin, Development, and Regulation of Norms," 96 *Michigan Law Review* 338, 412, 416, 426 (1997).

81. John Stuart Mill, *On Liberty* 6 (David Spitz ed., 1975).

82. Angus McLaren, *Sexual Blackmail: A Modern History* 3, 28, 8, 21, 124 (2002).

83. Lawrence M. Friedman, "Name Robbers: Privacy, Blackmail, and Assorted Matters in Legal History," 30 *Hofstra Law Review* 1093, 1106 (2002).

84. Gavison, "Privacy and the Limits of Law," 453.

85. Paul M. Schwartz, "Internet Privacy and the State," 32 *Connecticut Law Review* 815, 842–43 (2000).

86. Allen, *Uneasy Access*, 36.

87. Gavison, "Feminism," 43.

88. DeCew, *In Pursuit of Privacy*, 94.

89. Laura Gowing, *Domestic Dangers: Women, Words, and Sex in Early Modern London* 2–3, 109, 188–89 (1996).

90. Post, "Social Foundations of Privacy," 968.

91. Homer, *The Odyssey* bk. 12, ll. 190–98, at 214 (Robert Fitzgerald trans., Vintage Books 1990).

92. See Michael Sullivan & John T. Lysaker, "Between Impotence and Illusion: Adorno's Art of Theory and Practice," 57 *New German Critique* 87 (1992).

93. Alan Wolfe, "Public and Private in Theory and Practice: Some Implications of an Uncertain Boundary," in *Public and Private Thought and Practice: Perspectives on a Grand Dichotomy* 182, 186–87 (Jeff Weintraub & Krishan Kumar eds., 1997); see also Allen, *Uneasy Access*, 40 ("Privacy can be used for good or ill, to help or to harm").

5. A Taxonomy of Privacy

1. In 1967, Alan Westin identified four "basic states of individual privacy": (1) solitude, (2) intimacy, (3) anonymity, and (4) reserve ("the creation of a psychological barrier against unwanted intrusion"). Alan F. Westin, *Privacy and Freedom* 31–32 (1967). These categories focus mostly on spatial distance and separateness and fail to capture the many different dimensions of informational privacy. In 1992, Ken Gormley surveyed the law of privacy. See generally Ken Gormley, "One Hundred Years of Privacy," 1992 *Wisconsin Law Review* 1335 (1992). His categories—tort privacy, Fourth Amendment privacy, First Amendment privacy, fundamental-decision privacy, and state constitutional privacy—are based on different areas of law rather than on a more systematic conceptual account of privacy. Id. at 1340. In 1998, Jerry Kang defined privacy as a union of three overlapping clusters of ideas: (1) physical space ("the extent to which an individual's territorial solitude is shielded from invasion by unwanted objects or signals"); (2) choice ("an individual's ability to make certain significant decisions without interference"); and (3) flow of personal information ("an individual's control over the processing—i.e., the acquisition, disclosure, and use—of personal information"). Jerry Kang, "Information Privacy in Cyberspace Transactions," 50 *Stanford Law Review* 1193, 1202–03 (1998). Kang's understanding of privacy is quite rich, but the breadth of his categories limits their usefulness in law. The same is true of the three categories identified by philosopher Judith DeCew: (1) "informational privacy," (2) "accessibility privacy," and (3) "expressive privacy." Judith W. DeCew, *In Pursuit of Privacy: Law, Ethics, and the Rise of Technology* 75–77 (1997).

2. William L. Prosser, "Privacy," 48 *California Law Review* 383, 389 (1960).

3. Samuel D. Warren & Louis D. Brandeis, "The Right to Privacy," 4 *Harvard Law Review* 193, 195–96 (1890).

4. Of course, there remains the issue of what constitutes valid consent because there are many occasions in which people affirmatively give out information that should not be assumed to be consensual. See Julie E. Cohen, "Examined Lives: Informational Privacy and the Subject as Object," 52 *Stanford Law Review* 1373, 1397–98 (2000) (arguing that "people are demonstrably bad at" assessing the risk of future harms that may flow from the piecemeal, otherwise consensual collection

of their private data); Paul M. Schwartz, "Privacy and Democracy in Cyberspace," 52 *Vanderbilt Law Review* 1609, 1661–64 (1999) (discussing the legal fiction of consent in the context of the Internet, specifically the use of boilerplate consent forms that do not require user agreement before taking effect).

5. See Anita L. Allen, *Why Privacy Isn't Everything* 2, 146 (2003) (discussing tort theories available as recourse for the invasion of privacy in the context of sexual harassment claims).

6. I thank Peter Swire for suggesting and helping develop this diagram.

7. George Orwell, *Nineteen Eighty-four* 2 (Plume ed. 2003) (1949).

8. Samuel H. Hofstadter, *The Development of the Right of Privacy in New York* 1–2 (1954) (citing the Mishna and the Code of Maimonides, book 12). Jeffrey Rosen observes, "Jewish law, for example, has developed a remarkable body of doctrine around the concept of *hezzek re'iyyah*, which means 'the injury caused by seeing' or 'the injury caused by being seen.' . . . [I]f your neighbor constructs a window that overlooks your home or courtyard, you are entitled to an injunction that not only prohibits your neighbor from observing you but also orders the window to be removed." Jeffrey Rosen, *The Unwanted Gaze* 19 (2000).

9. Clay Calvert, *Voyeur Nation* 36–38 (2000); Avishai Margalit, "Privacy in the Decent Society," 68 *Social Research* 255, 259 (2001). In another version of the story, Tom is not blinded by others but is inexplicably struck blind upon looking at her after Lady Godiva asked the townspeople not to look. BBC, "Beyond the Broadcast, Making History: Lady Godiva of Coventry," http://www.bbc.co.uk/education/beyond/factsheets/makhist/makhist6_prog9d.shtml (last visited Jan. 21, 2006).

10. S.C. Code Ann. §16-17-470(A) (2003); see also Ga. Code Ann. §16-11-61 (2003) (criminalizing being a "peeping Tom" when "on or about the premises of another"); La. Rev. Stat. Ann. §14:284 (2004) (defining "Peeping Tom" and setting forth the penalty); N.C. Gen. Stat. §14-202 (Supp. 2004) (criminalizing peeping as a Class 1 misdemeanor); Va. Code Ann. §18.2-130 (2004) (criminalizing peeping or spying into a "dwelling or enclosure").

11. For example, in California, "[a]ny person who installs or who maintains . . . any two-way mirror permitting observation of any restroom, toilet, bathroom, washroom, shower, locker room, fitting room, motel room, or hotel room is guilty of a misdemeanor." Cal. Penal Code §653n (West 1988).

12. 4 William Blackstone, *Commentaries* *169.

13. Orin S. Kerr, "The Fourth Amendment and New Technologies: Constitutional Myths and the Case for Caution," 102 *Michigan Law Review* 801, 841 (2004).

14. Federal Communications Act of 1934, Pub. L. No. 90-351, §2520, 48 Stat. 1103 (codified as amended at 47 U.S.C. §605); Omnibus Crime Control and Safe Streets Act of 1968, Pub. L. No. 90-351, ch. 119, 82 Stat. 212 (codified as amended at 18 U.S.C. §§2510–2522); Electronic Communications Privacy Act of 1986, Pub. L. No. 99-508, 100 Stat. 1848 (codified as amended at 18 U.S.C. §§2510–2520, 2701–2711, 3121–3127).

15. The list of countries with wiretap laws is too long to include here. For a discussion of specific laws, see Electronic Privacy Information Center & Privacy International, *Privacy and Human Rights* (2005).

16. European Union Directive on Privacy and Electronic Communications (2002), Directive 2002/58/EC.

17. See Kang, "Information Privacy," 1193, 1260 ("Simply put, surveillance leads to self-censorship"); Peter P. Swire, "Financial Privacy and the Theory of High-Tech Government Surveillance," 77 *Washington University Law Quarterly* 461, 473 (1999) ("If I know I am under surveillance, I might . . . restrict my activities, so that nothing embarrassing or otherwise harmful could be detected").

18. Judge Richard Posner notes, "[N]orms are more effective when people are under the observation of their peers." Richard A. Posner, *The Problematics of Moral and Legal Theory* 75 (1999); see also James B. Rule, *Private Lives and Public Surveillance* 28 (1974) (finding that surveillance is helpful to a government "or any other agency seeking to obtain compliance from a mass clientele in a large-scale social setting").

19. John Gilliom, *Overseers of the Poor: Surveillance, Resistance, and the Limits of Privacy* 3 (2001).

20. Jeffrey Rosen, *The Naked Crowd: Reclaiming Security and Freedom in an Anxious Age* 36 (2004).

21. Cohen, "Examined Lives," 1426.

22. See Schwartz, "Privacy and Democracy in Cyberspace," 1656.

23. Stanley I. Benn, "Privacy, Freedom, and Respect for Persons," in *Nomos XIII: Privacy* 1, 7, 10 (J. Roland Pennock & John W. Chapman eds., 1971).

24. David Lyon, *The Electronic Eye: The Rise of Surveillance Society* 62–67 (1994).

25. Michel Foucault, *Discipline and Punish* 200 (Alan Sheridan trans., Vintage Books 2d ed. 1995) (1977).

26. Lyon, *Electronic Eye*, 63.

27. Daniel J. Solove, *The Digital Person: Technology and Privacy in the Information Age* 185 (2004). For a more extensive account of King's experience with the FBI, see David J. Garrow, *The FBI and Martin Luther King, Jr.* (1981).

28. 533 U.S. 27, 40 (2001).

29. Id. (internal quotation marks omitted); see also Andrew E. Taslitz, "The Fourth Amendment in the Twenty-First Century: Technology, Privacy, and Human Emotions," 65 *Law and Contemporary Problems* 125, 144 (2002) ("Central to the Court's reasoning was that the thermal imager revealed information concerning activities *inside the home*").

30. 488 U.S. 445, 449 (1989) (alteration in original) (internal quotation marks omitted).

31. 476 U.S. 227, 238–39 (1986).

32. 468 U.S. 705, 714 (1984).

33. United States v. Knotts, 460 U.S. 276, 277, 281 (1983).

34. See, e.g., Marc Jonathan Blitz, "Video Surveillance and the Constitution of Public Space: Fitting the Fourth Amendment to a World That Tracks Image and Identity," 82 *Texas Law Review* 1349, 1357 (2004) ("[C]ontemporary Fourth Amendment jurisprudence differentiates pervasive video surveillance from more familiar mass suspicionless searches in one crucial respect: by holding that it is not a 'search' at all"); Christopher Slobogin, "Public Privacy: Camera Surveillance of Public Places and the Right to Anonymity," 72 *Mississippi Law Journal* 213, 233 (2002) ("Meaningful legal strictures on government use of public surveillance cameras in Great Britain, Canada, and the United States are non-existent").

35. Solove, *Digital Person*, 42–44.

36. Restatement (Second) of Torts §652B (1977).

37. 206 A.2d 239, 241–42 (N.H. 1964); see also Wolfson v. Lewis, 924 F. Supp. 1413, 1431 (E.D. Pa. 1996) (finding media surveillance of a couple's activities in their home to be actionable under intrusion tort); Rhodes v. Graham, 37 S.W.2d 46, 47 (Ky. 1931) (holding that wiretapping a person's phone gives rise to a tort action because it violates his right "to the privacy of his home as against the unwarranted invasion of others").

38. See, e.g., Furman v. Sheppard, 744 A.2d 583, 586 (Md. Ct. Spec. App. 2000) (holding that the defendant was not liable under intrusion tort for trespassing into a private club to engage in video surveillance of the plaintiff because the club was not a secluded place); Forster v. Manchester, 189 A.2d 147, 149–50 (Pa. 1963) (finding no intrusion liability when a private investigator followed and filmed the plaintiff because the surveillance was conducted in public).

39. Nader v. General Motors Corp., 225 N.E.2d 765, 767, 771, 769 (N.Y. 1970).

40. See ABA Criminal Justice Section's Standards Comm., ABA Criminal Justice Standards on Electronic Surveillance Relating to Technologically-Assisted Physical Surveillance §2-6.1(d) to (g) (Draft 3d ed. 1997) (recommending that the law begin to address the harms of public surveillance).

41. Westin, *Privacy and Freedom*, 31.

42. Justice William O. Douglas observed in another case, "Monitoring, if prevalent, certainly kills free discourse and spontaneous utterances." United States v. White, 401 U.S. 745, 762 (1971) (Douglas, J., dissenting).

43. Quoted in Leonard W. Levy, *Origins of the Fifth Amendment* 273 (1968).

44. John Adams, as quoted in John H. F. Shattuck, *Rights of Privacy* xiii–xiv (1976), and Charles J. Sykes, *The End of Privacy: Personal Rights in the Surveillance Society* 14–15 note (1999) (capitalization in original quote altered).

45. U.S. Const. amend. V.

46. David M. O'Brien, *Privacy, Law, and Public Policy* 92–93 (1979) (emphasis omitted).

47. Brown v. Walker, 161 U.S. 591, 637 (1896) (Field, J., dissenting).

48. Ullmann v. United States, 350 U.S. 422, 445 (1956) (Douglas, J., dissenting).

49. Charles Fried, "Privacy," 77 *Yale Law Journal* 475, 488 (1968).

50. Mark Berger, "Europeanizing Self-Incrimination: The Right to Remain Silent in the European Court of Human Rights," 12 *Columbia Journal of European Law* 339, 341 (2006). Some examples include India, Canada, and New Zealand. See India Constitution art. 20, §3; Canadian Charter of Rights and Freedoms §11(c); New Zealand Bill of Rights Act §25(d). Jewish law also protected against self-incrimination, forbidding punishment based on self-incriminating statements gleaned through interrogation, as well as confession. See Samuel J. Levine, "An Introduction to Self-Incrimination in Jewish Law, with Applications to the American Legal System: A Psychological and Philosophical Analysis," 28 *Loyola Los Angeles International and Comparative Law Review* 257 (2006).

51. International Covenant on Civil and Political Rights art. 14(3)(g), Dec. 19, 1996, 999 U.N.T.S. 171.

52. Murray v. United Kingdom, 22 ECHR 29 (1996).

53. See Daniel J. Solove, "Privacy and Power: Computer Databases and Metaphors for Information Privacy," 53 *Stanford Law Review* 1393, 1401 (2001).

54. Robert Ellis Smith, *Ben Franklin's Web Site: Privacy and Curiosity from Plymouth Rock to the Internet* 62, 63 (2000).

55. See, e.g., Miranda v. Arizona, 384 U.S. 436, 467 (1966) (explaining the Fifth Amendment protections against self-incrimination in the context of custodial interrogation).

56. Charles I, Letter to the High Commission, Feb. 4, 1637, quoted in R. Carter Pittman, "The Colonial and Constitutional History of the Privilege Against Self-Incrimination in America," 21 *Virginia Law Review* 763, 770–71 (1935).

57. Levy, *Origins of the Fifth Amendment*, 43–82.

58. Ellen Schrecker, *Many Are the Crimes: McCarthyism in America* 369–70 (1998).

59. 360 U.S. 109, 127, 134, 144 (1959) (Black, J., dissenting) (emphasis added).

60. As John Henry Wigmore noted, "The simple and peaceful process of questioning breeds a readiness to resort to bullying and to physical force and torture." 8 John Henry Wigmore, *Evidence in Trials at Common Law* §2251 n.1(c) (John T. McNaughton ed., 4th ed. 1961).

61. Peter Brooks, *Troubling Confessions: Speaking Guilt in Law and Literature* 40 (2000). The interrogation of Dimitri Karamazov in Fyodor Dostoevsky's *The Brothers Karamazov* is an excellent literary example of how interrogation distorts the truth even when the interrogators bear no deliberate motivation to distort. See Richard H. Weisberg, *The Failure of the Word* 55–58 (1984) (commenting on "Dostoevsk[y]'s belief that the legal investigator, like the novelist himself, is motivated by an essentially personalized vision of reality").

62. 364 U.S. 479, 488–90 (1960).

63. Baird v. State Bar, 401 U.S. 1, 6–7 (1971). If the government has other purposes for asking such information, however, questions about political views and organizations are permissible. See Law Students Civil Rights Research Council, Inc. v. Wadmond, 401 U.S. 154, 165–66 (1971) (remarking that questions about membership and intent to further a subversive organization's illegal aims were constitutionally proper); Barenblatt v. United States, 360 U.S. 109, 127–28 (1959) (holding that a person could be compelled to disclose before the House Un-American Activities Committee whether he was a member of the Communist Party because questions were related to a "valid legislative purpose").

64. *Baird*, 401 U.S. at 6.

65. See Harriet R. Galvin, "Shielding Rape Victims in the State and Federal Courts: A Proposal for the Second Decade," 70 *Minnesota Law Review* 763, 765–66 (1986) (discussing how rape shield laws reversed the common-law doctrine that allowed a defendant to inquire into the complainant's tendency to engage in extramarital sexual relations).

66. See 42 U.S.C. §12112(d)(2) (limiting the legality of inquiries during the preemployment period); id. at §12112(d)(4) (prohibiting inquiries during the employment period). Drug testing is not considered a "medical examination" under the ADA. Id. at §12114(d)(1).

67. Wis. Stat. Ann. §103.15(2) (West 2002).

68. Mass. Gen. Laws Ann. ch. 151B, §4(9), (9A) (LexisNexis 1999).

69. See, e.g., Cal. Gov't Code §12940(o) (West 2005); Conn. Gen. Stat. Ann. §46a-60(11)(A) (West 2004); Del. Code Ann. tit. 19, §711(e) (Supp. 2004); N.Y. Exec. Law §296.19(a)(1) (McKinney 2004).

70. See, e.g., Ariz. Rev. Stat. Ann. §12-2235 (2005) (privileging, in civil actions, any patient communication to a physician or surgeon regarding "any physical or mental disease or disorder or supposed physical or mental disease or disorder or as to any such knowledge obtained by personal examination of the patient"); Cal. Evid. Code §954 (West 1995) ("[T]he client . . . has a privilege to refuse to disclose, and to prevent another from disclosing, a confidential communication between client and lawyer"); 735 Ill. Comp. Stat. Ann. 5/8-803 (West 2005) (rendering privileged any "confession or admission" made to an accredited practitioner of a religious denomination in her official capacity). As Catherine Ross contends, privileges protect against "forced betrayal." Catherine J. Ross, "Implementing Constitutional Rights for Juveniles: The Parent-Child Privilege in Context," 14 *Stanford Law and Policy Review* 85, 86 (2003).

71. William J. Stuntz, "Self-Incrimination and Excuse," 88 *Columbia Law Review* 1227, 1234 (1988) (footnotes omitted).

72. See Brown v. Walker, 161 U.S. 591, 605–06 (1896) ("The design of the constitutional privilege [against self-incrimination] is not to aid the witness in vindicating his character, but to protect him against being compelled to furnish evidence to convict him of a criminal charge").

73. 350 U.S. 422, 430, 439 (1956).

74. Id. at 450, 452 (Douglas, J., dissenting).

75. Stuntz, "Self-Incrimination and Excuse," 1228.

76. See *In re* Grand Jury, 103 F.3d 1140, 1146 (3d Cir. 1997) ("The overwhelming majority of all courts—federal or state—have rejected such a privilege").

77. *In re* A & M, 403 N.Y.S.2d 375, 380 (App. Div. 1978). When Monica Lewinsky's mother was subpoenaed to testify against her by Independent Counsel Kenneth Starr in his investigation of President Bill Clinton, there was an enormous public outcry. See Ruth Marcus, "To Some in the Law, Starr's Tactics Show a Lack of Restraint," *Washington Post*, Feb. 13, 1998, at A1 (providing reactions from prosecutors who believed that Starr's tactics were unwarranted). Critics have likened the tactic of having parents and children testify about each other to some of the infamous horrors of totalitarian societies, such as Nazi Germany, where the government sought to make family members divulge information about each other. See, e.g., J. Tyson Covey, "Making Form Follow Function: Considerations in Creating and Applying a Statutory Parent-Child Privilege," 1990 *University of Illinois Law Review* 879, 890; Wendy Meredith Watts, "The Parent-Child Privileges: Hardly a New or Revolutionary Concept," 28 *William and Mary Law Review* 583, 590–94 (1987).

78. Sometimes this quote has been attributed to Aristotle, although it is not written in any of his texts. Euclid is credited with a similar quote: "The whole is greater than the part," which he stated in *Elements* in the third century b.c.

79. Priscilla M. Regan, *Legislating Privacy: Technology, Social Values, and Public Policy* 82 (1995).

80. R. E. Smith, *Ben Franklin's Web Site*, 309–11. But cf. Note, "Privacy and Efficient Government: Proposals for a National Data Center," 82 *Harvard Law Review* 400, 412 (1968) (criticizing the congressional task force for undertaking "only a surface treatment" of the privacy issue and arguing that "Congress should give very careful consideration to essential legal and technological safeguards for the privacy interest").

81. David H. Flaherty, *Protecting Privacy in Surveillance Societies* 165–69 (1989).

82. Solove, *Digital Person*, 44–47.

83. See Cohen, "Examined Lives," 1398 ("A comprehensive collection of data about an individual is vastly more than the sum of its parts").

84. See Steven L. Nock, *The Costs of Privacy: Surveillance and Reputation in America* 73 (1993).

85. Solove, *Digital Person*, 1–10.

86. H. Jeff Smith, *Managing Privacy: Information Technology and Corporate America* 121 (1994) (footnote omitted).

87. United States Dep't of Justice v. Reporters Comm. for Freedom of the Press, 489 U.S. 749, 763, 764 (1989).

88. See, e.g., Cordell v. Detective Publ'ns, 307 F. Supp. 1212, 1218 (E.D. Tenn. 1968) ("The Court is of the opinion that the plaintiff may not complain of public disclosure of private facts when the material facts [of concern] are not private but are matters of public record and are in the public domain").

89. Restatement (Second) of Torts §652D cmt. b.

90. Id. at §652B cmt. c.

91. See, e.g., Cutshall v. Sundquist, 193 F.3d 466, 481 (6th Cir. 1999) (concluding that *Reporters Committee* was not applicable to a Megan's Law challenge). But see Doe v. Poritz, 662 A.2d 367, 411 (N.J. 1995) (following *Reporters Committee* and recognizing a privacy interest with respect to a sex offender community-notification statute).

92. 124 F.3d 1079, 1094 (9th Cir. 1997).

93. 170 F.3d 396, 400, 405 (3d Cir. 1999), *aff'd on reh'g sub nom.* Paul P. v. Farmer, 227 F.3d 98 (3d Cir. 2000) (stating that the holding of *Reporters Committee* dealt with the implication of a privacy interest protected by an exemption to the Freedom of Information Act, not by the Constitution, as in the case of *Paul P.*).

94. A.A. v. New Jersey, 176 F. Supp. 2d 274, 305 (D.N.J. 2001), *aff'd* 341 F.3d 206 (3d Cir. 2003).

95. Mark Twain, *Puddn'head Wilson* 108 (Sidney E. Berger ed., 1980) (1894).

96. Richard Sobel, "The Demeaning of Identity and Personhood in National Identification Systems," 15 *Harvard Journal of Law and Technology* 319, 349–50 (2002) (footnote omitted).

97. Id. at 350.

98. U.S. Dep't of Health, Educ., & Welfare, *Records, Computers, and the Rights of Citizens* xxxii (1973).

99. Doyle v. Wilson, 529 F. Supp. 1343, 1348 (D. Del. 1982).

100. See U.S. General Accounting Office, *Social Security: Government and Commercial Use of the Social Security Number Is Widespread* (Feb. 1999).

101. Colin J. Bennett, *Regulating Privacy: Data Protection and Public Policy in Europe and the United States* 47–65 (1992).

102. *Privacy and Human Rights* 233.

103. Id. *at* 48.

104. Roger Clarke, *Smart Card Technical Issues Starter Kit*, ch. 3 (April 8, 1998), available at http://www.anu.edu.au/people/Roger.Clarke/DV/SCTISK3.html. Clarke observes, "In the context of information systems, the purpose of identification is more concrete: it is used to link a stream of data with a person." Roger Clarke, "Human Identification in Information Systems: Management Challenges

and Public Policy Issues," 7 *Information, Technology, and People* 6, 8 (1994), available at http://www.anu.edu.au/people/Roger.Clarke/DV/HumanID.html.

105. For a history of criminal identification techniques, see Simon A. Cole, *Suspect Identities: A History of Fingerprinting and Criminal Identification* 4–5 (2001).

106. See generally John D. Woodward, Jr., Nicholas M. Orlans, & Peter T. Higgins, *Biometrics: Identity Assurance in the Information Age* (2003) (commenting that reliable identification improves public safety and the safety of business transactions).

107. See Communications Disclaimer Requirements, 11 C.F.R. §110.11 (2005) (requiring disclaimers on "general public political advertising"). The identification requirement was originally part of the Federal Election Campaign Act of 1971, Pub. L. No. 92-225, 86 Stat. 3 (1972) (codified as amended at 2 U.S.C. §§431–456 (2000 & Supp. II 2002)), which required identification for any expenditure with the purpose of influencing an election. The Court in *Buckley v. Valeo* held that the provision can only apply to speech that "expressly advocate[s] the election or defeat of a clearly identified candidate." 424 U.S. 1, 79–80 (1976).

108. 2 U.S.C. §441d(a)(3) (2000 & Supp. II 2002).

109. See Clarke, "Human Identification in Information Systems," 32–34 (describing proponents of this view).

110. Article 8 of the convention provides for the protection of "the right to respect for [an individual's] private and family life, his home and his correspondence." Convention for the Protection of Human Rights and Fundamental Freedoms art. 8, Nov. 4, 1950, 213 U.N.T.S. 221.

111. B. v. France, 232 ECHR 33, 36, 52 (1992). The science-fiction movie *Gattaca* also illustrates these points. Vincent, the protagonist, is linked to his high risk of developing heart problems, and this renders him unfit for all but the most menial jobs. *Gattaca* (Columbia Pictures 1997).

112. Solove, *Digital Person*, 1.

113. Clarke, "Human Identification in Information Systems," 20.

114. Richard Sobel observes, "Identity systems and documents have a long history of uses and abuses for social control and discrimination." Richard Sobel, "The Degradation of Political Identity Under a National Identification System," 8 *Boston University Journal of Science and Technology Law* 37, 48 (2002). Indeed, one of the primary reasons that governments created passports and identity cards was to restrict movement, alter patterns of migration, and control the movements of poor people and others viewed as undesirable. Marc Garcelon, "Colonizing the Subject: The Genealogy and Legacy of the Soviet Internal Passport," in *Documenting Individual Identity* 83, 86 (Jane Caplan & John Torpey eds., 2001).

115. Sobel, "Degradation of Political Identity," 49.

116. R. E. Smith, *Ben Franklin's Web Site*, 41, 43.

117. McIntyre v. Ohio Elections Comm'n, 514 U.S. 334, 343 n.6 (1995).

118. Gary Marx notes that anonymity can "facilitate the flow of information and communication on public issues" and "encourage experimentation and risk taking without facing large consequences, risk of failure, or embarrassment since one's identity is protected." Gary T. Marx, "Identity and Anonymity: Some Conceptual Distinctions and Issues for Research," in *Documenting Individual Identity*, 311, 316, 318; see also A. Michael Froomkin, "Flood Control on the Information Ocean: Living with Anonymity, Digital Cash, and Distributed Databases," 15 *Journal of*

Law and Communications 395, 408 (1996) ("Not everyone is so courageous as to wish to be known for everything they say, and some timorous speech deserves encouragement").

119. One of the most famous examples of an anonymous whistleblower is Deep Throat, Bob Woodward and Carl Bernstein's confidential source who helped them unearth the Watergate scandal. See Carl Bernstein & Bob Woodward, *All the President's Men* 71–73, 130–35 (1974).

120. See Julie E. Cohen, "A Right to Read Anonymously: A Closer Look at 'Copyright Management' in Cyberspace," 28 *Connecticut Law Review* 981, 1012–14 (1996) (arguing that reader anonymity is an important First Amendment value and that anonymous reading protects people from being associated with the ideas about which they read).

121. Talley v. California, 362 U.S. 60, 65 (1960); see also Watchtower Bible & Tract Soc. v. Village of Stratton, 536 U.S. 150, 166–67 (2002) (stating that anonymity protects people who engage in "unpopular causes"); McIntyre v. Ohio Elections Comm'n, 514 U.S. 334, 341–42 (1995) ("The decision in favor of anonymity may be motivated by fear of economic or official retaliation, by concern about social ostracism, or merely by a desire to preserve as much of one's privacy as possible").

122. Hiibel v. Sixth Judicial District Court, 542 U.S. 177, 189, 190–91 (2004).

123. Id. at 196 (Stevens, J., dissenting) (quoting id. at 191 (majority opinion)).

124. Franz Kafka, "The Burrow," in *The Complete Stories*, 325, 326 (Willa Muir and Edwin Muir trans., 1971).

125. Jennifer 8 Lee, "Fighting Back when Someone Steals Your Name," *New York Times*, Apr. 8, 2001, §3, at 8.

126. Solove, *Digital Person*, 110.

127. Janine Benner, Beth Givens, & Ed Mierzwinski, *Nowhere to Turn: Victims Speak Out on Identity Theft* pt. II, §§1, 4 (2000), http://www.privacyrights.org/ar/idtheft2000.htm.

128. Solove, *Digital Person*, 110.

129. Tom Zeller, Jr., "An Ominous Milestone: 100 Million Data Leaks," *New York Times*, Dec. 18, 2006.

130. Lynn M. LoPucki, "Human Identification Theory and the Identity Theft Problem," 80 *Texas Law Review* 89, 94 (2001).

131. Identification via password, however, can enhance security without linking the individual to immutable characteristics such as biometric identifiers.

132. See Nock, *Costs of Privacy*, 53 (recounting the rise of credit bureaus). For a comprehensive account of the credit reporting system, see Evan Hendricks, *Credit Scores and Credit Reports* (2004).

133. See Solove, *Digital Person*, 111–12, 115–19 (noting that investigation and prosecution of identity-theft cases are not top priorities for law-enforcement agencies, and that victims are slow to realize that their identity has been stolen).

134. Whalen v. Roe, 429 U.S. 589, 599, 605 (1977).

135. Fraternal Order of Police, Lodge No. 5 v. City of Philadelphia, 812 F.2d 105, 118 (3d Cir. 1987).

136. U.S. Dep't of Health, Educ., & Welfare, *Records*, 41.

137. Asia-Pacific Economic Cooperation, Privacy Framework principle 22 (2004); Organization for Economic Cooperation and Development (OECD),

Guidelines on the Protection of Privacy and Transborder Flows of Personal Data para. 11 (1980); Directive of the European Parliament and the Council of Europe on the Protection of Individuals with Regard to the Processing of Personal Data and on the Free Movement of Such Data art. 17 (1995).

138. Convention for the Protection of Individuals with Regard to Automatic Processing of Personal Data, Council of Europe Treaties No. 108, art. 7 (Jan. 28, 1981).

139. The provisions are Privacy Act, 5 U.S.C. §552a(e) (10); Children's Online Privacy Protection Act, 15 U.S.C. §6502(b) (1) (D); Gramm-Leach-Bliley Act, 15 U.S.C. §§6801(b), 6805(b) (2); Health Insurance Portability and Accountability Act, 42 U.S.C. §1320d-2(d) (2); and Computer Fraud and Abuse Act, 18 U.S.C. §1030. For the Federal Trade Commission's security regulations, see 16 C.F.R. §314 (2005).

140. See Daniel J. Solove, "The New Vulnerability: Data Security and Personal Information," 11-12 (2004), available at http://ssrn.com/abstract=583483 (arguing that the law fails to adequately guard sensitive information, and that a reconceptualization of the legal duties information keepers owe their customers is necessary).

141. See, e.g., Electronic Communications Privacy Act of 1986, 18 U.S.C. §2707(c) (2000) (setting a minimum $1,000 fine per violation); Video Privacy Protection Act of 1988, 18 U.S.C. §2710(c) (2000) (setting liquidated damages of $2,500 as the minimum amount). The Privacy Act of 1974 also contains a liquidated-damages provision; however, the Supreme Court interpreted it to apply only when the plaintiff demonstrates actual damages. See Doe v. Chao, 540 U.S. 614, 616 (2004) (construing 5 U.S.C. §552a(g) (4) (2000)).

142. Pisciotta v. Old National Bankcorp, 499 F.3d 629, 639 (7th Cir. 2007).

143. 15 U.S.C. §45.

144. In the Matter of Microsoft Corp., No. 012–3240 (Dec. 24, 2002).

145. *In re* Guess.com, Inc., No. 022-3260 (July 30, 2003).

146. Arthur R. Miller, *The Assault on Privacy: Computers, Data Banks, and Dossiers* 34 (1971).

147. Regan, *Legislating Privacy*, 86; Robert Gellman, "Does Privacy Law Work?" in *Technology and Privacy: The New Landscape* 193, 198–99 (Philip E. Agre & Marc Rotenberg eds., 1997).

148. See Gary T. Marx, *Undercover: Police Surveillance in America* 208–11 (1988) (citing instances of government agencies—including the Selective Service and the Internal Revenue Service—using databases supplied by private businesses to investigate instances of draft dodging and tax fraud).

149. Computer Matching and Privacy Protection Act (CMPPA) of 1988, Pub. L. No. 100-503, 102 Stat. 2507 (codified at 5 U.S.C. §552a (2000)).

150. U.S. Dep't of Health, Educ., & Welfare, *Records*, 41–42.

151. The statutory provisions are Privacy Act, 5 U.S.C. §552a(e) (3) (B); Fair Credit Reporting Act, 15 U.S.C. §1681b; Driver's Privacy Protection Act, 18 U.S.C. §2722(a); Cable Communications Policy Act, 47 U.S.C. §551(e); Gramm-Leach-Bliley Act, 15 U.S.C. §6802(c); Video Privacy Protection Act, 18 U.S.C. §2710(e).

152. Federal Election Compaign Act, 2 U.S.C. §438(a)(4); Health Insurance Portability and Accountability Act regulations, 45 C.F.R. §164.508(a).

153. EU Data Protection Directive, art. 6.

154. Convention for the Protection of Individuals with Regard to Automatic Processing of Personal Data, Council of Europe Treaties No. 108, art. 5b (Jan. 28, 1981).

155. APEC Privacy Framework, principle 19; OECD Guidelines, para. 9, 10.

156. Australian Institute of Private Detectives Ltd v. Privacy Commissioner, [2004] FCA 1440 (5 November 2004) (discussing 17 Clause 2.1 of Schedule 3 to the Privacy Act).

157. Information Protection Act, art. 24.1; see Korean Personal Information Dispute Mediation Committee, [2004] KRPIDMC 1, http://www.worldlii.org/kr/cases/KRPIDMC/2004/1.html (assessing damages for a company's disclosure of a person's résumé on its website); Personal Information Protection and Electronic Documents Act, S.C. 2000 ch. 5 (Can.).

158. United Nations Guidelines Concerning Computerized Personal Data Files, adopted by the General Assembly on Dec. 14, 1990.

159. Pamela Sankar, "DNA-Typing: Galton's Eugenic Dream Realized?" in *Documenting Individual Identity*, 273, 278–79.

160. Schwartz, "Privacy and Democracy in Cyberspace," 1683.

161. Dwyer v. American Express Co., 652 N.E.2d 1351, 1354 (Ill. App. 1995).

162. Sheets v. Salt Lake County, 45 F.3d 1383, 1388 (10th Cir. 1995).

163. Anderson v. Blake, 469 F.3d 910 (10th Cir. 2006).

164. Franz Kafka, *The Trial* 115 (Breon Mitchell trans., 1998).

165. U.S. Dep't of Health, Educ., & Welfare, *Records*, 29.

166. Id. at 41.

167. Constitution of the Argentine Nation, quoted in Donald C. Dowling, Jr., & Jeremy M. Mittman, "International Privacy Law," in *Proskauer on Privacy* 14-1, 14-39 (Christopher Wolf ed., 2006).

168. Constitution of Brazil art. 5; Federal Law No. 8,078, art. 43, Sept. 11, 1990, discussed in *Privacy and Human Rights*, 290.

169. Ruby v. Canada (Solicitor General), [2000] 3 F.C. 589 [F.C.A.].

170. EU Data Protection Directive, art. 12; OECD Guidelines para. 12, 13; APEC Privacy Framework, principles 23, 24.

171. See Mobil Oil Corp. v. Rubenfeld, 339 N.Y.S.2d 623, 632 (Civ. Ct. 1972) (defining a fiduciary relationship as one "founded on trust or confidence").

172. Meinhard v. Salmon, 164 N.E. 545, 546 (N.Y. 1928).

173. Moore v. Regents of the Univ. of Cal., 793 P.2d 479, 483 (Cal. 1990) (en banc).

174. The statutory provisions are Privacy Act, 5 U.S.C. §552a(d); Cable Communications Policy Act, 47 U.S.C. §551(d); Fair Credit Reporting Act, 15 U.S.C. §1681g(a); and Children's Online Privacy Protection Act, 15 U.S.C. §6502(b) (1) (B) (i).

175. See, e.g., Fair Credit Reporting Act, 15 U.S.C. §1681i(a) (5) (A).

176. Gramm-Leach-Bliley Act, 15 U.S.C. §6802(b).

177. Mark Twain, *The Autobiography of Mark Twain* xxxv (Charles Neider ed. 1990).

178. Benjamin Franklin, *Poor Richard's Almanac* (July 1735), quoted in John Bartlett, *Bartlett's Familiar Quotations* 309:15 (Justin Kaplan ed., Little, Brown, 16th ed. 1992).

179. McCormick v. England, 494 S.E.2d 431, 432, 435, 438 (S.C. Ct. App. 1997).

180. See, e.g., Peterson v. Idaho First Nat'l Bank, 367 P.2d 284, 290 (Idaho 1961) (recognizing a breach-of-confidentiality tort for disclosure by a bank). For more information on the breach-of-confidentiality tort, see generally Alan B. Vickery, Note, "Breach of Confidence: An Emerging Tort," 82 *Columbia Law Review* 1426, 1426 (1982).

181. See Hammonds v. Aetna Cas. & Sur. Co., 243 F. Supp. 793 (N.D. Ohio 1965) (holding an insurance company liable for inducing a physician to disclose confidential information).

182. Neil M. Richards & Daniel J. Solove, "Privacy's Other Path: Recovering the Law of Confidentiality," 96 *Georgetown Law Journal* 123 (2007); Raymond Wacks, *Privacy and Press Freedom* 48–58 (1995).

183. Barrymore v. News Group Newspapers Ltd., [1997] F.S.R. 600, 601 (Ch.).

184. A v. B, [2003] Q.B. 195, 207, 216.

185. See Mark S. Hayes, "Privacy Law in Canada," in *Proskauer on Privacy* 13-1, 13-41 (Christopher Wolf ed., 2006) (discussing Canada's breach-of-confidence tort); David J. Seipp, "English Judicial Recognition of a Right to Privacy," 3 *Oxford Journal of Legal Studies* 325, 366 (1983) (discussing Scotland's recognition of breach of confidence); Hosking v. Runting, [2004] NZCA 34, at [46] (Mar. 25, 2004) (discussing New Zealand's breach-of-confidentiality tort); Australian Broadcasting Corp. v. Lenah Game Means, [2001] 208 CLR 199 (discussing Australia's breach-of-confidentiality tort).

186. Simonsen v. Swenson, 177 N.W. 831, 832 (Neb. 1920).

187. Id. at 831, 832.

188. Tarasoff v. Regents of the Univ. of Cal., 551 P.2d 334, 339–40, 347 (Cal. 1976) (en banc).

189. United States v. Miller, 425 U.S. 435, 437, 442–43 (1976).

190. Smith v. Maryland, 442 U.S. 735, 743 (1979).

191. Solove, *Digital Person*, 201–09.

192. See, e.g., Brex v. Smith, 146 A. 34, 36 (N.J. Ch. 1929) (finding an "implied obligation" for banks to keep customers' bank records confidential unless compelled by a court to disclose them).

193. The states are California, Colorado, Florida, Hawaii, Idaho, Illinois, Montana, New Jersey, Pennsylvania, Utah, and Washington. See Stephen E. Henderson, "Learning from All Fifty States: How to Apply the Fourth Amendment and Its State Analogs to Protect Third Party Information from Unreasonable Search," 55 *Catholic University Law Review* 373, 395 (2006).

194. Distt. Registrar & Collector, Hyderabad & Anr v. Canara Bank Etc, [2004] INSC 668, available at http://www.commonlii.org/in/cases/INSC/2004/668.html.

195. Peterson v. Idaho First Nat'l Bank, 367 P.2d 284, 290 (Idaho 1961).

196. See, e.g., Barnett Bank of W. Fla. v. Hooper, 498 So. 2d 923, 926 (Fla. 1986) (recognizing that banks establish fiduciary relationships with customers when they enter into transactions); Ind. Nat'l Bank v. Chapman, 482 N.E.2d 474, 482 (Ind. Ct. App. 1985) (finding an implied contract not to disclose personal financial information between a bank and its customers); Suburban Trust Co. v. Waller, 408 A.2d 758, 762 (Md. Ct. Spec. App. 1979) ("[A] bank implicitly warrants to maintain, in strict confidence, information regarding its depositor's affairs"); Richfield

Bank & Trust Co. v. Sjogren, 244 N.W.2d 648, 651 (Minn. 1976) (recognizing a duty of confidentiality for banks); McGuire v. Shubert, 722 A.2d 1087, 1091 (Pa. Super. Ct. 1998) (finding a duty for a bank to keep its customers' account information confidential).

197. Henry James, *The Reverberator* 62 (1888).

198. Restatement (Second) of Torts §652D (1977); see Warren & Brandeis, "Right to Privacy," 195–96.

199. 429 U.S. 589, 598–99 (1977).

200. See, e.g., Doe v. Borough of Barrington, 729 F. Supp. 376, 382 (D.N.J. 1990) (holding that it was a violation of the plaintiff's constitutional right to information privacy for police to disclose to neighbors that the plaintiff's husband was infected with AIDS).

201. Privacy Act of 1974, 5 U.S.C. §552a(e) (10) (prohibiting agencies from disclosing information about an individual without her prior written consent); Family Educational Rights and Privacy Act of 1974, 20 U.S.C. §1232g(b) (1) (requiring educational agencies or institutions that receive government funding not to disclose education records without written consent); Cable Communications Policy Act of 1984, 47 U.S.C. §§551(b)–(c) (limiting the extent to which a cable service may collect or disclose personally identifiable information about subscribers); Video Privacy Protection Act of 1988, 18 U.S.C. §2710(b) (1) (creating civil liability for video stores that disclose personally identifiable information about any customer); Driver's Privacy Protection Act of 1994, 18 U.S.C. §§2721–2725 (restricting the use of personal information contained in state motor-vehicle records); Health Insurance Portability and Accountability Act of 1996, 42 U.S.C. §1320d-2 (protecting the privacy of personal health information in transactions).

202. See, e.g., Cal. Health & Safety Code §199.21 (West 1990) (repealed 1995) (prohibiting, inter alia, disclosure of HIV test results); N.Y. Pub. Health Law §17 (McKinney 2001) (permitting the release of medical records of minors relating to sexually transmitted diseases and abortion upon written request, but prohibiting disclosure to parents without consent); 71 Pa. Stat. Ann. §1690.108 (West 1990) (prohibiting disclosure of all records prepared during alcohol- or drug-abuse treatment).

203. Argentine Civil Code art. 1071, incorporated by Law No. 21.173, quoted in *Privacy and Human Rights*, 217.

204. Privacy Act 1978 RSS c P-24 (Saskatchewan) s 2; Privacy Act 1990 RSNL c P-22 (Newfoundland and Labrador) s 3(1) ; Privacy Act 1996 RSBC c 373 (British Columbia) s 1(1); Privacy Act CCSM s P125 (Manitoba) s 2(1).

205. Jeanne M. Hauch, "Protecting Private Facts in France: The Warren & Brandeis Tort Is Alive and Well and Flourishing in Paris," 68 *Tulane Law Review* 1219, 1222, 1231–32 (1994).

206. Jorge A. Vargas, "Privacy Rights Under Mexican Law: Emergence and Legal Configuration of a Panoply of New Rights," 27 *Houston Journal of International Law* 73, 111 (2004).

207. Hosking v. Runting, [2005] 1 NZLR 1, [117].

208. Cap. 217, 9-8, quoted in D. S. Choi & S. C. Park, "Korea," in *International Libel and Privacy Handbook* 7-1, 7-2 (Charles J. Glasser, Jr., ed., 2006).

209. Lawrence W. Beer, "Freedom of Expression: The Continuing Revolution," 53 *Law and Contemporary Problems* 36, 54–55 (1990); see also Serge Gutwirth, *Privacy and the Information Age* 26 (Raf Casert trans., 2002).

210. Dan Rosen, "Private Lives and Public Eyes: Privacy in the United States and Japan," 6 *Florida Journal of International Law* 141, 153 (1990).

211. Eugene Volokh, "Freedom of Speech and Information Privacy: The Troubling Implications of a Right to Stop People from Speaking About You," 52 *Stanford Law Review* 1049, 1050–51 (2000); see also Thomas I. Emerson, *The System of Freedom of Expression* 556 (1970) ("[T]he right of privacy depends upon guaranteeing an individual freedom from intrusion and freedom to think and believe, not freedom from discussion of his opinions, actions or affairs").

212. Richard A. Posner, *The Economics of Justice* 271 (1981).

213. Warren & Brandeis, "Right to Privacy," 210–11.

214. See Daniel J. Solove, "The Virtues of Knowing Less: Justifying Privacy Protections Against Disclosure," 53 *Duke Law Journal* 967, 990–92 (2003).

215. Cohen, "Right to Read Anonymously," 1012–13.

216. 816 A.2d 1001, 1008 (N.H. 2003).

217. Diane L. Zimmerman, "Requiem for a Heavyweight: A Farewell to Warren and Brandeis's Privacy Tort," 68 *Cornell Law Review* 291, 334 (1983).

218. See, e.g., Kathleen Guzman, "About Outing: Public Discourse, Private Lives," 73 *Washington University Law Quarterly* 1531, 1568 (1995) ("Outers offer up the victim as a 'sacrificial lamb' to portray themselves as purifying redeemers, able to solve the problems of discrimination").

219. John P. Elwood, "Outing, Privacy, and the First Amendment," 102 *Yale Law Journal* 747, 773 (1992) ("Even under the best of circumstances, the relationship between outing a particular figure and effecting a societal change is simply too attenuated to override the outing target's privacy rights").

220. John D'Emilio & Estelle B. Freedman, *Intimate Matters: A History of Sexuality in America* 285–86 (2d ed. 1997).

221. See J. Rosen, *Unwanted Gaze*, 200 ("[C]hanges in media technology have increased the risk of mistaking information for knowledge"); Lawrence Lessig, "Privacy and Attention Span," 89 *Georgetown Law Journal* 2063, 2068–69 (2001) (arguing that access to limited amounts of information only "creates the impression of knowledge"); Solove, "Virtues," 1037 ("Much misunderstanding occurs because of the disclosure of private information").

222. See Solove, "Virtues," 1041–43 (describing the stigma attached to those with certain diseases and illnesses).

223. U.S. Dep't of Health, Educ., & Welfare, *Records*, 112.

224. Cefalu v. Globe Newspaper Co., 391 N.E.2d 935, 939 (Mass. App. Ct. 1979).

225. 469 N.E.2d 1025, 1028 (Ohio Ct. App. 1984) (quoting Jackson v. Playboy Enters., 574 F. Supp. 10, 13 (S.D. Ohio 1983)).

226. 201 Cal. Rptr. 665, 666, 669 (Ct. App. 1984).

227. Duran v. Detroit News, Inc., 504 N.W.2d 715, 720 (Mich. Ct. App. 1993) (finding her identity to be "open to the public eye" because her work in Colombia had been disclosed in newspaper articles, and because she had occasionally used her real name in the United States); see also Fisher v. Ohio Dep't of Rehab. & Corr., 578 N.E.2d 901, 903 (Ohio Ct. Cl. 1988) (holding that the disclosure of a public conversation between a plaintiff and her fellow employees was not a privacy violation).

228. Times Mirror Co. v. Superior Court, 244 Cal. Rptr. 556, 561 (Ct. App. 1988); see also Multimedia WMAZ, Inc. v. Kubach, 443 S.E.2d 491, 500 (Ga. Ct.

App. 1994) (finding that the plaintiff's disclosure of his infection status to family, friends, and members of an HIV support group did not render the information public); Y.G. v. Jewish Hosp., 795 S.W.2d 488, 500 (Mo. Ct. App. 1990) (holding that disclosure to doctors and other participants of the plaintiff's in vitro fertilization did not render that information public).

229. See Lior Jacob Strahilevitz, "A Social Networks Theory of Privacy," 72 *University of Chicago Law Review* 919, 974 (2005).

230. Quoted in Norbert Elias, *The Civilizing Process* 112 (1994).

231. DeMay v. Roberts, 9 N.W. 146, 148–49 (Mich. 1881).

232. Nat'l Archives & Records Admin. v. Favish, 541 U.S. 157, 171, 168 (2004) (quoting 5 U.S.C. §552(b) (7) (C) (2000)) (internal quotation marks omitted). Courts have also allowed tort suits based on the dissemination of autopsy photos. See Reid v. Pierce County, 961 P.2d 333, 339–42 (Wash. 1998) (en banc) (holding that relatives of deceased persons maintained a cause of action for invasion of privacy when coroner's office employees disseminated autopsy photos).

233. Earnhardt v. Volusia County Office of the Medical Examiner, No. 2001-30373-CICI, at 7 (7th Judicial Circuit, July 9, 2001).

234. Judgement of June 16, 1858, Trib. Pr. Inst. de la Seine, 1858 D.P. III 62 (Fr.) (l'affaire Rachel), quoted in Hauch, "Protecting Private Facts in France," 1233.

235. See, e.g., Anita L. Allen, "Lying to Protect Privacy," 44 *Villanova Law Review* 161, 177 (1999) ("Sex is an area in which we encounter our desires, prejudices and shame, and cloak these emotions in privacy").

236. See Elias, *Civilizing Process,* 114 ("The social reference of shame and embarrassment recedes more and more from consciousness. Precisely because the social command not to show oneself exposed or performing natural functions now operates with regard to everyone[,] . . . it seems to the adult a command of his own inner self").

237. Martha C. Nussbaum, *Hiding from Humanity: Disgust, Shame, and the Law* 115–16 (2004).

238. See William Ian Miller, *The Anatomy of Disgust* 177 (1997) ("The civilizing process, according to [Norbert] Elias, means the expansion of the private sphere at the expense of the public. The new norms demand private spaces in which one prepares, grooms, and does the things that would disgust others if they were to be witnessed"); Carl D. Schneider, *Shame, Exposure, and Privacy* 49 (W. W. Norton 1992) (1977) ("The open display of bodily functions—defecating, great pain, the process of dying—threatens the dignity of the individual, revealing an individual vulnerable to being reduced to his bodily existence, bound by necessity").

239. Certain activities, such as defecation, we view as uncivilized to perform in front of others. William Ian Miller observes, "Clearly defecation is degrading and contaminating. It is hedged in with rules about appropriateness as to place. And to violate those rules is a cause for disgrace and shame." Miller, *Anatomy of Disgust,* 147, 178.

240. Rochelle Gurstein, *The Repeal of Reticence* 11 (1996).

241. One victim of Chicago's invasive strip-search policy testified that "the incident caused her emotional distress that manifested itself in reduced socializing, poor work performance, paranoia, suicidal feelings, depression, and an inability to

disrobe in any place other than a closet." Joan W. v. City of Chicago, 771 F.2d 1020, 1021–22 (7th Cir. 1985).

242. Restatement (Second) of Torts §652D (1977).

243. Eugene Volokh explains that this difference may be because the information revealed via exposure is less useful to those to whom the information is given than that revealed via disclosure. Volokh, "Freedom of Speech," 1094.

244. Daily Times Democrat v. Graham, 162 So. 2d 474, 478 (Ala. 1964).

245. McNamara v. Freedom Newspapers, Inc., 802 S.W.2d 901, 905 (Tex. App. 1991).

246. Aesop, *Fables,* in 17 *The Harvard Classics* (Joseph Jacobs trans., New York, P. F. Collier & Son 1909–14).

247. See Solove, *Digital Person,* 131–32 (observing that digital filing requirements and the conversion of paper files to digital format will lead to significant online accessibility of court records).

248. Judicial Conference Comm. on Court Admin. & Case Mgmt., *Report on Privacy and Public Access to Electronic Case Files* (2001), http://www.privacy.uscourts .gov/Policy.htm.

249. Robert Gellman, "Public Records, Public Policy, and Privacy," *Human Rights,* Winter 1999, at 7, 9.

250. Solove, *Digital Person,* 131–32; see also Gellman, "Public Records," 7 (warning that although "[p]rivacy protections were inherent in the technology of paper," digitization has led to increased accessibility).

251. Peter A. Winn, "Online Court Records: Balancing Judicial Accountability and Privacy in an Age of Electronic Information," 79 *Washington Law Review* 307, 315 (2004).

252. Restatement (Second) of Torts §652D cmt. b.

253. See, e.g., Cline v. Rogers, 87 F.3d 176, 179 (6th Cir. 1996) (holding that the constitutional right to information privacy did not apply to the disclosure of police records because "one's criminal history is arguably not a private 'personal matter' at all, since arrest and conviction information are matters of public record"); Doe v. City of New York, 15 F.3d 264, 268–69 (2d Cir. 1994) (finding that "an individual cannot expect to have a constitutionally protected privacy interest in matters of public record" but that plaintiff's HIV status was not a matter of public record); Scheetz v. Morning Call, Inc., 946 F.2d 202, 207 (3d Cir. 1991) (holding that because information about the victim's claims of spousal abuse potentially "would have wound up on the public record," the victim did not have a privacy interest in the claims).

254. Walls v. City of Petersburg, 895 F.2d 188, 193–94 (4th Cir. 1990).

255. United States Dep't of Justice v. Reporters Comm. for Freedom of the Press, 489 U.S. 749, 780, 764 (1989).

256. Angus McLaren, *Sexual Blackmail: A Modern History* 17 (2002).

257. Id. at 20 (quoting "Central Criminal Court," *Times* (London), June 20, 1895, at 3).

258. Id. at 17, 21.

259. See Leo Katz, *Ill-Gotten Gains* 140–45 (1996) (discussing various philosophers' interpretations of the connection between blackmail and coercion and the difficulties of formulating a complete theory). The term "blackmail" originated in Tudor times and referred to extortion in general. McLaren, *Sexual*

Blackmail, 12. "Modern blackmail first emerged when criminals in the eighteenth century recognized that the laws against sodomy provided them with the means by which they could extort money from those whom they could entrap." Id. at 3.

260. See 31A Am. Jur. 2d, "Extortion, Blackmail, and Threats" §20 (2002) (recognizing that although statutes differ in form, the use of a threat to extract something is at the heart of blackmail). For a discussion of how blackmail laws protected reputations in different periods of American history, see Lawrence M. Friedman, "Name Robbers: Privacy, Blackmail, and Assorted Matters in Legal History," 30 *Hofstra Law Review* 1093, 1112–13 (2002) (observing that blackmail went "against the American grain" of allowing second chances and fresh starts).

261. Walter Block & Gary M. Anderson, "Blackmail, Extortion, and Exchange," 44 *New York Law School Law Review* 541, 541 (2001).

262. Joseph Isenbergh, "Blackmail from A to C," 141 *University of Pennsylvania Law Review* 1905, 1914 (1993) (noting that in any given case, individuals who have obtained valuable information are most likely to disclose it in the presence of a law forbidding bargaining for secrecy with data subjects, though in the long run, such laws will deter potential blackmailers from digging for valuable information).

263. Richard A. Posner, "Blackmail, Privacy, and Freedom of Contract," 141 *University of Pennsylvania Law Review* 1817, 1818–20 (1993).

264. Block & Anderson, "Blackmail," 544–47.

265. Jennifer Gerarda Brown, "Blackmail as Private Justice," 141 *University of Pennsylvania Law Review* 1935, 1971 (1993).

266. Richard A. Epstein, "Blackmail, Inc.," 50 *University of Chicago Law Review* 553, 565 (1983).

267. Wendy J. Gordon, "Truth and Consequences: The Force of Blackmail's Central Case," 141 *University of Pennsylvania Law Review* 1741, 1761 (1993).

268. Richard H. McAdams, "Group Norms, Gossip, and Blackmail," 144 *University of Pennsylvania Law Review* 2237, 2243–64 (1996).

269. See Restatement (Second) of Torts §13 (1965) (defining battery); id. at §21 (defining assault).

270. Henrik Ibsen, *Hedda Gabler,* in *Hedda Gabler and Other Plays* 362 (Una Ellis-Fermor trans., Penguin Books 1961).

271. See, e.g., Cal. Penal Code §518 (West 1999) (defining extortion as "the obtaining of property from another, with his consent, or the obtaining of an official act of a public officer, induced by a wrongful use of force or fear").

272. Edison v. Edison Polyform Mfg. Co., 67 A. 392, 394 (N.J. 1907).

273. Roberson v. Rochester Folding Box Co., 64 N.E. 442, 442, 442–43, 447–48 (N.Y. 1902).

274. Editorial, "The Right of Privacy," *New York Times,* Aug. 23, 1902, at 8, reprinted in Denis O'Brien, "The Right of Privacy," 2 *Columbia Law Review* 437, 438 (1902).

275. Editorial, *New York Times,* Aug. 12, 1902.

276. Comment, "An Actionable Right to Privacy? Roberson v. Rochester Folding Box Co.," 12 *Yale Law Journal* 35, 36 (1902).

277. Denis O'Brien, "Right of Privacy," 437.

278. See, e.g., Irwin R. Kramer, "The Birth of Privacy Law: A Century Since Warren and Brandeis," 39 *Catholic University Law Review* 703, 717 (1990) (noting

that the statutes "made it both a tort and a misdemeanor . . . to use another's name, portrait, or picture for commercial purposes without the subject's consent").

279. N.Y. Civ. Rights Law §§50, 51 (McKinney 1992).

280. Restatement (Second) of Torts §652C & cmt. c (1977).

281. Hauch, "Protecting Private Facts in France," 1223.

282. Ruth Redmond-Cooper, "The Press and the Law of Privacy," 34 *International and Comparative Law Quarterly* 769, 772 (1985); James Whitman, "The Two Western Cultures of Privacy: Dignity Versus Liberty," 113 *Yale Law Journal* 1151, 1175 (2004).

283. Bruce W. Sanford, *Libel and Privacy* §2.4, at 43 (2d ed. 1991). For more on the law of appropriation in Germany and France, see Ansgar Ohly & Agnès Lucas-Schloetter, *Privacy, Property, and Personality: Civil Law Perspectives on Commercial Appropriation* (2005).

284. Von Hannover v. Germany, [2004] ECHR 294 (23 June 2004), at ¶50.

285. Aubry v. Éditions Vice-Versa, Inc., [1998] 1 S.C.R. 591.

286. See generally Robert C. Post, "Rereading Warren and Brandeis: Privacy, Property, and Appropriation," 41 *Case Western Reserve Law Review* 647 (1991) (contrasting the "property" and "dignity" rationales for the tort of appropriation).

287. Edward J. Bloustein, "Privacy as an Aspect of Human Dignity: An Answer to Dean Prosser," 39 *New York University Law Review* 962, 987 (1964).

288. Prosser, "Privacy," 406.

289. Jonathan Kahn, "Bringing Dignity Back to Light: Publicity Rights and the Eclipse of the Tort of Appropriation of Identity," 17 *Cardozo Arts and Entertainment Law Journal* 213, 223 (1999). A new tort, known as the "right of publicity," has emerged to redress violations of property rights in one's name or likeness. See, e.g., Thomas McCarthy, *The Rights of Publicity and Privacy* §5.63 (1991) ("Simplistically put, while the appropriation branch of the right of privacy is invaded by an injury to the psyche, the right of publicity is infringed by an injury to the pocketbook").

290. David A. Elder, *The Law of Privacy* §6:1, at 375 (1991) (quoting McQueen v. Wilson, 161 S.E.2d 63, 66 (Ga. Ct. App. 1968), *rev'd on other grounds*, 162 S.E.2d 313 (Ga. 1968)).

291. See Andrew J. McClurg, "A Thousand Words Are Worth a Picture: A Privacy Tort Response to Consumer Data Profiling," 98 *Northwestern University Law Review* 63, 109, 114 (2003) (arguing that Prosser's characterization of appropriation as vindicating property interests obscured the dignitary interests the tort protected, and noting that "[m]odern courts are prone to subsuming the privacy claim under the label of publicity").

292. Pavesich v. New England Life Ins. Co., 50 S.E. 68, 68, 69, 70, 80 (Ga. 1905).

293. Roberson v. Rochester Folding Box Co., 64 N.E. 442, 449 (N.Y. 1902) (Gray, J., dissenting).

294. Edison v. Edison Polyform Mfg. Co., 67 A. 392, 392 (N.J. 1907). The court granted the injunction. Id. at 395.

295. Onassis v. Christian Dior–New York, Inc., 472 N.Y.S.2d 254, 257 (Sup. Ct. 1984).

296. Quoted in Beate Rössler, *The Value of Privacy* 14–15 (2005).

297. Arthur Miller, *The Crucible* 133 (Penguin Books 1995) (1953).

298. Van Vechten Veeder, "The History and Theory of Defamation," 3 *Columbia Law Review* 546, 563 (1903).

299. Rodney A. Smolla, *Law of Defamation*, at 1–4 (2d ed. 1999).

300. Restatement (Second) of Torts §558(a) (1977).

301. Id. at §559.

302. Id. at §652E; Gary T. Schwartz, "Explaining and Justifying a Limited Tort of False Light Invasion of Privacy," 41 *Case Western Reserve Law Review* 885, 885 (1991) (noting that Warren and Brandeis's article led to decisions that Prosser later labeled the false-light tort). Although there is a significant amount of overlap between the two torts, false light has a more expansive view of the harm caused by distortion. While defamation requires proof of reputational harm, false light does not, and plaintiffs can be compensated solely for emotional distress. Id. at 887.

303. Restatement (Second) of Torts §652E cmt. b.

304. Constitution of the Republic of Hungary art. 59; Poland, The Constitutional Act of 1997, art. 47; Constitution of the Portuguese Republic art. 26; Constitution of the Russian Federation art. 23 (1993); Constitution of the Democratic Socialist Republic of Sri Lanka art. 14(1) (1978); quoted in *Privacy and Human Rights*, 543, 812, 828, 850, 951.

305. United Nations Universal Declaration of Human Rights, GA Res 217A(III), UN Doc A/Res/810 (1948).

306. Janmejay Rai & Barunesh Chandra, "India," in *International Libel and Privacy Handbook* 7-1, 7-2 (Charles J. Glasser, Jr., ed., 2006).

307. Supreme Court, May 27, 1997, Minshu 51-5-2024; quoted in *International Libel and Privacy Handbook* 8-1, 8-2 (Charles J. Glasser, Jr., ed., 2006).

308. Quoted in Daniel Buchanan, *Japanese Proverbs and Sayings* 120 (1965).

309. Peter F. Carter-Ruck & Rupert Eliott, *Carter-Ruck on Libel and Slander* 18 (5th ed. 1997); Maryann McMahon, "Defamation Claims in Europe: A Survey of the Legal Armory," 19 *Communications Lawyer* 24 (2002).

310. The statutory provisions are Privacy Act, 5 U.S.C. §552a(d); Fair Credit Reporting Act, 15 U.S.C. §1681i; and Family Educational Rights and Privacy Act, 20 U.S.C. §1232g(a) (2).

311. See Dep't of Health, Educ., & Welfare, *Records*, xx–xxiii; OECD Privacy Guidelines; European Union Data Protection Directive, art. 6. For more background on the OECD Privacy Guidelines, see Joel R. Reidenberg, "Restoring Americans' Privacy in Electronic Commerce," 14 *Berkeley Technology Law Journal* 771, 773–81 (1999).

312. Arlette Farge, "The Honor and Secrecy of Families," in *A History of Private Life*, vol. 3, *Passions of the Renaissance* 571, 585 (Roger Chartier ed. & Arthur Goldhammer trans., 1989). Heinrich Böll's novella *The Lost Honor of Katharina Blum* is a remarkable account of the harm of distortion. See Heinrich Böll, *The Lost Honor of Katharina Blum* (Leila Vennewitz trans., 1975) (featuring a character whose life is ruined by the publication of misleading information).

313. Robert C. Post, "The Social Foundations of Defamation Law: Reputation and the Constitution," 74 *California Law Review* 691, 711 (1986).

314. William Shakespeare, *The Tragedy of Othello, the Moor of Venice* act 3, sc. 3, ll. 158–64 (Edward Pechter ed., W. W. Norton 2004) (1623).

315. Emily Dickinson, *Poems by Emily Dickinson* (1890), quoted in *Emily Dickinson* 17–18 (J. M. Brinnin ed., 1960).

316. The notion that the home was one's "castle" was articulated as early as 1499. See Note, "The Right to Privacy in Nineteenth Century America," 94 *Harvard Law Review* 1892, 1894 (1981) (dating the first mention to a report written in 1499) (the note was published anonymously but written by historian David Seipp); see also Semayne's Case, 77 Eng. Rep. 194, 195 (K.B. 1605) ("[T]he house of every one is to him as his . . . castle and fortress").

317. 4 William Blackstone, *Commentaries* *223.

318. Nuisance involves "an invasion of another's interest in the private use and enjoyment of land." Restatement (Second) of Torts §822 (1977). William Blackstone defined private nuisance as "any thing done to the hurt or annoyance of the lands, tenements, or hereditaments of another." 3 William Blackstone, *Commentaries* *216.

319. Thomas M. Cooley, *A Treatise on the Constitutional Limitations Which Rest upon the Legislative Power of the States of the American Union* 306 (1868).

320. U.S. Const. amend. IV ("The right of the people to be secure in their persons, houses, papers, and effects, against unreasonable searches and seizures, shall not be violated").

321. Restatement (Second) of Torts §652B.

322. Craig M. Bradley, *The Failure of the Criminal Procedure Revolution* 95–143 (1993).

323. Vargas, "Privacy Rights Under Mexican Law," 105.

324. Canadian Charter of Rights and Freedoms, 1982, c. 11, §8.

325. *Privacy and Human Rights*, 217.

326. Hosking v. Runting, [2004] NZCA 34, at [106] (Mar. 25, 2004).

327. Warren & Brandeis, "Right to Privacy," 193.

328. Galella v. Onassis, 487 F.2d 986, 994 (2d Cir. 1973) (quoting Galella v. Onassis, 353 F. Supp. 196, 228 (S.D.N.Y. 1972)).

329. Dorothy J. Glancy, "The Invention of the Right to Privacy," 21 *Arizona Law Review* 1, 25 (1979).

330. See, e.g., Janette Dillon, *Shakespeare and the Solitary Man* 3–13 (1981) (discussing approaches to solitude before Shakespeare's time, which viewed a solitary life as running counter to the good of the community). Solitude, which became a coveted aspect of existence by the end of the seventeenth century, was viewed by many as dangerous and undesirable during the Middle Ages. See Michel Rouche, "Private Life Conquers State and Society," in *A History of Private Life*, vol. 1, *From Pagan Rome to Byzantium* 419, 434–35 (Paul Veyne ed. & Arthur Goldhammer trans., 1987) (describing the concern a ninth-century abbot had for the hermit's solitary life).

331. Aristotle, *Ethica Nicomachea* §1169b, ll. 18–19 (W. D. Ross trans., Clarendon Press 1925) (n.d.).

332. See Michael A. Weinstein, "The Uses of Privacy in the Good Life," in *Nomos XIII: Privacy*, 88, 91–93 (discussing critiques of solitude).

333. Govind v. State of Madhya Pradesh & Anr, [1975] INSC 74; [1975] 3 SCR 946; [1975] 2 SCC 148; AIR 1975 SC 1378 (Mar. 18, 1975), available at http://www.commonlii.org/in/cases/INSC/1975/75.html.

334. Hannah Arendt, *The Human Condition* 71 (1958).

335. According to philosopher Philip Koch, solitude "gives respite and restoration, a time and a place to lick the wounds of social strife." Philip Koch, *Solitude* 5

(1994); see also Westin, *Privacy and Freedom,* 35 ("[N]o individual can play indefinitely, without relief, the variety of roles that life demands. . . . Privacy in this aspect gives individuals, from factory workers to Presidents, a chance to lay their masks aside for rest. To be always 'on' would destroy the human organism").

336. For Thoreau, solitude fosters better social relationships because "we live thick and are in each other's way, and stumble over one another, and I think that we thus lose some respect for one another." Henry David Thoreau, *Walden,* in *Walden and Other Writings* 113 (Barnes & Noble Books 1993) (1854).

337. Many social, political, and religious leaders began their influential public work with preparations performed in private. See, e.g., Joseph Bensman & Robert Lilienfeld, *Between Public and Private: The Lost Boundaries of the Self* 37 (1979) (describing how a "religious hero['s]" retreat to privacy would inspire followers on his return to the public life); Richard H. Weisberg, "It's a Positivist, It's a Pragmatist, It's a Codifier! Reflections on Nietzsche and Stendhal," 18 *Cardozo Law Review* 85, 92 (1996) (noting that for Nietzsche, "[t]he great legislator is himself (or herself) conceived of as one whose act of social codification begins with a private program of creative self-fulfillment"). Sixteenth-century French essayist Michel de Montaigne contended that solitude—even for public figures—is not self-indulgent, for "[t]hey have only stepped back to make a better jump, to get a stronger impetus wherewith to plunge deeper into the crowd." Michel de Montaigne, "Of Solitude," in *The Complete Essays of Montaigne* 174, 182 (Donald M. Frame trans., 1958).

338. See, e.g., Restatement (Second) of Torts §652B cmt. c (1977) ("The defendant is subject to liability . . . only when he has intruded into a private place, or has otherwise invaded a private seclusion that the plaintiff has thrown about his person or affairs").

339. Irwin Altman, *The Environment and Social Behavior: Privacy, Personal Space, Territory, Crowding* 52–54, 96, 87–89 (Irvington 1981) (1975).

340. Robert C. Post, "The Social Foundations of Privacy: Community and Self in the Common Law Tort," 77 *California Law Review* 957, 966–68, 971–73 (1989).

341. See, e.g., Shulman v. Group W Prods., Inc., 955 P.2d 469, 491 (Cal. 1998) (holding that a car-accident victim had a privacy interest in her conversation with medical rescuers at the accident scene); Stressman v. Am. Black Hawk Broad. Co., 416 N.W.2d 685, 687–88 (Iowa 1987) (holding that broadcasting video of the plaintiff eating at a restaurant might have violated her privacy interest and noting that "the mere fact a person can be seen by others does not mean that person cannot legally be 'secluded' " (quoting Huskey v. Nat'l Broad. Co., 632 F. Supp. 1282, 1287–88 (N.D. Ill. 1986)).

342. Sanders v. American Broad. Co., 978 P.2d 67, 72 (Cal. 1999).

343. Margaret Atwood, *The Handmaid's Tale* 63 (1986).

344. Griswold v. Connecticut, 381 U.S. 479, 484 (1965).

345. Eisenstadt v. Baird, 405 U.S. 438, 453 (1972) (emphasis omitted).

346. Roe v. Wade, 410 U.S. 113, 153 (1973).

347. See, e.g., Pierce v. Soc'y of Sisters, 268 U.S. 510, 534–35 (1925) (invalidating an Oregon law requiring parents to send their children to public school because it "unreasonably interfere[d] with the liberty of parents . . . to direct the upbringing and education of children under their control").

348. Laurence H. Tribe, *American Constitutional Law* 1352 (2d ed. 1988).

349. Louis Henkin, "Privacy and Autonomy," 74 *Columbia Law Review* 1410, 1410–11 (1974).

350. Neil M. Richards, "The Information Privacy Project," 94 *Georgetown Law Journal* 1087, 1095, 1108 (2006).

351. Whalen v. Roe, 429 U.S. 589, 599–600 (1977).

352. See, e.g., *In re* Crawford, 194 F.3d 954, 958 (9th Cir. 1999) ("We agree . . . that the indiscriminate public disclosure of [certain personal information] may implicate the constitutional right to informational privacy"); Walls v. City of Petersburg, 895 F.2d 188, 192 (4th Cir. 1990) ("Personal, private information in which an individual has a reasonable expectation of confidentiality is protected by one's constitutional right to privacy"); Kimberlin v. U.S. Dep't of Justice, 788 F.2d 434, 438 (7th Cir. 1986) ("Whether or not Kimberlin has a privacy interest in the information . . . depends upon whether he has a reasonable expectation of privacy in the information"); Barry v. City of New York, 712 F.2d 1554, 1559 (2d Cir. 1983) ("Most courts considering the question . . . appear to agree that privacy of personal matters is a [constitutionally] protected interest"); J.P. v. DeSanti, 653 F.2d 1080, 1090 (6th Cir. 1981) ("Our opinion does not mean . . . there is *no* constitutional right to non-disclosure of private information"); United States v. Westinghouse Elec. Corp., 638 F.2d 570, 577 (3d Cir. 1980) (recognizing that *Whalen* protects "the right not to have an individual's private affairs made public by the government"); Plante v. Gonzalez, 575 F.2d 1119, 1132 (5th Cir. 1978) ("There is another strand to the right to privacy properly called the right to confidentiality").

353. Whalen, 429 U.S. at 600.

354. Id. at 600–02.

355. John Stuart Mill, *On Liberty* 13 (David Spitz, ed. 1975).

356. Sir James Fitzjames Stephen, *Liberty, Equality, Fraternity* 161–62 (1967 ed.) (1873).

357. Union Pac. Ry. Co. v. Botsford, 141 U.S. 250, 251–52 (1891).

358. Richards, "Information Privacy Project," 1108.

359. Stanley v. Georgia, 394 U.S. 557, 564 (1969).

360. Olmstead v. United States, 277 U.S. 438, 478 (1928) (Brandeis, J., dissenting), quoted in Stanely v. Georgia, 394 U.S. at 564.

361. Id. at 565.

362. Post, "Social Foundations of Privacy," 973.

363. Lawrence v. Texas, 539 U.S. 558, 578, 567, 562 (2003).

364. Id. at 572 (quoting Model Penal Code §213.2 cmt. 2 (1980) and citing Model Penal Code Commentary 277–78 (Tentative Draft No. 4, 1955)). For an interesting discussion of *Lawrence* and public versus private places, see Lior Jacob Strahilevitz, "Consent, Aesthetics, and the Boundaries of Sexual Privacy After *Lawrence v. Texas*," 54 *DePaul Law Review* 671 (2005).

365. McLaren, *Sexual Blackmail*, 6, 8.

6. Privacy: A New Understanding

1. Quoted in Joanne B. Freeman, "Slander, Poison, Whispers, and Fame: Jefferson's 'Anas' and Political Gossip in the Early Republic," 15 *Journal of the Early Republic* 25, 31 (1995).

2. Rodney A. Smolla, *Law of Defamation* 9-14, 9-19, 9-17 (2d ed. 2000).

3. Eric H. Reiter, "Personality and Patrimony: Comparative Perspectives on the Right to One's Image," 76 *Tulane Law Review* 673, 676–78 (2002).

4. Paul Sieghart, quoted in Colin J. Bennett, *Regulating Privacy: Data Protection and Public Policy in Europe and the United States* 28 (1992).

5. Samuel D. Warren & Louis D. Brandeis, "The Right to Privacy," 4 *Harvard Law Review* 193, 193, 194, 197 (1890).

6. Id. at 196.

7. Nancy Levit, "Ethereal Torts," 61 *George Washington Law Review* 136, 141 (1992); see also James M. Fischer, *Understanding Remedies* 124 (1999) (courts were reluctant to award damages for emotional distress because of "concerns over genuineness, reliability, and the specter of unlimited liability for trivial losses").

8. Smolla, *Law of Defamation*, 11–41 to 11–43.

9. Restatement (Second) of Torts §46.

10. Levit, "Ethereal Torts," 150.

11. See Glen Weissenberger, *Federal Evidence* §501 (4th ed. 2001); Upjohn Co. v. United States, 449 U.S. 383, 389 (1981) (attorney-client); Jaffee v. Redmond, 518 U.S. 1 (1996) (psychotherapist-patient).

12. Sweezy v. New Hampshire, 354 U.S. 234, 250 (1957) ("Merely to summon a witness and compel him, against his will, to disclose the nature of his past expressions and associations is a measure of governmental interference in these matters"); Shelton v. Tucker, 364 U.S. 479, 490 (1960) (striking down statute requiring teachers to provide a list to the government of all the groups they were members of); Baird v. State Bar, 401 U.S. 1, 6 (1971) ("[W]hen a State attempts to make inquiries about a person's beliefs or associations, its power is limited by the First Amendment. Broad and sweeping state inquiries into these protected areas . . . discourage citizens from exercising rights protected by the Constitution").

13. NAACP v. Alabama, 357 U.S. 449, 462 (1958).

14. Alexis de Tocqueville, 2 *Democracy in America* 196 (Phillips Bradley ed. 1945).

15. For a comparison of privacy law and environmental law, see Dennis D. Hirsch, "Protecting the Inner Environment: What Privacy Regulation Can Learn from Environmental Law," 41 *Georgia Law Review* 1 (2006).

16. Daniel J. Solove, *The Digital Person: Technology and Privacy in the Information Age* 99 (2004).

17. See, e.g., Laird v. Tatum, 408 U.S. 1, 1, 13 (1972) (confronting the alleged "chilling effect" that army surveillance had on "lawful and peaceful civilian political activity").

18. Frederick Schauer, "Fear, Risk and the First Amendment: Unraveling the 'Chilling Effect,'" 58 *Boston University Law Review* 685, 693 (1978) (emphasis omitted).

19. Daniel J. Solove, "The First Amendment as Criminal Procedure," 82 *New York University Law Review* 112, 119–23, 154–59 (2007).

20. Robert Merton, *Social Theory and Social Structure* 375 (1957).

21. Joel R. Reidenberg, "Privacy Wrongs in Search of Remedies," 54 *Hastings Law Journal* 877, 882–83 (2003).

22. Priscilla M. Regan, *Legislating Privacy: Technology, Social Values, and Public Policy* 225 (1995).

23. Privacy Act, 5 U.S.C. §552a.

24. Robert Gellman, "Does Privacy Law Work?" in *Technology and Privacy: The New Landscape* (Philip E. Agre & Marc Rotenberg eds., 1997).

25. 306 F.3d 170, 180–82 (4th Cir. 2002), *cert. granted* (June 27, 2003).

26. See Doe v. Chao, 540 U.S. 614 (2004).

27. U.S. West, Inc. v. Fed. Communications Comm'n, 182 F.3d 1224, 1235 (10th Cir. 1999).

28. Solove, *Digital Person*, 93–101; Daniel J. Solove, "Identity Theft, Privacy, and the Architecture of Vulnerability," 54 *Hastings Law Journal* 1227 (2003).

29. Dyer v. Northwest Airlines Corp., 334 F. Supp. 2d 1196, 1200 (D.N.D. 2004). Another court reached a similar conclusion. See *In re* Northwest Airlines Privacy Litigation, 2004 WL 1278459 (D.Minn. 2004).

30. 293 A.D.2d 598, 599–600 (N.Y. App. Div. 2002).

31. John M. Roberts & Thomas Gregor, "Privacy: A Cultural View," in *Nomos XIII: Privacy* 199, 203–14 (J. Roland Pennock & J. W. Chapman eds., 1971).

32. Dan Rosen, "Private Lives and Public Eyes: Privacy in the United States and Japan," 6 *Florida Journal of International Law* 141, 172–73 (1990).

33. James Whitman, "The Two Western Cultures of Privacy: Dignity Versus Liberty," 113 *Yale Law Journal* 1151, 1160, 1163, 1171, 1204, 1164, 1221 (2004).

34. Joel R. Reidenberg, "Setting Standards for Fair Information Practices in the U.S. Private Sector," 80 *Iowa Law Review* 497, 500 (1995).

35. Francesca Bignami, "European Versus American Liberty: A Comparative Analysis of Anti-terrorism Data-Mining," 48 *Boston College Law Review* 609, 682–86 (2007).

36. See Marc Rotenberg, "Fair Information Practices and the Architecture of Privacy (What Larry Doesn't Get)," 2001 *Stanford Technology Law Review* 1 (2001).

37. Bennett, *Regulating Privacy*, 96.

38. Board of Education v. Earls, 536 U.S. 822, 828–29 (2002).

39. Id. at 832, 833.

40. Id. at 834.

41. Nat'l Fed'n of Fed. Employees v. Cheney, 884 F.2d 603 (D.C. Cir. 1989) (sustaining U.S. Army's drug-testing program).

42. Vernonia School District v. Acton, 515 U.S. 646, 682 (1995).

43. Earls, 536 U.S. at 848 (Ginsburg, J., dissenting).

44. See id. at 833 (majority opinion).

45. John M. Poindexter, "Finding the Face of Terror in Data," *New York Times*, Sept. 10, 2003, at A25.

46. Shane Harris, "TIA Lives On," *National Journal*, Feb. 23, 2006.

47. GAO Report, *Data Mining: Federal Efforts Cover a Wide Range of Uses* 2 (May 2004).

48. Jacqueline Klosek, *The War on Privacy* 51 (2007).

49. Leslie Cauley, "NSA Has Massive Database of Americans' Phone Calls," *USA Today*, May 11, 2006, at A1; Susan Page, "Lawmakers: NSA Database Incomplete," *USA Today*, June 30, 2006, at A1.

50. Cauley, "NSA Has Massive Database."

51. Daniel J. Solove, Marc Rotenberg, & Paul M. Schwartz, *Information Privacy Law* 603–04 (2d ed. 2006).

52. Richard A. Posner, "Our Domestic Intelligence Crisis," *Washington Post*, Dec. 21, 2005, at A31.

53. Richard A. Posner, *Not a Suicide Pact: The Constitution in a Time of National Emergency* 97 (2006).

54. Solove, *Digital Person*, 165–209; see also Daniel J. Solove, "Digital Dossiers and the Dissipation of Fourth Amendment Privacy," 75 *Southern California Law Review* 1083 (2002).

55. Roger Clarke, "Information Technology and Dataveillance" 3 (1987), http://www.anu.edu.au/people/Roger.Clarke/DV/CACM88.html.

56. Christopher Slobogin, "Transaction Surveillance by the Government," 75 *Mississippi Law Journal* 139 (2005).

57. Solove, "First Amendment as Criminal Procedure," 112.

58. Solove, *Digital Person*, 27–55.

59. George Orwell, *Nineteen Eighty-four* (Plume ed. 2003) (originally published in 1949).

60. Franz Kafka, *The Trial* 158–59 (Breon Mitchell trans., 1998) (originally published in 1937).

61. Solove, *Digital Person*, 221.

62. Peck v. United Kingdom [2003] ECHR 44 (2003), at ¶15.

63. Id. at ¶¶53, 59, 62.

Index